Workbook

Modern Automotive Technology

James E. Duffy
Automotive Writer

Publisher
THE GOODHEART-WILLCOX COMPANY, INC.
Tinley Park, Illinois

Important Safety Notice

Proper service and repair methods are critical to the safe, reliable operation of automobiles. The procedures described in this workbook are designed to assist you in using a manufacturer's service manual. A service manual will provide the procedures and specifications needed to do competent work.

The text contains safety precautions which must be followed to prevent personal injury or part damage. The precautions are general, however, and do not cover some special hazards. Refer to a service manual when in doubt about any service operation!

Introduction

The **Modern Automotive Technology Workbook** is two products in one: a text study guide and a shop activity guide. It is designed to help you learn the essential aspects of auto technology. It does this by highlighting the most important content in the textbook and supplementing the information with in-shop activities (jobs).

The first portion of the workbook serves as a study guide for the textbook chapters. The exercises reinforce the material in the textbook, ensuring that you understand both the written and illustrated aspects of automotive technology.

Illustrations are used heavily in the workbook. After answering written questions on a subject or assembly, you will be asked to identify similar or related parts on a simplified illustration. This will help you more fully grasp the written material.

The jobs in the back of the workbook are supplemental hands-on tasks. They provide detailed instructions for a variety of shop activities, such as servicing cylinder heads and brake assemblies. Other jobs cover shop safety, checking vehicle fluids, using service manuals, and servicing ignition systems. All jobs will help you develop the practical skills needed when starting work in an automotive repair facility.

As a student of automotive technology, you will find this workbook an essential tool for making your study easier and more interesting. Good luck!

James Duffy

Contents

Text   *Workbook*

Section 5—Electrical Systems

Section 6—Cooling and Lubrication Systems

Section 7—Emission Control Systems

Section 8—Engine Performance

Section 9—Engine Service and Repair

Section 10—Drive Trains and Axles

Text   *Workbook*

Section 11—Suspension, Steering, and Brakes

Section 12—Heating and Air Conditioning

Section 13—Accessory Systems

Workbook Jobs

Instructions for Answering Workbook Questions

Each chapter in the workbook correlates with the same chapter in the textbook. Before answering the questions in the workbook, study the assigned chapter of the text and answer the review questions. Read the objectives at the beginning of each workbook chapter. This will help you review the important concepts covered in the chapter. Try to complete as many of the questions as possible *without* referring to the textbook. Then, use the text to complete the remaining questions.

Various types of questions are presented in the workbook, including multiple-choice, fill-in-the blank, short answer, matching, and identification. The sequence of questions corresponds to the sequence of material in the textbook chapter. The following are examples of completed workbook questions.

Matching

Match the air conditioning terms listed below to the corresponding descriptions.

1. Uses cooling action of vaporizing refrigerant to cool the air inside the vehicle.

2. Fan that forces air through the evaporator and into the passenger compartment.

3. Causes refrigerant to change from a gaseous state to a liquid state, causing it to give off its stored heat.

4. Removes moisture from and stores refrigerant.

5. Shuts the compressor off when the evaporator temperature nears freezing.

6. Substance that carries heat through the system to lower the air temperature in the vehicle.

7. Pump that pressurizes refrigerant and forces it through the system.

8. Expansion valve or tube that causes refrigerant pressure and temperature to drop, cooling the evaporator.

(A) Refrigerant
(B) Compressor
(C) Condenser
(D) Flow-control device
(E) Evaporator
(F) Receiver-drier or accumulator
(G) Blower
(H) Thermostatic switch

1. __(E)__

2. __(G)__

3. __(C)__

4. __(F)__

5. __(H)__

6. __(A)__

7. __(B)__

8. __(D)__

Fill-in-the-blank

9. _____ action normally makes the cylinders wear more at right angles to the centerline of the piston pins.

9. _Piston thrust_

Multiple-choice

10. _____ is a type of driveline with an open drive shaft that operates a rear axle assembly mounted on springs.
    (A) Constant velocity
    (B) Torque tube
    (C) Variable velocity
    (D) Hotchkiss

10. _(D)_____

Short Answer

11. What does *static imbalance* cause a tire to do? _It causes the tire to vibrate up and down._

Identification

12. Label the parts of the planetary gearset assembly.

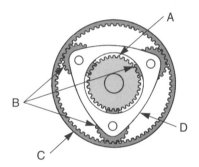

(A) _Sun gear_____
(B) _Planet gears_____
(C) _Ring gear_____
(D) _Planet carrier_____

Instructions for Completing Workbook Jobs

The jobs in the workbook are designed to supplement the textbook through various hands-on activities. Before beginning any job, read the objective and instructions carefully. Ask your instructor for any possible changes in the job procedures and for help as needed.

It is also important to read the related chapters in the text and to review pertinent safety information before you begin. Always answer the job questions with complete sentences. Work neatly!

The Automobile

Name: _____ Date: _____

Instructor: _____ Score: _____ Textbook pages 1–21

Objective: After completing this workbook assignment, you will be able to identify and explain the most important parts of a vehicle.

Parts, Assemblies, and Systems

1. A(n)_____ is a set of fitted parts designed to complete a function.   1._____

2. Identify the following automotive systems and parts. Use arrows to indicate air, fuel, and exhaust flow. Also, use arrows to show drive train operation.

(A) _____

(B) _____

(C) _____

(D) _____

(E) _____

(F) _____

(G) _____

(H) _____

(I) _____

(J) _____

(K) _____

(L) _____

(M) _____

(N) _____

(O) _____

(P) _____

3. List and describe three of the seven modern automotive body types.

(A)_____

_____

_____

(B)_____

_____

_____

(C)_____

_____

_____

Match the terms on the right with the following statements.

4. Transfers the energy of combustion to the connecting rod.

5. Keep(s) combustion pressure and oil from leaking between the piston and cylinder wall.

6. Metal casting that holds all the other parts in place.

7. Links the piston to the crankshaft.

8. Hollow area between the top of the piston and the bottom of the cylinder head.

9. Controls the opening of the valves.

10. Ride(s) on the camshaft and transfers motion to the other parts of the valve train.

11. Keep(s) the valves closed when they do not need to be open.

12. Changes the reciprocating motion of the piston and rod into useful rotary motion.

13. Open and close to control the flow of the air-fuel mixture and the exhaust gases.

14. Covers and seals the top of the cylinder.

(A) Cylinder head

(B) Piston

(C) Valve springs

(D) Valves

(E) Rings

(F) Lifters

(G) Block

(H) Connecting rod

(I) Crankshaft

(J) Combustion chamber

(K) Camshaft

4. _____

5. _____

6. _____

7. _____

8. _____

9. _____

10. _____

11. _____

12. _____

13. _____

14. _____

Computer System

15. Explain the function of an automotive *computer system.* _____

_____

_____

_____

_____

16. Name the three major parts of an automotive computer system and describe their functions.

(A)_____

_____

(B)_____

_____

(C)_____

_____

Name _____

Fuel System

17. What are the functions of a modern automotive *fuel system?* _____

_____

_____

_____

_____

18. Define *air-fuel ratio.* _____

_____

_____

_____

19. The _____ fuel system uses engine vacuum to draw fuel into the engine.   19. _____

20. Modern gasoline injection systems use a control module, _____, and electrically-operated injectors to meter fuel into the engine.   20. _____

21. Define *throttle valve.* _____

_____

_____

Electrical System

22. What purpose does the *ignition coil* serve? _____

_____

_____

_____

23. The ignition system's control module _____ sensor signals in order to trigger the ignition coil.   23. _____

24. The _____ system has a powerful electric motor that rotates the engine crankshaft until the engine fires and runs on its own power.   24. _____

25. A(n) _____ provides the electricity for the starting system.   25. _____

26. Identify the components and operations of the automotive ignition system illustrated below. Draw in any missing wires and use arrows to show current flow.

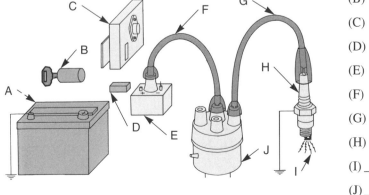

(A) _____

(B) _____

(C) _____

(D) _____

(E) _____

(F) _____

(G) _____

(H) _____

(I) _____

(J) _____

Cooling and Lubrication Systems

27. What are the functions of an automotive *cooling system?* _____

_____

_____

_____

_____

28. The _____ forces coolant through the inside of the engine, hoses, and radiator.

28. _____

29. A(n) _____ draws cool air through the radiator.

29. _____

30. What purpose does the cooling system *thermostat* serve? Where is it normally located? _____

_____

_____

_____

_____

_____

31. Describe the functions of the automotive *lubrication system.* _____

_____

_____

_____

_____

32. Identify the parts of the cooling system illustrated below.

(A) _____

(B) _____

(C) _____

(D) _____

(E) _____

(F) _____

(G) _____

(H) _____

33. The _____ pulls oil out of the pan and pushes it to various moving parts of   33._____
    the engine.

Exhaust and Emission Control Systems

34. Define *automotive engine exhaust system.*_____

    _____

    _____

35. Emission control systems are used to reduce the amount of _____   35._____
    substances produced by an engine.

36. Label the basic parts of the exhaust system illustrated below.

(A) _____

(B) _____

(C) _____

(D) _____

(E) _____

(F) _____

Drive Train Systems

Match the terms on the right with statements 37–45.

37. Transfers turning force from the engine crank-shaft to the drive wheels.

38. Allows the driver to engage or disengage the engine and manual transmission or transaxle.

39. Uses various gear combinations, or ratios, to multiply engine speed and torque to accommodate driving conditions.

40. Lets the driver change gear ratios to better accommodate driving conditions.

41. Uses an internal hydraulic system and, sometimes, electronic controls to shift gears.

42. Transfers power from the transmission to the rear axle assembly.

43. Contains a differential and two axles.

44. A set of gears and shafts that transmits power from the drive shaft to the axles.

45. Consists of a transmission and a differential in a single housing.

(A) Rear axle assembly

(B) Clutch

(C) Drive train

(D) Transmission

(E) Drive shaft

(F) Differential

(G) Axles

(H) Torque converter

(I) Transaxle

(J) Automatic transmission

(K) Manual transmission

37._____

38._____

39._____

40._____

41._____

42._____

43._____

44._____

45._____

Suspension, Steering, and Brake Systems

46. The suspension, steering, and brake systems are the _____ parts of the chassis.

46. _____

47. Describe the purpose of an automotive *suspension system.* _____

_____

_____

_____

_____

_____

48. The steering system allows the driver to control _____ by turning the wheels right or left.

48. _____

49. The brake system produces _____ to slow or stop the vehicle.

49. _____

50. Label the parts of the brake system illustrated below.

(A) _____

(B) _____

(C) _____

(D) _____

(E) _____

(F) _____

(G) _____

(H) _____

Accessory and Safety Systems

51. List five common components of an automotive accessory system. _____

_____

_____

_____

_____

52. List three automotive safety systems. _____

_____

_____

_____

Automotive Careers and ASE Certification

Name: _____ Date: _____

Instructor: _____ Score: _____ Textbook pages 22–32

Objective: After completing your workbook assignment, you will be able to describe the type of jobs available in automotive technology and explain certification tests.

The Automotive Technician

1. An automotive technician makes a living _____ cars, vans, and light trucks.
    (A) diagnosing
    (B) servicing
    (C) repairing
    (D) All of the above.

1._____

2. A master automotive technician requires skills commonly used by _____.
    (A) machinists
    (B) plumbers
    (C) electricians
    (D) All of the above.

2._____

3. A service station attendant requires little _____ experience.

3._____

4. What is an *apprentice technician* and what does he or she do? _____

_____

_____

_____

_____

5. What is a *specialized technician?* _____

_____

6. A(n) _____ technician troubleshoots, services, and repairs automobile engines.
    (A) transmission
    (B) engine
    (C) steering and suspension
    (D) None of the above.

6._____

7. A transmission technician sometimes services _____ assemblies.

7._____

8. Describe the responsibilities of a *steering and suspension technician.* _____
_____
_____
_____
_____
_____
_____

9. List three of the automotive systems an electrical system technician must be able to repair.
_____
_____
_____

10. What is a *tune-up technician?* _____
_____
_____
_____
_____

Match the positions listed on the right with the descriptions on the left.

11. Normally capable of repairing automotive brake systems.

12. In charge of all the other technicians in the service facility.

13. Handles customer complaints.

14. Prepares shop work orders on cars entering the garage for repairs.

15. Designs new automotive systems and parts.

(A) Master technician

(B) Shop service manager

(C) Automotive engineer

(D) Shop supervisor

(E) Service writer

11. _____

12. _____

13. _____

14. _____

15. _____

Preparing for a Career in Automotive Technology

16. Why must automobile technicians have above-average math and English skills? _____
_____
_____

17. What are *cooperative training programs?* _____
_____
_____

18. What are some of the responsibilities of a technician who accepts employment at an automotive repair facility?
_____
_____
_____
_____

Name _____

Chapter 2   Automotive Careers and ASE Certification   17

ASE Certification

19. What is the function of the ASE board of directors? _____
_____
_____
_____

20. What is *automobile technician certification?* _____
_____
_____
_____

21. List the eight automotive technology test categories of the ASE certification test. _____
_____
_____
_____
_____
_____

22. How many tests can be taken at each ASE certification testing session?   22. _____
    (A) Two
    (B) Four
    (C) Five
    (D) None of the above.

23. ASE-certified master automobile technician status is granted when _____   23. _____
areas have been passed.
    (A) at least two
    (B) four out of eight
    (C) six out of eight
    (D) all eight

24. What are the requirements for ASE certification? _____
_____
_____
_____

25. When are ASE certification tests given? _____
_____

26. List three tips that might help you pass the ASE test.

    (A) _____
_____

    (B) _____
_____

    (C) _____
_____

27. The ASE tests are designed to measure your knowledge of what three things? _____

_____

_____

_____

_____

_____

28. What types of questions are used in ASE certification tests? _____

_____

_____

_____

_____

29. Identify the following type of ASE question. Answer the question and explain why you chose your particular answer.

29. _____

The fuel in a gasoline injection system is sprayed into the combustion chamber by these parts:
   (A) injectors.
   (B) valves.
   (C) spark plugs.
   (D) glow plugs.

_____

_____

_____

_____

_____

_____

30. Once you are certified in any area, you must take a recertification test every _____ years to maintain your certification.

30. _____

Entrepreneurship

31. Define *entrepreneur.* _____

_____

_____

_____

_____

32. Most successful entrepreneurs have a quality known as _____.

32. _____

Basic Hand Tools

Name: _____Date: _____

Instructor: _____Score: _____Textbook pages 33–45

Objective: After completing this chapter, you will be able to properly organize tools and select the correct tool for a specific job.

Tool Rules

1. Why should you buy quality tools? _____
   _____
   _____

2. _____ or _____ maintained tools will hurt an automotive technician's   2._____
   on-the-job performance.   _____

Tool Storage

3. Name the three basic parts to a toolbox. _____
   _____

4. A toolbox's _____ is for holding frequently used tools.   4._____

5. In what part of a toolbox are large power tools normally kept?   5._____

6. What is the basic function of tool holders? _____
   _____

Wrenches

7. _____ is determined by measuring across the wrench jaws.   7._____

8. What type of wrench is designed for use with a hammer?   8._____

9. Which of the following statements best describes an open-end wrench?   9._____
   (A) Has adjustable jaws.
   (B) Can be used on a ratchet.
   (C) Has both box and open jaws.
   (D) Has an open jaw on both ends.

10. Why is each end of an open-end wrench set at an angle? _____
    _____
    _____

11. Box-end wrenches are available with either _____ or _____ openings.

11. _____
    _____

12. Identify the wrenches illustrated below.

(A) _____

(B) _____

(C) _____

(D) _____

13. A socket is a cylinder-shaped, box-end tool for removing and installing _____ and _____.

13. _____
    _____

14. Define *speed handle*. _____
_____
_____

15. A(n) _____ is a swivel that lets the socket wrench reach around obstructions.

15. _____

16. A(n) _____ wrench is an adjustable wrench used to grasp cylindrical objects.

16. _____

17. A(n) _____ wrench is used to turn set screws on pulleys, gears, and knobs.

17. _____

Screwdrivers

18. A(n) _____ screwdriver has a single blade that fits into a slot in the screw head.

18. _____

19. A(n) _____ screwdriver has two crossing blades that fit into a star-shaped screw slot.

19. _____

20. A(n) _____ looks like a screwdriver, but it has a sharp, pointed tip.

20. _____

21. How do you choose the correct screwdriver for the job? _____
_____
_____

22. Heavy-duty screwdrivers with a(n) _____ can withstand light hammering and prying.

22. _____

Pliers

23. Pliers are used for _____ various parts.
    (A) gripping
    (B) cutting and crimping
    (C) holding and bending
    (D) All of the above.

23. _____

24. _____ pliers are the most common pliers used by an automotive technician.   24. _____

25. _____ pliers are excellent for handling extremely small parts or reaching into highly restricted areas.   25. _____

Hammers

26. A(n) _____ hammer is the most common type of hammer used in automotive work.   26. _____

27. When should a brass hammer be used? _____

_____

28. What type of hammer should be used when installing wheel covers?   28. _____

Chisels and Punches

29. For what purpose are chisels used? _____

_____

30. A(n) _____ punch is used to drive pins, shafts, and metal rods part of the way out of a hole.   30. _____

31. List the rules that should be followed when using chisels and punches. _____

_____

_____

_____

_____

_____

_____

Files

32. A(n) _____ file with large cutting edges should be used on soft materials, such as plastic, brass, and aluminum.   32. _____

33. A(n) _____ file with small cutting edges is needed to produce a smoother surface and to cut harder materials, like cast iron or steel.   33. _____

34. List at least three safety rules that should be followed when working with a file. _____

_____

_____

_____

Saws

35. What type of saw is most frequently used by a technician?   35. _____

36. Name at least two of the rules to remember when using a hacksaw. _____

_____

_____

Holding Tools

37. List the rules to follow when using a vise. _____

_____

_____

_____

38. C-clamps _____.
    (A) come in many different sizes
    (B) can be used when cutting or welding
    (C) hold parts on a work surface
    (D) All of the above.

38._____

39. Name some of the types of stands or holding fixtures that can be used when servicing an automobile.

_____

_____

_____

_____

Cleaning Tools

40. Why is dirt considered a major enemy of a vehicle?_____

_____

_____

41. Name two types of cleaning tools that help the technician remove carbon, rust, dirt, grease, old gaskets, and dried oil from parts.

41._____

42. _____ are used to remove light rust and dirt on parts.

42._____

Probe and Pickup Tools

43. What is the purpose of pickup and probing tools? _____

_____

_____

44. A(n) _____ probe will allow you to see an oil leak behind the engine.

44._____

Pry Bars

45. How are pry bars helpful during automotive servicing? _____

_____

_____

46. Pry bars are commonly used when adjusting engine _____.

46 ._____

47. Why should you always use caution when using a pry bar during vehicle servicing?_____

_____

_____

Chapter 4

Power Tools and Equipment

Name: _____ Date: _____

Instructor: _____ Score: _____ Textbook pages 46–58

Objective: After studying this chapter, you will be able to select and use power tools properly.

Compressed-Air System

1. What is an *air compressor?* _____

   _____

2. What is the usual air pressure in a shop's compressed air system?   2. _____

3. Define *quick disconnect connectors.* _____

   _____

   _____

4. A(n) _____ is used to set a specific pressure in the compressed-air system.   4. _____

5. Identify the components of the compressed-air system illustrated below.

(A) _____   (F) _____

(B) _____   (G) _____

(C) _____   (H) _____

(D) _____   (I) _____

(E) _____

Air Tools

6. Air tools are also referred to as _____ tools.   6. _____

7. Why should you always lubricate an air tool before operation? _____

   _____

   _____

8. Air wrenches provide a very fast means of installing or removing _____.

8._____

9. A(n) _____ or _____ on the impact wrench controls the direction of rotation.

9._____

_____

10. Why should you be careful when loosening or tightening fasteners with an air wrench? _____

_____

_____

11. What is an *air ratchet?* _____

_____

_____

12. An air ratchet normally has a _____ drive.
    (A) 1/4″
    (B) 3/8″
    (C) 1/2″
    (D) 7/8″

12._____

13. Describe the differences between an *impact socket* and a *conventional socket.* _____

_____

_____

_____

14. Why shouldn't an impact wrench be used in place of a torque wrench? _____

_____

_____

15. For what purpose(s) is an air hammer used? _____

_____

16. Never turn an air hammer on unless the tool is pressed tightly against the _____.

16._____

17. For what purpose(s) is an *air-powered blowgun* used? _____

_____

_____

_____

18. What is the application of a *solvent gun?* _____

_____

_____

19. Why is an air drill excellent for many repair jobs? _____

_____

_____

20. A(n) _____ is used in an air or electric drill and can quickly remove old gasket material, carbon deposits, and rust with a minimum amount of effort.

20._____

21. A(n) _____ pad is another type of cleaning tool that can be used in an air drill.

21._____

22. To be safe, you should always adjust an air drill to the _____ speed when using a rotary brush.

22._____

Electric Tools

23. Bench grinders can be used for _____ operations.
    (A) grinding
    (B) polishing operations
    (C) cleaning
    (D) All of the above.

23. _____

24. A bench grinder usually has _____ wheel(s).

24. _____

25. List four safety rules to follow when using a bench grinder.

    _____

    _____

    _____

    _____

26. Drills use drill bits, or _____, to drill holes in metal and plastic parts.

26. _____

27. A drill bit is _____, or mounted, in a drill.

27. _____

28. A special key, called a(n) _____ key is used to tighten the drill bit in the drill.

28. _____

29. What are drill bits normally made of? _____

    _____

30. The size of a drill is an indication of the capacity of its _____.

30. _____

31. What is a *drill press?* _____

    _____

    _____

32. What rules should be followed when using a drill press? _____

    _____

    _____

    _____

    _____

    _____

33. Identify the parts of the drill press.

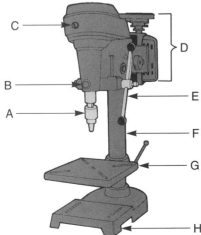

(A) _____

(B) _____

(C) _____

(D) _____

(E) _____

(F) _____

(G) _____

(H) _____

Hydraulic Tools

34. Hydraulic tools are powered by _____.   34._____

35. Where can you place a floor jack without causing vehicle damage? _____

_____

36. _____ are designed to hold transmissions during removal or installation.   36._____

37. Besides removing and installing engines, what are the other possible applications of a portable engine crane?

_____

38. A(n) _____ is used to install or remove gears, pulleys, bearings, seals, and   38._____
    other parts requiring a high pushing force.

Shop Equipment

39. An arbor press works like a(n) _____, however, it is all _____.   39._____

_____

40. It is not safe to work under a vehicle held up by only a jack. The vehicle   40._____
    must be supported on _____ during repairs.

41. A(n) _____ is used to hold an engine once it is removed from the vehicle   41._____
    for rebuilding or repair.

42. What is the purpose of a *cold solvent?* _____

_____

_____

43. A(n) _____ is used to remove heavy deposits of dirt, grease, and oil from the   43._____
    outside of large assemblies, such as engines, transmissions, and transaxles.

44. A(n) _____ can be used to cut, bend, and weld metal parts.   44._____
    (A) arc welder
    (B) soldering gun
    (C) oxyacetylene torch
    (D) hydraulic press

45. A(n) _____ is used to join wires.   45._____

46. Why should you always connect the battery charger leads to the battery before turning on the charger?

_____

_____

_____

47. A(n) _____ provides a portable source of light when working on a vehicle.   47._____

48. _____ are used to start a vehicle that has a dead battery.   48._____

49. A(n) _____ lets the technician easily roll under vehicles without getting   49._____
    dirty.

50. Describe the function of a roll-around cart. _____

_____

_____

51. _____ are placed over fenders, upper grille, or other body sections to pro-   51._____
    tect the paint or finish from nicks, scratches, and grease.

Chapter 5

The Auto Shop and Safety

Name: _____ Date: _____

Instructor: _____ Score: _____ Textbook pages 59–67

Objective: After studying this chapter, you will be able to list the important safety rules for the auto shop.

Auto Shop Layout

1. What does an auto shop's repair area normally include? _____

   _____

   _____

   _____

2. A(n) _____ is a small work area where a car can be parked for repairs.   2._____

3. List the rules that should be followed when using a lift._____

   _____

   _____

   _____

   _____

   _____

4. Describe how a vehicle should be pulled onto an alignment rack. _____

   _____

   _____

   _____

5. The _____ is part of the shop area used to store shop tools, small equip-   5._____
   ment, and supplies.

6. The _____ is used for seminars, demonstrations, and other technician   6._____
   training activities.

7. Why is it important to engage the safety catch before working under a vehicle?_____

   _____

   _____

   _____

Shop Safety

8. Most accidents which occur in the auto shop are the result of broken _____.

8. _____

9. What should you look for when thinking of safety in the auto shop?_____

_____

_____

_____

_____

_____

_____

_____

10. Why is it important from a safety point of view to remember that you are surrounded by other technicians in the shop?

_____

_____

_____

_____

_____

_____

_____

_____

11. Identify the potential dangers present around an automobile.

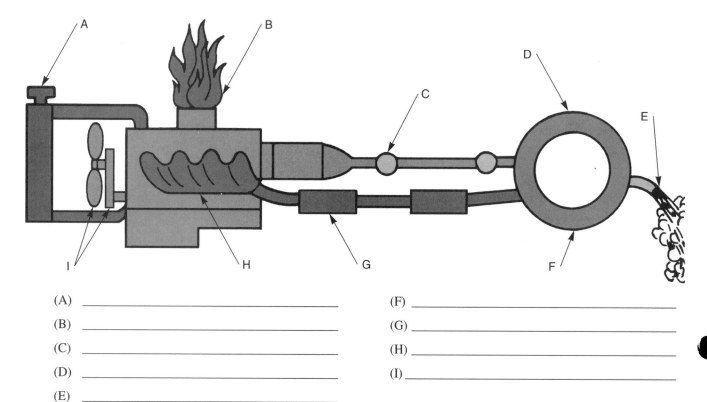

(A) _____   (F) _____

(B) _____   (G) _____

(C) _____   (H) _____

(D) _____   (I) _____

(E) _____

Types of Accidents

12. List six types of accidents that can occur in the auto shop._____

_____

_____

_____

_____

_____

13. What should you do if an accident or injury occurs in the auto shop? _____

_____

_____

_____

14. _____ is the most dangerous and underestimated flammable in an auto shop.   14._____

15. How should you carry an air bag? _____

_____

_____

_____

16. A(n) _____ should be worn when working around any airborne impurities.   16._____

17. The _____ on an electric power tool prevents current from accidentally passing through your body.   17._____

18. When lifting heavy objects in the shop, you should lift with your _____ and *not* your _____.   18._____

_____

19. Label the names of the protective gear you should wear when handling solvents and other caustic materials.

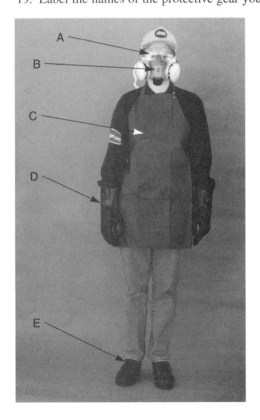

(A) _____

(B) _____

(C) _____

(D) _____

(E) _____

General Safety Rules

20. When should eye protection be worn in the auto shop? _____

_____

_____

_____

_____

_____

_____

21. Why shouldn't you carry shop tools in your pocket? _____

_____

_____

_____

_____

_____

22. _____ dust is a cancer-causing agent found in brake and clutch dust.   22. _____

23. Why must you respect running engines? _____

_____

_____

_____

_____

_____

_____

24. Never work under a car not supported by _____.   24. _____

25. The _____ on an automobile can turn on even with the ignition key off.   25. _____

26. When should the shop ventilation fan be turned on? _____

_____

_____

_____

_____

_____

_____

Chapter 6

Automotive Measurement and Math

Name: _____ Date: _____

Instructor: _____ Score: _____ Textbook pages 68–82

Objective: After studying this chapter, you will be able to understand basic math skills and how they are applied to automotive measurements.

Measuring Systems

1. The two measuring systems are the _____ system and the _____ system.

1._____

_____

2. Which measuring system is used by most countries?

2._____

3. Our customary system originated from sizes taken from parts of the _____.

3._____

4. The metric system uses a power of _____ for all basic units.

4._____

5. A measuring system _____ is needed when changing from one measuring system to another.

5._____

6. Fractions are only accurate to about _____ of an inch.

6._____

7. What are the equivalent metric values for the following?
   (A) 1″ = __?__ mm
   (B) 3.5″ = __?__ mm
   (C) 1 psi = __?__ kPa
   (D) 1/2 quart = __?__ liter
   (E) 55 mph = __?__ km/h

(A) _____

(B) _____

(C) _____

(D) _____

(E) _____

Measuring Tools

8. A(n) _____ or scale, is frequently used to make low-precision linear measurements.

8._____

9. A(n) _____ normally has lines or divisions representing millimeters.

9._____

10. A(n) _____ or tape rule, is sometimes needed for large distance measurements during body, suspension, and exhaust system repairs.

10._____

11. _____ look like a drafting compass, but have straight, sharply pointed tips.

11._____

31

12. Describe the applications of an *outside caliper.*_____

_____

_____

_____

_____

13. Explain how to use an *inside caliper.*_____

_____

_____

_____

_____

14. Label the parts of the vernier caliper illustrated below.

(A) _____

(B) _____

(C) _____

(D) _____

(E) _____

(F) _____

15. List three types of *mikes* used in automotive service and repair.

15._____

_____

_____

16. A(n) _____ micrometer is used for measuring external dimensions, diameters, or thicknesses.

16._____

17. Describe how to use an *inside micrometer.* _____

_____

_____

_____

_____

_____

_____

18. A(n) _____ gauge is used to measure internal part bores or openings.

18._____

19. When using a micrometer, you should _____.
    (A) grasp the frame in your palm and turn the thimble with your finger
    (B) check the accuracy after a long period of use
    (C) never drop or overtighten a micrometer
    (D) All of the above.

19. _____

20. List two basic types of feeler gauges. _____

_____

21. What are the automotive service applications of a *dial indicator?* _____

_____

_____

_____

22. Specifications are normally given in _____ when measuring rotation of a part or an angle formed by a part.

22. _____

23. What are the equivalent temperatures for the following?
    (A) 212°F = __?__ °C
    (B) 0°C = __?__ °F
    (C) 98.6°F = __?__ °C

    (A) _____

    (B) _____

    (C) _____

Other Measurements and Measuring Tools

24. What are the three general types of torque wrenches? _____

_____

25. Name some of the automotive service applications of a *pressure gauge.* _____

_____

_____

_____

_____

26. A(n) _____ gauge can be used to measure the vacuum in an engine's intake manifold.

26. _____

27. Identify the following types of torque wrenches.

A

B

C

(A) _____

(B) _____

(C) _____

Using Basic Mathematics

28. The result of an addition problem is called the _____.

28._____

29. Solve the following addition problem.

       654
       765
       644
    + 342

29._____

30. The amount that is left after subtracting is called the _____.

30._____

31. Solve the following subtraction problem.

       876
    − 645

31._____

32. The number being divided in a division problem is called the _____.

32._____

33. A car parts store pays $980.00 for ten U-joints. How much does each U-joint cost?

33._____

34. The result of a multiplication problem is called the _____.

34._____

35. A customer is told that the six fuel injectors in his/her car need to be replaced. Each injector costs $46.00. What will it cost to replace the six injectors?

35._____

36. Look at the following fraction. Which number is the denominator?

    $\frac{5}{8}$

36._____

37. Solve the following decimal problems.

    (A)   2.5
            765.7
            543.6
         + 298.0

    (B)   342.80
         × 542.54

    (A) _____

    (B) _____

    (C)   63.70
         − 42.90

    (D) 70.105 ÷ 35 =

    (C) _____

    (D) _____

Chapter 7

Using Service Information

Name: _____ Date: _____

Instructor: _____ Score: _____ Textbook pages 83–93

Objective: After completing this chapter, you will be able to properly use automotive service manuals and other sources of automotive service information.

Service Manuals

1. Explain the following types of service manuals.

    (A) Manufacturer's manual: _____

    _____

    _____

    (B) Specialized manual: _____

    _____

    _____

    (C) General repair manual: _____

    _____

    _____

2. The _____ section of a service manual helps you with a vehicle's identification, basic maintenance, lubrication, and other general subjects.

    2._____

3. Where is a *vehicle identification number (VIN)* normally located? _____

    _____

    _____

4. The _____ sections of a service manual cover the vehicle's major systems.

    4._____

5. What purpose(s) do *service illustrations* serve? _____

    _____

    _____

    _____

    _____

6. What do the following abbreviations stand for?

   (A) A/C: _____

   (B) A/T:_____

   (C) EGR:_____

   (D) GND: _____

   (E) IC:_____

   (F) MAP: _____

   (G) PCV:_____

   (H) WOT. _____

7. Name four basic types of diagnostic charts. _____

   _____

   _____

   _____

Service Publications

8. What information is normally contained in an *owner's manual?* _____

   _____

   _____

9. How is a *flat rate manual* used?_____

   _____

   _____

   _____

10. _____ help the technician stay up-to-date with recent technical changes, repair problems, and other service-related information.

    10._____

11. Name three methods for storing computerized service data._____

    _____

    _____

12. A(n) _____ is connected to the computer and used to access the _____ or other on-line service through a phone line.

    12._____

    _____

13. _____ allow a service facility to find service information that is *not* available in the manuals or electronic media they have on hand.

    13._____

14. List five types of information that may be available on a service facility computer system.

    _____

    _____

    _____

    _____

    _____

    _____

Chapter 8

Basic Electricity and Electronics

Name: _____ Date: _____

Instructor: _____ Score: _____ Textbook pages 94–107

Objective: After studying this chapter, you will be able to understand the basic principle related to automotive electricity and electronics.

Electricity

1. _____ is the movement of electrons from atom to atom.

1._____

2. What is an *insulator?* _____
_____
_____
_____

3. _____ is the flow of electrons through a conductor.

3._____

4. Explain the *electron theory of current.* _____
_____
_____
_____
_____

5. Define *voltage.* _____
_____
_____
_____

6. _____ is needed to control the flow of current in a circuit.

6._____

7. What does a *simple circuit* consist of?_____
_____
_____

8. A(n) _____ circuit has more than one load connected in a single electrical path.

8._____

9. A(n) _____ circuit has more than one electrical path.

9._____

10. Identify the parts and draw in the missing wires of the following frame ground circuit. Use arrows to show current flow.

B

C

(A) _____

(B) _____

(C) _____

A

11. What is *Ohm's law?* _____

_____

_____

_____

■ Using Ohm's law, solve the following problems.

12. If a circuit has 12 volts and 2 ohms, what is the current in this circuit?   12._____

13. If a circuit has 6 amps and 2 ohms, what is the voltage in this circuit?   13._____

14. If a circuit has 12 volts and .2 amps, what is the resistance in this circuit?   14._____

15. Name four automotive components that operate on the magnetic field principle. _____

_____

_____

_____

16. A(n) _____ allows an electric circuit to be turned on or off.   16._____

17. A(n) _____ circuit is an accidental low-resistance connection that results   17._____
in excessive current flow.

18. A(n) _____ protects a circuit against damage caused by a short circuit.   18._____

19. A(n) _____ is a small section of wire designed to burn in half when excess   19._____
current is present in the circuit.

Automotive Electronics

20. In electronic systems, the components are _____ and do *not* have _____   20. _____
parts.

_____

21. What is a *semiconductor?* _____

_____

_____

_____

_____

22. A(n) _____ only allows current to flow in one direction.   22._____

23. A transistor acts as a(n) _____ switch or current amplifier.   23._____

24. In your own words, how does a *transistor* operate? _____

_____

_____

_____

_____

_____

_____

25. _____ are used to absorb unwanted electrical pulses in a circuit.   25._____

26. Explain the difference between an integrated circuit and a printed circuit. _____

_____

_____

_____

_____

27. A(n) _____ is designed to use a very small current to control a very large   27._____
current.

Automotive Wiring

28. Define *primary wire.* _____

_____

_____

29. A(n) _____ wire is only used in a vehicle's ignition system for spark plug   29._____
or coil wires.

30. How much current does a starting motor normally draw?   30._____

31. _____ connect electrical components to the chassis or ground of the car.   31._____

32. _____ are multiwire terminals that connect several wires together.   32._____

33. What type of solder should be used when performing electrical repairs?   33._____

34. Identify the following wire terminals and connectors.

(A) _____

(B) _____

(C) _____

(D) _____

(E) _____

(F) _____

(G) _____

(H) _____

(I) _____

(J) _____

(K) _____

(L) _____

(M) _____

35. Explain how to use a *soldering gun.* _____

_____

_____

_____

_____

Basic Electrical Tests

36. What is a *jumper wire* used for? _____

_____

_____

_____

_____

37. How is a *test light* used? _____

_____

_____

_____

_____

38. A modern inductive _____ is clipped over the wire insulation to measure amps.

38. _____

39. To prevent damage, an ohmmeter must never be connected to a source of _____.

39. _____

40. What is another name for a *multimeter?*

40. _____

41. A(n) _____ displays voltage readings as a trace, or white line, on a display screen.

41. _____

42. How is a *scanner* used as a diagnostic tool in automotive repair? _____

_____

_____

_____

_____

_____

Chapter 9

Fasteners, Gaskets, Seals, and Sealants

Name: _____ Date: _____

Instructor: _____ Score: _____ Textbook pages 108–122

Objective: After studying this chapter, you will be able to select and use automotive fasteners properly.

Fasteners

1. Bolt _____ is measured across the outside diameter of the bolt threads.

2. Bolt _____ is measured from the bottom of the bolt head to the threaded end of the bolt.

3. What are the three basic types of threads? _____

_____

_____

4. With *right-hand threads*, the fastener must be turned _____ to tighten.

5. _____ refers to the amount of pull a fastener can withstand before breaking.

6. Define *bolt description.* _____

_____

_____

7. Identify the common types of nuts used in a vehicle.

A

B

C

D

E

F

G

H

I

J

1._____

2._____

4._____

5._____

(A) _____
(B) _____
(C) _____
(D) _____
(E) _____
(F) _____
(G) _____
(H) _____
(I) _____
(J) _____

41

8. A(n) _____ washer prevents the bolt or nut from digging into the part.

8. _____

9. A(n) _____ washer keeps a bolt or nut from loosening under stress and vibration.

9. _____

10. _____ screws are similar to bolts, are threaded their full length, and are relatively small.

10. _____

11. _____ screws are commonly used on plastic and sheet metal parts.

11. _____

12. Define *torque specifications.* _____

_____

_____

13. _____ is a bolt-tightening method that requires a specific bolt torque, followed by turning the bolt a specific number of degrees.

13. _____

14. Why is it important to use the proper *bolt tightening sequence* when torquing bolts on an engine?

_____

_____

_____

_____

15. Which of the following is *not* a basic rule to follow when using a torque wrench?
    (A) Pull only on the handle of the torque wrench.
    (B) Use swivel joints whenever possible.
    (C) Read the scale while looking straight down at it.
    (D) Tighten bolts and nuts in four steps.

15. _____

16. List three types of the tools that can be used to remove damaged fasteners. _____

_____

_____

Gaskets and Seals

17. What is the function of *gaskets* and *seals?* _____

_____

_____

_____

18. _____ sealers are used on permanent assemblies and for filling uneven surfaces.

18. _____

19. _____ sealers are for semipermanent assemblies.

19. _____

20. Name two types of *form-in-place gaskets.* _____

_____

_____

21. What purpose does a *seal* serve? _____

_____

_____

_____

Chapter 10

Vehicle Maintenance, Fluid Service, and Recycling

Name: _____ Date: _____

Instructor: _____ Score: _____ Textbook pages 123–139

Objective: After studying this chapter, you will be able to explain how to do the most common maintenance operations on a vehicle and describe the safety precautions associated with vehicle fluids.

Vehicle Maintenance

1. Define *vehicle maintenance.* _____

_____

_____

_____

_____

_____

_____

_____

2. A car's warranty may become void if _____ are used.
   (A) incompatible fluids
   (B) incorrect service procedures
   (C) improper intervals
   (D) All of the above.

2. _____

3. Should the engine be warm or cold when you check the oil level in an automotive engine?

3. _____

4. The oil level should be between _____ and _____ marks on the dipstick.

4. _____

   _____

5. Identify the fluid checkpoints in the following illustration.

(A) _____

(B) _____

(C) _____

(D) _____

(E) _____

(F) _____

6. What causes *oil foaming?* _____

_____

_____

_____

_____

_____   7. _____

7. Which of the following is *not* one of the procedures to follow when changing the oil in an automotive engine?
    (A) Warm up the engine.
    (B) Place a catch pan under the oil drain plug.
    (C) Wipe some clean oil on the O-ring and install the new filter.
    (D) Using an oil filter wrench, screw the new filter on.

8. _____

8. The gear selector should be in _____ when checking the fluid level in an automatic transmission or transaxle.

9. _____

9. When changing the fluid and filter in an automatic transmission, you should _____.
    (A) warm the engine and transmission
    (B) position the new pan gasket using an approved sealer
    (C) start all the pan bolts with your fingers
    (D) All of the above.

10. _____

10. When checking a manual transmission's fluid level, warm fluid should be even with the _____.

11. Where is the *fill plug* normally located on an automotive differential? _____

_____

_____

12. Why should engine *coolant* be changed periodically? _____

_____

_____   13. _____

13. Power steering fluid _____.
    (A) feels like transmission fluid
    (B) can be red in color
    (C) can be amber or clear in color
    (D) All of the above.

14. _____

14. The fluid level in an automotive master cylinder should be checked _____.
    (A) every other year
    (B) every other month
    (C) at least twice a year
    (D) None of the above.

15. _____

15. Some manual transmission clutches use a(n) _____ system to disengage the clutch.

16. How do you check the fluid level in an *automotive manual steering box?* _____

_____

_____   17. _____

17. The technician or owner can check an automobile's windshield washer fluid by looking through the side of the plastic _____.

18. _____

18. New cars use _____ batteries, which do not require an electrolyte check.

19. When should an *air filter* be replaced? _____

_____

_____ 20. _____

20. Modern fuel systems often use _____ fuel filters between the fuel tank and
the engine.

21. Define *grease job.* _____

_____

_____

_____ 22. _____

22. A(n) _____ is used to force chassis grease into small fittings.   23. _____

23. List three types of automotive body lubricant.   _____

_____

24. Define *service interval.* _____

_____

_____

_____

25. Identify the possible locations of grease fittings in the following illustration.

   (A) _____   (C) _____

   (B) _____   (D) _____

General Inspection and Problem Location

26. When checking problem areas of a vehicle, what areas should the inspection include?

_____

_____

_____ 27. _____

27. List some of the common causes of automotive fluid leaks.   28. _____

28. Automotive fluid leaks tend to flow _____ and to the _____ of the vehicle.   _____

29. Describe how a *stethoscope* can be used to pinpoint the source of internal part noises.

_____

_____

_____

_____

_____

Recycling and Disposal of Auto Shop Wastes

30. Name at least four types of hazardous wastes produced by automotive maintenance.

_____

_____

_____

_____

31. Repair and maintenance facilities that generate _____ of hazardous waste monthly must file a Uniform Hazardous Waste Manifest before removing the wastes.

31._____

32. EPA regulations state that no manifest is needed for used _____ or _____ batteries if they are sent for recycling.

32._____

_____

33. _____ of used motor oil can be refined into two and one-half quarts of high-quality motor oil.

33._____

34. _____ has been classified as a hazardous waste due to heavy metal and chlorinated solvents that it picks up circulating through cooling systems.

34._____

35. List at least three recyclable materials that are commonly removed from service during maintenance and repair of vehicles.

_____

_____

_____

_____

_____

_____

_____

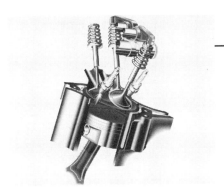

Engine Fundamentals

Name: _____ Date: _____

Instructor: _____ Score: _____ Textbook pages 141–157

Objective: After studying this chapter, you will be able to explain the basic operation and construction of a modern automotive engine.

Engine Operation

1. Why is an automotive engine called a *power plant?* _____
   _____
   _____

2. The _____ is the hollow area between the top of the piston and the bottom   2._____
   of the cylinder head.

3. How does an engine convert fuel into a useful form of energy? _____
   _____
   _____
   _____
   _____

4. Piston _____ is the distance the piston slides up or down from TDC/BDC.   4._____

5. Name the four strokes of an automotive engine. _____
   _____
   _____

6. The crankshaft must rotate _____ complete revolutions to complete the   6._____
   four-stroke cycle.

Engine Bottom End

7. The engine _____ forms the main body of the engine.   7._____

8. The _____ are large, round holes machined through the block from top to   8._____
   bottom.

9. Define *deck surface.* _____
   _____
   _____

10. _____ are coolant passages through the block that allow a solution of water and antifreeze to cool the cylinders.

10._____

11. The _____ are holes machined in the bottom of the block to hold the crankshaft.

11._____

12. _____ bolt to the bottom of the block and hold the crankshaft and main bearing inserts in place.

12._____

13. The _____ changes the up-and-down motion of the pistons into a rotating motion.

13._____

14. What is the purpose of crankshaft counterweights? _____

_____

_____

15. The _____ provides a mounting place for the camshaft drive mechanism, front damper, and fan belt pulleys.

15._____

16. What is the function of the *crankshaft flange?* _____

_____

_____

17. Engine main bearings are inserts that fit between the block main bore and crankshaft _____.

17._____

18. A main _____ limits how far the crankshaft can slide forward or rearward in the block.

18._____

19. What is *main bearing clearance?* _____

_____

_____

20. An engine's rear main _____ can be a one- or two-piece seal.

20._____

21. List three functions of an *engine flywheel.*

(1) _____

_____

(2) _____

_____

(3) _____

_____

22. The connecting rod transfers piston _____ and combustion pressure to the crankshaft _____.

22._____

_____

23. _____ clearance is the small space between the rod bearing and crankshaft journal.

23._____

24. Describe the purpose of an engine *piston.* _____

_____

_____

_____

_____

Name _____

25. Name six parts of an engine piston. _____

_____

_____

_____

_____

26. Identify the parts of the engine piston illustrated below.

(A) _____

(B) _____

(C) _____

(D) _____

27. Piston _____ must keep combustion pressure from entering the crankcase and must also keep _____ out of the combustion chamber.

27. _____

   _____

28. Name the two types of piston rings and explain their functions. _____

_____

_____

_____

_____

29. The split between the ends of a piston ring is called _____.

29. _____

Engine Top End

30. What is *engine top end?* _____

_____

_____

_____

31. _____ are small pockets formed in the cylinder heads where the fuel burns.

31. _____

32. The _____ route air or air and fuel into the combustion chambers.

32. _____

33. What components normally make up a *valve train?* _____

_____

_____

_____

_____

34. Describe the function of the engine *valve train.* _____

_____

_____

35. Where is an engine *camshaft* normally located? _____

_____

_____

36. A(n) _____ usually rides on the cam lobes and transfers motion to the rest   36. _____
    of the valve train.

37. _____ transfer motion between the lifters and the rocker arms.   37. _____

38. Which is usually larger, the intake valve or the exhaust valve?   38. _____

39. Define *valve face.* _____

_____

_____

_____

40. The valve _____ is a long shaft extending out of the valve head.   40. _____

41. Explain the function of *valve seals.* _____

_____

_____

_____

_____

42. On late-model engines, the fuel injectors and the throttle body mount on   42. _____
    the _____ manifold.

43. Explain the function of an *exhaust manifold.* _____

_____

_____

44. The _____ cover is a thin metal or plastic cover over the top of the cylinder   44. _____
    head.

Engine Front End

45. What is the function of an *engine front end?* _____

_____

_____

_____

46. A(n) _____ is needed to turn the camshaft at one-half engine speed.   46. _____

47. Explain the purpose of an automotive engine's *crank damper.* _____

_____

_____

_____

Chapter 12

Engine Design Classifications

Name: _____ Date: _____

Instructor: _____ Score: _____ Textbook pages 158–175

Objective: After studying this chapter, you will be able to describe and explain basic automotive engine designs and classifications.

Cylinder Arrangement

1. Define *cylinder arrangement.* _____
   _____
   _____
   _____
   _____

2. Name the four basic cylinder arrangements. _____
   _____
   _____

3. The cylinders of a(n) _____ engine are lined up in a single row.   3._____

4. A(n) _____ engine has only one bank of cylinders.   4._____

5. Cylinders of a(n) _____ engine lie flat on either side of the crankshaft. 5._____

Number of Cylinders

6. Normally, car and truck engines have either _____ cylinders.   6._____
   (A) 4, 5, or 6
   (B) 2, 4, or 6
   (C) 4, 6, or 8
   (D) 6, 10, or 12

7. A greater number of cylinders generally _____ (increases/decreases) engine   7._____
   smoothness and power.

8. A(n) _____ cylinder engine produces twice as many power strokes per   8._____
   crank revolution as a(n) _____ cylinder engine.   _____
   (A) 3, 8
   (B) 8, 4
   (C) 6, 10
   (D) None of the above.

Cylinder Numbering and Firing Order

9. Why do engine manufacturers number each engine cylinder? _____

_____

_____

10. Cylinder numbers are normally stamped on an engine's _____ rods or they   10. _____
    are sometimes cast into the _____.

11. Define *firing order.* _____

_____

_____

12. When is it important to know an engine's firing order? _____

_____

_____

_____

Cooling System Type

13. Explain how a *liquid cooling system* operates. _____

_____

_____

_____

14. _____ cooled engines are seldom used in passenger cars.   14. _____

15. An air cooling system circulates air over _____ on the cylinders to prevent   15. _____
    overheating.

Fuel Type

16. An engine can be classified by the type of _____ it burns.   16. _____

17. Name at least three types of fuels used in automotive engines.   17. _____

     _____

     _____

18. What are the two most common types of fuel for vehicles?   18. _____

     _____

Ignition Type

19. Explain the difference between a *spark* ignition engine and a *compression* ignition engine.

_____

_____

_____

_____

_____

Name _____

20. Gasoline engines use _____ ignition.

20._____

21. A diesel engine is a(n) _____ ignition engine.

21._____

Valve Location

22. A(n) _____ engine has both the intake and exhaust valves in the block.

22._____

23. A(n) _____ engine has both valves in the cylinder head.

23._____

24. Identify the parts of the valve-in-block arrangement illustrated below.

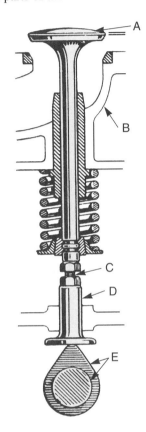

(A) _____

(B) _____

(C) _____

(D) _____

(E) _____

25. What type of valve-camshaft arrangement is illustrated below? Label the parts as indicated.

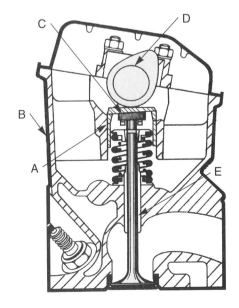

_____

(A) _____

(B) _____

(C) _____

(D) _____

(E) _____

26. What type of valve-camshaft arrangement is illustrated below? Label the parts as indicated.

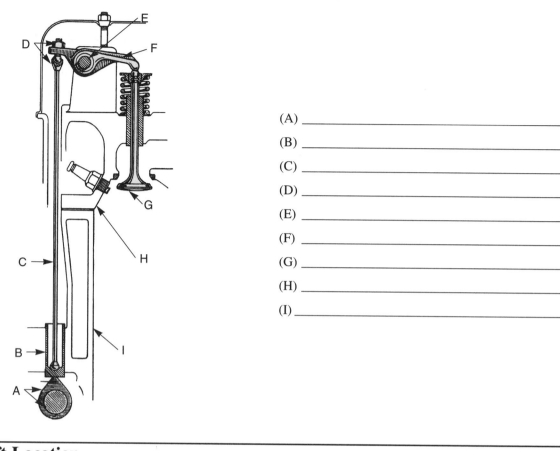

(A) _____

(B) _____

(C) _____

(D) _____

(E) _____

(F) _____

(G) _____

(H) _____

(I) _____

Camshaft Location

27. Name the two basic locations for the engine camshaft._____

_____

_____

_____

28. A(n) _____ engine uses pushrods to transfer motion to the rocker arms and valves and a(n) _____ engine has the camshaft in the cylinder head.

28._____

_____

29. A(n) _____ engine has only one camshaft per cylinder head.

29._____

30. The _____ arrangement is frequently used in engines equipped with four-valve combustion chambers.

30._____

Combustion Chamber Shape

31. List the three types of combustion chamber designs. _____

_____   _____

_____

32. The _____ combustion chamber has valve heads that are almost parallel to the top of the piston.

32._____

33. In a(n) _____ combustion chamber, the spark plug is located near the center.

33._____

Combustion Chamber Types

34. A(n) _____ combustion chamber is designed to cause the air-fuel mixture to swirl, or spin, as it enters from the _____ port.

34._____

_____

35. The extra valves in a(n) _____ combustion chamber increase flow in and out of the chamber.

35._____

36. A three-valve combustion chamber has ____ intake valve(s) and ____ exhaust valve(s).
    (A) 1, 2
    (B) 2, 1
    (C) 3, 3
    (D) None of the above.

36._____

_____

37. Briefly describe the operation of a *stratified charge combustion chamber.* _____

_____

_____

_____

_____

_____

_____

38. A(n) _____ combustion chamber has a single chamber fitted with an extra air valve.

38._____

Alternative Engines

▮ Fill in the blanks of the statements on the left with the correct term from the list on the right.

39. A(n) _____ engine uses a triangular rotor instead of conventional pistons.

(A) two-stroke engine

(B) two-stroke-cycle engine

39._____

40. A steam engine is a(n) _____ combustion engine.

(C) external

40._____

41. A(n) _____ only requires one revolution of the crankshaft for a complete power-producing cycle.

(D) Miller-cycle

41._____

42. A(n) _____ uses a mixture of fuel and oil.

(E) rotary

42._____

43. A(n) _____ is designed with a short compression stroke and a long power stroke to increase efficiency.

43._____

Typical Automotive Engines

44. Label the parts of the fuel-injected V-8 engine illustrated below. Indicate the type(s) of metal used in each part's construction.

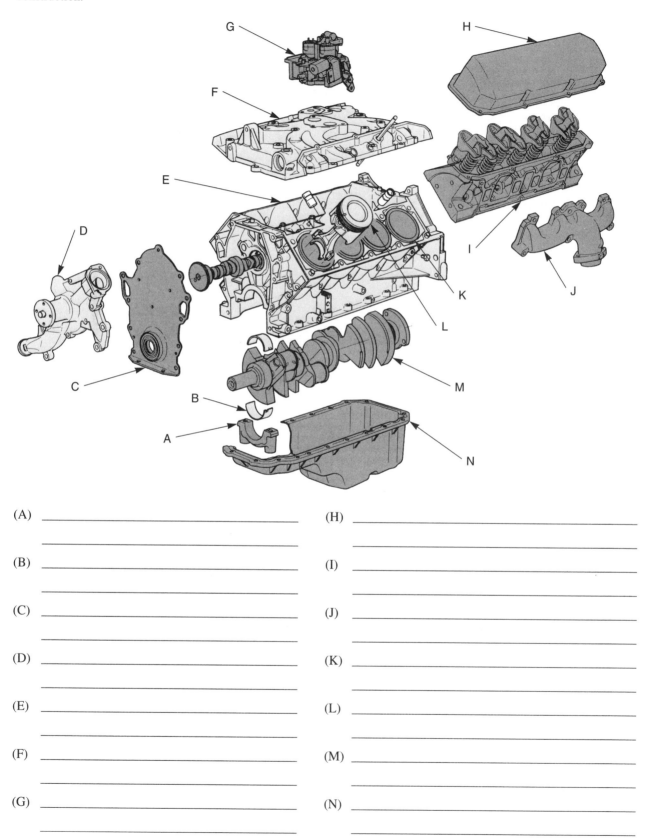

(A) _____

(B) _____

(C) _____

(D) _____

(E) _____

(F) _____

(G) _____

(H) _____

(I) _____

(J) _____

(K) _____

(L) _____

(M) _____

(N) _____

Chapter 13

Engine Top End Construction

Name: _____ Date: _____

Instructor: _____ Score: _____ Textbook pages 176–191

Objective: After studying this chapter, you will be able to understand the construction of an engine's top end and the parts that make up this engine section.

Cylinder Head Construction

1. Define *bare cylinder head.* _____
   _____
   _____

2. What is a bare cylinder head normally made of?   2. _____

3. The construction of a cylinder head varies with engine _____ and _____.   3. _____
   _____

4. A(n) _____ valve guide is part of the cylinder head casting.   4. _____

5. A(n) _____ valve guide is a separate sleeve forced into an oversize hole machined in the cylinder head.   5. _____

6. Name the two types of valve seats.   6. _____
   _____

7. Define *valve seat angle.* _____
   _____
   _____
   _____

8. The most common valve seat angles are _____.   8. _____
   (A) 25° and 35°
   (B) 45° and 35°
   (C) 45° and 30°
   (D) None of the above.

9. A(n) _____ angle is a 1/2°–1° difference between the valve seat face angle and the angle of the valve face.   9. _____

10. A diesel prechamber cup is pressed into the cylinder head and encloses the tips of the _____ and _____.   10. _____
    _____

11. Identify the two different types of valve guides and seats. Also, label the names of the related components.

(A) _____

(B) _____

(C) _____

(D) _____

(E) _____

(F) _____

(G) _____

(H) _____

(I) _____

(J) _____

Valve Train Construction

12. What is the function of an engine's *valve train?* _____

_____

_____

_____

13. Automotive engines commonly use _____ or _____ valves.

13. _____

_____

14. Define *valve face angle.* _____

_____

_____

_____

15. _____, hollow-stem valves are used when extra valve cooling action is needed.

15. _____

16. A stellite valve is often used in engines designed to burn _____ fuel.

16. _____

17. A(n) _____ valve seal is shaped like a cup and can be made of neoprene rubber or plastic.

17. _____

18. A(n) _____ valve seal is a small round seal that fits into an extra groove cut in the valve stem.

18. _____

19. A valve spring _____ is normally used with an O-ring type oil seal.

19. _____

20. Define *valve spring tension.* _____

_____

_____

_____

21. Valve spring _____ is the length of the valve spring when removed from the engine.

21._____

22. Define *valve spring open length.* _____

_____

_____

_____

_____

_____

_____

23. Valve spring _____ is the length of the valve spring when installed on the engine with the valve closed.

23._____

24. Valve _____ occurs when the valve fails to close entirely at high rpms because the spring is too weak.

24._____

25. A valve spring _____ is a very thin, accurately machined washer used to increase spring tension.

25._____

26. What is the function of *valve retainers* and *keepers?* _____

_____

_____

_____

_____

27. A valve spring _____ is a cup-shaped washer installed between the cylinder head and the bottom of the valve spring.

27._____

28. Explain the purpose of *valve rotators.* _____

_____

_____

_____

_____

_____

29. A valve _____ helps prevent stem and rocker arm wear.

29._____

30. What is the function of an engine's *camshaft?* _____

_____

_____

_____

_____

_____

31. Cam lobe shape can be used to control _____.
    (A) when each valve opens in relation to piston position
    (B) how long each valve stays open
    (C) how far each valve opens
    (D) All of the above.

31._____

32. Identify the top end components of the dual overhead cam engine illustrated below.

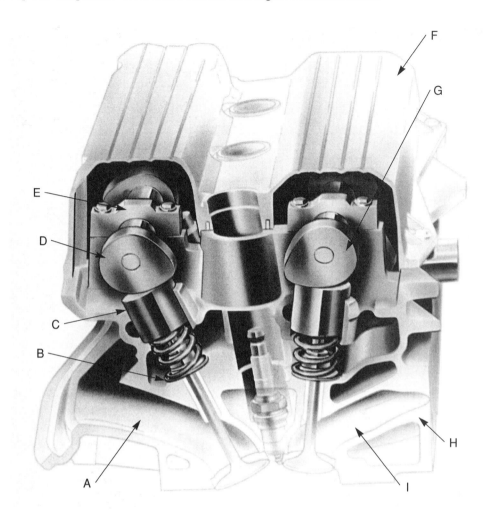

(A) _____   (F) _____

(B) _____   (G) _____

(C) _____   (H) _____

(D) _____   (I) _____

(E) _____

33. Camshaft _____ is how far the valves open.   33._____

34. Camshaft _____ determines how long the valve stays open.   34._____

35. Define *valve timing*. _____

_____

_____

_____

_____

_____

36. _____ is the time when both the intake and exhaust valves in the same   36._____
    cylinder are open.

37. Describe the purpose of a *camshaft thrust plate.* _____

_____

_____

_____

_____

38. The camshaft journals ride in the cam _____.   38. _____

39. Explain the term *cam housing.* _____

_____

_____

_____

40. A cam cover serves the same purpose as a(n) _____ cover on an overhead   40. _____
    valve engine.

41. Valve _____ ride on the camshaft lobes and transfer motion to the other   41. _____
    parts of the valve train.

42. _____ lifters are common because they operate quietly by maintaining zero   42. _____
    valve clearance.

43. _____ lifters are not self-adjusting and require periodic setting.   43. _____

44. A roller lifter can be either mechanical or _____.   44. _____

45. How is valve clearance normally adjusted on engine's equipped with OHC followers? _____

_____

_____

_____

_____

46. Identify the parts of the following hydraulic lifter illustrated below.

(A) _____

(B) _____

(C) _____

(D) _____

(E) _____

(F) _____

(G) _____

(H) _____

(I) _____

(J) _____

(K) _____

47. _____ are used in cam-in-block engines to transfer motion from the lifters to the rocker arms.

47._____

48. Describe the function of *rocker arms.* _____

_____

_____

_____

_____

49. Rocker arms are usually made of either _____ or _____.

49._____

_____

50. _____ rocker arms are used to change the valve train clearance.

50._____

Intake Manifold Construction

51. An intake manifold holds the _____ and has passages (runners) going to each cylinder head port.

51._____

52. What is an *intake manifold* normally made of? _____

_____

_____

_____

_____

_____

53. _____ are internal passages formed in the intake manifold to carry either the air-fuel mixture or air to the cylinder head ports.

53._____

54. Define *flame arrester.* _____

_____

_____

_____

_____

_____

55. A(n) _____ system has two sets of intake runners controlled by butterfly valves to aid engine efficiency and performance.

55._____

Exhaust Manifold Construction

56. Describe the function of an *exhaust manifold.* _____

_____

_____

_____

_____

57. A few high-performance or sports car engines use lightweight, free-flowing steel tubing exhaust manifolds called _____.

57._____

Chapter 14

Engine Bottom End Construction

Name: _____ Date: _____

Instructor: _____ Score: _____ Textbook pages 192–208

Objective: After studying this chapter, you will be able to describe and explain the construction of an engine's bottom end and its related parts.

Cylinder Block Construction

1. What are engine cylinder blocks normally made of?

2. A(n) _____ cylinder block dissipates heat better than a(n) _____ block.

3. Many vehicles use _____ blocks to reduce weight and increase fuel economy.

4. A(n) _____ is relatively thin and is not exposed to engine coolant.

5. A(n) _____ is exposed to engine coolant and must withstand combustion pressure and heat without the added support of the cylinder block.

6. Define *line boring.* _____

_____

_____

_____

_____

_____

_____

7. A(n) _____ main block only uses two cap screws to secure each main bearing cap to the _____.

8. _____ mains are used on high-performance engines.

1. _____

2. _____

_____

3. _____

4. _____

5. _____

7. _____

_____

8. _____

Piston Construction

9. Define *piston diameter.* _____

_____

_____

10. What is meant by the term *pinhole diameter?* _____

_____

_____

11. Define *ring groove width.* _____

_____

_____

12. A(n) _____ piston is machined slightly out-of-round when viewed from   12. _____
the top.

13. What is the purpose of *piston taper?* _____

_____

_____

14. _____ generally refers to the contour of the piston head.   14. _____

15. The head of a(n) _____ piston is almost flat and is parallel with the block's   15. _____
deck surface.

16. Define *valve reliefs.* _____

_____

_____

_____

17. A(n) _____ provides clearance between the piston and the crankshaft   17. _____
counterweights.

18. A(n) _____ piston is a two-piece design controlled by engine oil pressure.   18. _____

19. Identify the following piston dimensions.

(A) _____

(B) _____

(C) _____

(D) _____

(E) _____

(F) _____

(G) _____

(H) _____

Piston Ring Construction

20. Automotive pistons normally use _____ rings; _____, compression rings   20. _____
and _____ oil ring.

_____

_____

21. The _____ prevent pressure leakage into the crankcase and wipe oil from the cylinder walls.

21._____

22. Explain *ring seating.* _____

_____

_____

_____

23. Name the two basic oil ring designs.

23._____

_____

24. What is the function of a piston's *oil ring?* _____

_____

_____

_____

25. The piston _____ is the distance from the top of the ring to the bottom of the ring.

25._____

26. Piston ring _____ is the distance from the face of the ring to its inner wall.

26._____

27. Piston _____ is the distance between the ends of the ring when installed in the cylinder.

27._____

28. Hard ring coatings, such as _____, are used in new or freshly machined cylinders that are perfectly round.

28._____

29. When are *soft ring coatings* desirable? _____

_____

_____

Piston Pin Construction

30. What are piston pins normally made of?

30._____

31. _____ is a heating and cooling process that increases the wear resistance of the piston pin.

31._____

32. A(n) _____ piston pin is secured by snap rings and is free to rotate in both the rod and piston.

32._____

33. A press-fit piston pin is forced tightly into the connecting rod's _____.

33._____

34. What is the purpose of *piston pin offset?*_____

_____

35. A(n) _____ on the head of the piston is frequently used to indicate piston pin offset and the front of the piston.

35._____

Connecting Rod Construction

36. Most connecting rods are made of _____.

36._____

37. Explain *low-inertia parts.* _____

_____

_____

38. What is the purpose of a hole machined through the entire length of a drilled connecting rod?

_____

_____

39. _____ are used to ensure proper location of each connecting rod in the engine.

39._____

40. Define *powdered metal forging.* _____

_____

_____

_____

Crankshaft Construction

41. What are engine crankshafts usually made of?

41._____

42. Turbocharged or diesel engines are normally equipped with crankshafts made of _____.

42._____

43. Oil enters the crankshaft at the _____ and passes through holes in the main bearing journals.

43._____

44. With a V-type engine, _____ connecting rods bolt to each rod journal.

44._____

45. A(n) _____ crankshaft has weights formed opposite every crankpin.

45._____

46. A(n) _____ crankshaft only has weights formed on the center areas.

46._____

Engine Bearing Construction

47. Identify the three basic types of engine bearings.

(A) _____

(B) _____

(C) _____

48. _____ is the bearing's ability to withstand pounding and crushing during engine operation.

48._____

49. _____ is the bearing's ability to adjust to imperfections in the journal surface.

49._____

50. _____ refers to the bearing's ability to absorb dirt, metal, or other hard particles.

50._____

51. _____ is the bearing's ability to withstand being acted on by acids, water, and other impurities in the engine oil.

51._____

52. Define *bearing crush.* _____

_____

_____

_____

_____

_____

53. _____ is used on split-type engine bearings to hold the bearing in place during assembly.

53. _____

54. A(n) _____ bearing has the original dimensions specified by the engine manufacturer for a new, unworn, or unmachined crankshaft.

54. _____

55. An undersize bearing is designed to be used on a crankshaft journal that has been machined to a(n) _____ diameter.

55. _____

56. Connecting rod and main bearings are available in undersizes of _____.
    (A) 0.125″, 0.135″, 0.145″, 0.155″
    (B) 0.010″, 0.020″, 0.030″, 0.040″
    (C) 0.225″, 0.235″, 0.245″, 0.255″
    (D) 1.010″, 1.020″, 1.030″, 1.040″

56. _____

57. _____ or dowels position split bearings in their bores.

57. _____

58. Identify the following bottom end components.

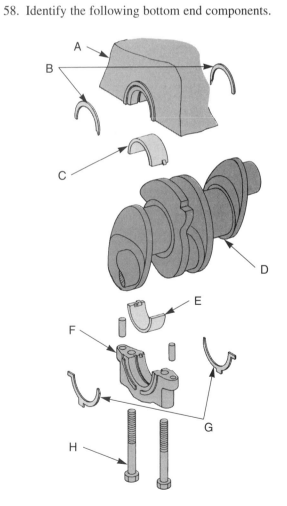

(A) _____

(B) _____

(C) _____

(D) _____

(E) _____

(F) _____

(G) _____

(H) _____

59. How are engine bearings lubricated? _____

_____

_____

_____

_____

_____

_____

60. What is the function of a *main thrust bearing?* _____

_____

_____

_____

_____

Rear Main Bearing Oil Seal Construction

61. Describe the purpose of a *rear main bearing oil seal.* _____

_____

_____

_____

_____

_____

_____

62. Name three types of rear main bearing oil seals.   62. _____

_____

_____

63. A(n) _____ rear oil seal is simply a woven rope filled with graphite.   63. _____

Additional Exercises

64. _____ means that some engine parts are selected and installed in a certain position to improve the fit or clearance between parts.   64. _____

65. _____ are used in some engines to cancel the vibrating forces produced by crankshaft, piston, and rod movement.   65. _____

Chapter 15

Engine Front End Construction

Name: _____ Date: _____

Instructor: _____ Score: _____ Textbook pages 209–215

Objective: After studying this chapter, you will be able to explain the construction and operation of an automotive engine's front end.

Vibration Damper Construction

1. Define *harmonic vibration*. _____

   _____

   _____

   _____

2. What can happen if harmonic vibration is *not* controlled in an automotive engine? _____

   _____

   _____

   _____

   _____

3. What device(s) controls harmonic vibration?　　　　　3._____

4. The crankshaft _____ is often part of the harmonic balancer.　　　　　5._____

5. Identify the parts of the vibration damper illustrated below.

(A) _____

(B) _____

(C) _____

(D) _____

Camshaft Drive Construction

6. What is the function of the *camshaft drive?* _____

_____

_____

_____

_____

7. A(n) _____ cam drive is commonly used for heavy-duty applications, such   7._____
   as taxicabs or trucks.

8. Define *cam drive timing marks.* _____

_____

_____

_____

_____

9. Identify the following type of camshaft drive and label its components.

(A) _____

(B) _____

(C) _____

(D) _____

(E) _____

(F) _____

(G) _____

(H) _____

10. What is the most common type of camshaft drive arrangement used on   10._____
    cam-in-block engines?

11. _____ is when the timing chain flaps back and forth because of excessive   11._____
    slack in the chain.

12. A(n) _____ may be used to take up the slack in the chain as it and the   12._____
    sprockets wear.

13. What is the purpose of an *auxiliary chain?* _____

_____

_____

_____

_____

14. Describe the function of an *engine front cover.* _____

_____

_____

_____

_____

_____

15. A(n) _____ prevents oil leakage between the crankshaft and cover.   15._____

16. What is an engine front cover normally made of?   16._____

17. Explain the function of an engine's *front end oil slinger.* _____

_____

_____

_____

_____

_____

_____

18. What basic components make up a *timing belt drive mechanism?* _____

_____

_____

_____

19. A(n) _____ provides a very smooth and accurate method of turning the camshaft.   19._____

20. A(n) _____ is a spring-loaded wheel that keeps the timing belt firmly seated on its sprockets.   20._____

21. A timing belt may also be used to drive the _____.   21._____
    (A) diesel injection pump
    (B) ignition distributor
    (C) oil pump
    (D) All of the above.

22. Describe the function of a *timing belt cover.* _____

_____

_____

_____

_____

_____

23. What is a timing belt cover normally made of?   23._____

24. *True* or *False?* A timing belt cover serves the same function as an engine front cover.   24._____

25. Identify the parts that are installed on the front of this OHC engine.

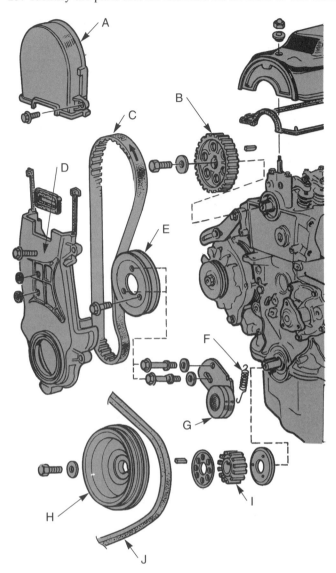

(A) _____

(B) _____

(C) _____

(D) _____

(E) _____

(F) _____

(G) _____

(H) _____

(I) _____

(J) _____

Engine Size and Performance Measurements

Name: _____ Date: _____

Instructor: _____ Score: _____ Textbook pages 216–223

Objective: After studying this chapter, you will be able to explain the most important measurements of engine size and performance.

Engine Size Measurement

1. How is *engine size* determined? _____
   _____
   _____
   _____
   _____

2. Define *cylinder bore*. _____
   _____
   _____

3. How is cylinder bore measured? _____
   _____
   _____

4. Cylinder bores vary in size from _____ to _____.   4. _____
                                                                  _____

5. Define *piston stroke*. _____
   _____
   _____
   _____

6. The amount of offset built into the _____ controls the piston stroke.   6. _____

7. If an engine's specs for bore and stroke are given as 4.00″ × 3.00″, what does it mean?
   _____
   _____
   _____
   _____

8. Generally, a larger _____ and a longer stroke make an engine more powerful.

8._____

9. Piston displacement is the volume the piston displaces as it travels from _____ to _____.

9._____

_____

10. A large cylinder diameter and large piston stroke produce a large piston _____.

10._____

11. If an engine has a bore of 3″ and a stroke of 4″, what is its piston displacement?

11._____

12. Engine displacement is the volume displaced by all the _____ in an engine.

12._____

13. If one piston displaces 30 cu. in. and the engine has four cylinders, what is the engine's displacement?

13._____

14. Engine displacement is usually matched to the _____ of the car.

14._____

15. Identify the bore and stroke areas of measurement indicated below.

(A) _____

(B) _____

(C) _____

(D) _____

(E) _____

(F) _____

Force, Work, and Power

16. Define *force*. _____

_____

_____

_____

17. If you use a hoist to lift a 600 lb. engine 5′ in the air, how much work has been done?

17._____

18. Define *power*. _____

_____

_____

_____

19. The metric unit for power is the _____.

19._____

20. How much power is needed for an engine to move a 4000 lb. car 2000′ in one minute?

20._____

21. Define *compression ratio.* _____

_____

_____

_____

_____

22. In a compression ignition engine, the BDC cylinder volume is _____ times   22._____
    as large as the TDC cylinder volume.
      (A) four
      (B) twelve
      (C) seventeen
      (D) fifty

23. Define *compression pressure.*_____

_____

_____

_____

24. Compression pressure is normally measured in _____.   24._____
      (A) Kilopascals
      (B) pounds per square inch
      (C) newtons
      (D) Both A and B.

25. What is the normal compression pressure for a modern automotive   25._____
    gasoline engine?

26. A(n) _____ is used to measure engine compression pressure.   26._____

27. What are possible indications that an engine's compression pressure is low? _____

_____

_____

_____

28. Define *engine torque.* _____

_____

_____

_____

29. Engine torque specifications are given in a(n) _____.   29._____

Horsepower

30. What is *engine horsepower?* _____

_____

_____

31. About how much horsepower would be needed for a small engine to lift   31._____
    1000 lb. a distance of 500′ in one minute?

32. _____ measures the usable power at the engine crankshaft.   32._____

33. A(n) _____ is used to measure the brake horsepower of modern car engines.

33. _____

34. A(n) _____ measures the horsepower delivered to the drive wheels.

34. _____

35. Define *indicated horsepower.* _____

_____

_____

_____

36. Explain *frictional horsepower.* _____

_____

_____

_____

37. _____ horsepower is the maximum power developed when an engine is loaded by all accessories.

37. _____

38. _____ horsepower is the engine power available with only basic accessories installed.

38. _____

39. _____ horsepower is simply a general rating of engine size.

39. _____

Engine Efficiency

40. What is meant by *engine efficiency?* _____ _____

_____

_____

_____

_____

_____

_____

41. Modern piston engines are only about _____ percent efficient.

41. _____

42. _____ is the ratio of air drawn into the cylinder and the maximum possible amount of air that could enter the cylinder.

42. _____

43. Define *mechanical efficiency.* _____

_____

_____

_____

_____

_____

44. Normally, _____ of an engine's power is lost to friction.
    (A) 10%–15%
    (B) 20%–30%
    (C) 35%–40%
    (D) 40%–55%

44. _____

45. Thermal efficiency measures the amount of _____ converted into crankshaft rotation.

45. _____

46. A gallon of gasoline has about _____ Btu (British thermal units) of heat energy.

46. _____

Chapter 17

Computer System Fundamentals

Name: _____ Date: _____

Instructor: _____ Score: _____ Textbook pages 225–249

Objective: After studying this chapter, you will be able to describe and explain the basic operating principles and components of modern computer systems.

Cybernetics

1. Define *cybernetics.* _____
_____
_____
_____

2. The human nervous system uses _____ signals to control the body.   2._____

3. The nerve cells in the tip of your finger are comparable to a(n) _____ in a computer system.   3._____

4. The brain makes decisions much like computer _____ produce logical outputs.   4._____

5. Name three reasons why computers are used in modern vehicles.

   (1) _____
   _____

   (2) _____
   _____

   (3) _____
   _____

Digital Electronics

6. Define *digital electronics.* _____
_____
_____
_____

7. What two numbers are used in the binary numbering system?   7._____

8. In a computer's binary system, what number represents *off?*   8._____

9. Define *gate*. _____

_____ _____

_____

_____

10. A(n) _____ gate will reverse its input.   10._____

11. A(n) _____ gate requires voltage (1) at both inputs to produce a voltage (1)   11._____
    at the output.

12. A NAND gate's output is opposite that of a(n) _____ gate.   12._____

13. A(n)_____ gate will produce an output if either output is energized.   13._____

14. A(n) _____ is a chart that shows what the output of a gate will be with dif-   14._____
    ferent inputs.

15. Why are gates often called *logic devices?* _____

_____

_____

_____

Integrated Circuits

16. What is an *integrated circuit?* _____

_____

_____

_____

Computer Signals

17. Define *computer signal.* _____

_____

_____

_____

18. _____ signals are on-off signals, like those produced by a rapidly flipping   18._____
    switch.

19. A(n) _____ signal gradually changes in strength.   19._____

20. Define *pulse width.* _____

_____

_____

_____

21. What is meant by *signal amplitude?* _____

_____

_____

22. _____ is the percentage of *on* time compared to total cycle time.   22._____

Computer System Operation

23. Describe and explain the three stages of computer system operation.

(1) _____

_____

_____

_____

(2) _____

_____

_____

_____

(3) _____

_____

_____

_____

24. A computer system block diagram is a simple service manual drawing that shows how the _____ interact.
    (A) sensors, actuators, and computer
    (B) computer and wiring harness
    (C) actuators and brake system
    (D) All of the above.

24. _____

Sensors

25. Most vehicle sensors, or transducers, change a(n) _____ condition into an electrical signal.

25. _____

26. What is an *active sensor?*_____

_____

_____

27. How does a *passive sensor* receive voltage? _____

_____

_____

▨ Match the following sensor type to the particular automotive sensor.

28. Switching sensor

29. Magnetic sensor

30. Piezoelectric sensor

31. Optical sensor

32. Direction sensor

(A) Steering system sensor

(B) Knock sensor

(C) Speed sensor

(D) Transmission sensor

(E) Crankshaft sensor

(F) Distributor sensor

28. _____

29. _____

30. _____

31. _____

32. _____

33. _____ sensors measure the amount of oxygen in the engine's exhaust gases before and after the catalytic converter.

33. _____

34. A(n) _____ sensor measures outside air pressure in relation to vacuum inside the engine intake manifold.

34._____

35. A(n) _____ sensor measures the outside air pressure around the engine.

35._____

36. A(n) _____ sensor measures the opening angle of the throttle valves to detect how much power is requested by the driver.

36._____

37. A(n) _____ sensor measures engine rpm for ignition system operation.

37._____

38. A(n) _____ sensor measures crankshaft position, rotation, and speed.

38._____

39. _____ involves using the computer itself instead of designated sensors to monitor component and circuit operation.

39._____

Computers

40. Define *computer.*_____

_____

_____

_____

_____

_____

41. Which of the following is another name for an automotive computer?
    (A) Central processing unit (CPU)
    (B) Electronic control unit (ECU)
    (C) Engine control module (ECM)
    (D) All of the above.

41._____

42. A(n) _____ control module is used to monitor and control the engine, transmission, and other systems.
    (A) powertrain
    (B) vehicle
    (C) engine
    (D) None of the above.

42._____

43. A high-power control module is a computer used to _____ from a few sensors and the main computer.
    (A) control or increase current flow
    (B) process output signals
    (C) Both A and B.
    (D) Neither A nor B.

43._____

44. The _____ is a small computer that uses inputs to operate a digital dash display.

44._____

45. The suspension system module uses vehicle _____ to control ride stiffness or shock absorber action.
    (A) speed
    (B) steering sensor inputs
    (C) suspension
    (D) All of the above.

45._____

46. Name three possible locations for an automotive computer._____

_____

_____

_____

Name _____

■ Match the computer parts listed on the right to the statement on the left that best describes it.

47. Serves as a temporary storage area for data.

48. Metal or plastic enclosure that protects electronic components from induced currents and physical damage.

49. Converts battery and other voltages into lower voltages.

50. Integrated circuit that stores data for the microprocessor.

51. Increases strength of signals from input devices.

52. Fiber board with flat metal conductors printed on its surface that connects and holds components.

53. Alter signals for use by the computer and its actuators.

54. Integrated circuit that produces a constant pulse rate to coordinate computer operations.

55. Multipin terminal that attaches to the vehicle's wiring harness.

56. Power transistor that steps up current or provides a ground path to operate actuators or modules.

57. Integrated circuit that makes decisions or calculations for the computer.

(A) Voltage regulator

(B) Amplifiers

(C) Conditioners

(D) Buffer

(E) Microprocessor

(F) Memory

(G) Clock

(H) Output driver

(I) Circuit board

(J) Harness connector

(K) Computer housing

47. _____

48. _____

49. _____

50. _____

51. _____

52. _____

53. _____

54. _____

55. _____

56. _____

57. _____

58. What type of computer memory can be altered by the technician in the field?

58. _____

59. _____ is a memory chip that allows the computer to have an adaptive strategy.

59. _____

60. The information stored in _____ allows the computer to maintain normal vehicle performance with abnormal inputs from sensors.

60. _____

61. Define *computer network*. _____

_____

_____

_____

_____

_____

62. What is meant by *multiplexing?* _____

_____

_____

_____

_____

_____

Actuators

63. What is the function of *actuators?*_____

_____

_____

_____

64. Where can *actuators* be located in an automotive computer system?_____

_____

_____

_____

65. When the computer turns on an actuator, it normally provides the device with a(n) _____.

65._____

66. A(n) _____ is often used as an actuator when a high-current load must be controlled by the computer.

66._____

67. An idle speed motor is normally a reversible _____ motor.

67._____

68. The fuel _____ uses a solenoid valve to control fuel flow.

68._____

69. The fuel _____ uses an electric motor that drives a pumping mechanism to force fuel out of the tank and to the engine.

69._____

70. The _____ solenoid controls airflow into the engine to help control idle speed.

70._____

71. _____ solenoids open and close small ports to control exhaust gas flow back into engine to control emissions.

71._____

72. Identify the operations and components in the following computer-controlled door lock circuit.

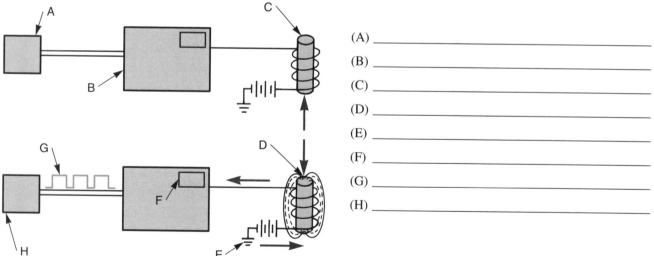

(A) _____

(B) _____

(C) _____

(D) _____

(E) _____

(F) _____

(G) _____

(H) _____

Chapter 18

On-Board Diagnostics and Scan Tools

Name: _____ Date: _____

Instructor: _____ Score: _____ Textbook pages 250–271

Objective: After studying this chapter, you will have a basic understanding of automotive on-board computer self-diagnostic capabilities and scan tools applications.

On-Board Diagnostic Systems

1. An automotive computer system scans its input and output circuits to detect an incorrect _____.
    (A) current
    (B) voltage
    (C) resistance
    (D) All of the above.

1._____

2. A vehicle's engine _____ module can detect engine misfiring and air-fuel mixture problems.

2._____

3. Explain why on-board diagnostics is considered a time-saver when servicing automotive computer systems.

_____

_____

_____

_____

_____

_____

_____

_____

4. What does *OBD I* stand for? _____

_____

_____

5. OBD II is designed to _____.
    (A) keep the vehicle running efficiently for at least 100,000 miles
    (B) detect part deterioration
    (C) monitor the condition of hardware that affects emissions
    (D) All of the above.

5._____

6. OBD II systems can produce over _____ engine performance-related trouble codes.

6._____

7. Define *malfunction indicator light*. _____

_____

_____

_____

8. An MIL is flashing continuously in an OBD II equipped vehicle. Technician A says this problem is not critical but should be repaired. Technician B says this flashing MIL means the trouble could damage the catalytic converter and is, therefore, considered critical. Who is right?
    (A) A only.
    (B) B only.
    (C) Both A and B.
    (D) Neither A nor B.

8. _____

9. Explain *trouble code conversion*. _____

_____

_____

_____

10. _____ are digital signals produced and stored by the computer when an operating parameter is exceeded.

10. _____

11. A(n) _____ is an acceptable minimum and maximum value.

11. _____

12. _____ percent of all engine performance problems are caused by faults in the computer or one of its sensors.
    (A) Fifteen
    (B) Twenty
    (C) Sixty
    (D) Eighty

12. _____

13. Identify the common problems that can affect an engine's performance and computer operation.

(A) _____   (F) _____

(B) _____   (G) _____

(C) _____   (H) _____

(D) _____   (I) _____

(E) _____

Scanning Computer Problems

14. What is a *scan tool?* _____

_____

_____

_____

_____

15. A(n) _____ tool is another name for a scan tool.

15. _____

16. What are *scan tool program cartridges?* _____

_____

_____

_____

17. A(n) _____ cartridge provides data for one or more vehicle manufacturers.

17. _____

18. Describe the function of a *data link connector.* _____

_____

_____

_____

_____

_____

19. Name at least three of the most common locations for the data link connector.

_____

_____

_____

20. The standardized DLC connector used with OBD II systems has _____ pins.

20. _____

    (A) four

    (B) sixteen

    (C) eighteen

    (D) None of the above.

21. Sometimes it is necessary to use a(n) _____ in order for the scan tool connector to communicate with different pin configurations.

21. _____

22. What are *scan tool prompts?* What purpose do they serve? _____

_____

_____

_____

23. Why does a scan tool require *VIN* information? _____

_____

_____

24. Why should you always correct the cause of the *lowest number* diagnostic trouble code first?

_____

_____

_____

_____

25. OBD II requires all auto manufacturers to use a set of standardized _____   25. _____
    trouble codes.

26. What does the *letter* in all OBD II trouble codes represent? _____

_____

_____

_____

27. What does the *first digit* of an OBD II trouble code indicate? _____

_____

_____

_____

28. The *second number* in the OBD II code indicates the _____ of the system   28. _____
    where the fault is located.

29. What do the *last two digits* of an OBD II trouble code indicate? _____

_____

_____

_____

30. Define *hard failure.* _____

_____

_____

31. Define *soft failure.* _____

_____

_____

▪ Match the descriptions on the left with the types of computer system failures on the right.

32. The circuit or component has a fixed value, no   (A) High-input failure   32. _____
    output, or an output that is out of specifications.
                                                            (B) General circuit failure
33. Produces a voltage, current, or signal frequency   33. _____
    below normal operating parameters.   (C) Improper range/performance
                                                               failure
34. Results when the signal reaching the on-board   34. _____
    computer has more voltage, more current, or a   (D) Low-input failure
    higher frequency than normal.

35. Occurs when a sensor or actuator is producing   35. _____
    values slightly lower or higher than normal.

Name _____

36. What are *diagnostic scan values?* _____

_____

_____

_____

_____

37. How is the computer's *engine-off/key-on diagnostics mode* activated?_____

_____

_____

_____

_____

38. What should be done if you work in the engine-off/key-on diagnostic mode for over 30 minutes?

_____

_____

_____

_____

39. List the procedures used to perform a wiggle test. _____

_____

_____

_____

_____

_____

_____

40. What is the function of engine-on/key-on diagnostics?_____

_____

_____

_____

_____

41. A(n) _____ test involves activating various switches while using a scan tool.   41._____

Energizing OBD I Systems without a Scan Tool

42. List at least two methods of activating on-board diagnostics of a vehicle using an OBD I system without using a scan tool.

_____

_____

_____

_____

_____

_____

43. List five different ways to read computer trouble codes without the use of a scan tool.

   (1) _____

   _____

   (2) _____

   _____

   (3) _____

   _____

   (4) _____

   _____

   (5) _____

   _____

44. A(n) _____ code is read by counting the number of needle deflections between each pause.

44. _____

45. You should use only a(n) _____ test light or multimeter when testing computer circuits.

45. _____

46. A(n) _____ trouble code is produced by indicator lights on the side of the computer.

46. _____

47. What is the purpose of a trouble code chart? _____

   _____

   _____

   _____

48. Normally, trouble codes will be automatically erased after _____ engine starts or warm-ups.
   (A) 30–50
   (B) 50–60
   (C) 70–80
   (D) 80–90

48. _____

49. Describe three methods used to erase trouble codes from the computer.

   (1) _____

   _____

   _____

   (2) _____

   _____

   _____

   (3) _____

   _____

   _____

50. While determining the trouble code on a GMC automobile, a technician watches the engine light flash four times, pause, then flash three more times. What trouble code is indicated?

50. _____

Chapter 19

Computer System Service

Name: _____ Date: _____

Instructor: _____ Score: _____ Textbook pages 272–288

Objective: After studying this chapter, you will be able to test and replace an automotive computer, its sensors, actuators, and other system related components.

Preliminary Visual Inspection

1. What does a preliminary visual inspection involve? _____

    _____

    _____

    _____

2. A trouble code indicates a coolant temperature sensor circuit problem. Technician A checks the sensor resistance and the wiring going to the sensor. Technician B checks the coolant level and the thermostat. Who is right?

    (A) A only.
    (B) B only.
    (C) Both A and B.
    (D) Neither A nor B.

2. _____

3. An engine fails to start properly. Technician A tests the computer for problems. Technician B checks the engine for mechanical problems. Who is right?

    (A) A only.
    (B) B only.
    (C) Both A and B.
    (D) Neither A nor B.

3. _____

4. How can *contaminated engine oil* trigger a computer trouble code? _____

    _____

    _____

    _____

    _____

    _____

    _____

5. _____ can be damaged by static electricity.   5._____
   (A) Computers
   (B) Transistors
   (C) Removable PROM chips
   (D) All of the above.

6. List at least three rules to remember when working with semiconductor devices and their wiring.

_____

_____

_____

_____

_____

_____

Computer System Circuit Problems

7. What is the most difficult aspect of making computer system repairs? _____

_____

8. What questions should you ask yourself when attempting to locate computer system problems?

_____

_____

_____

_____

_____

_____

_____

9. Define *stress testing.*_____

_____

_____

_____

Sensor and Actuator Problems

10. Name some of the problems that can occur with computer system actuators, sensors, and their circuits.

_____

_____

_____

_____

11. What should be done if a sensor's test value is too high or too low? _____

_____

_____

12. Name two testing instruments normally used to locate sensor or actuator   12._____
    malfunctions.

_____

13. ____ connections are the most common cause of electrical-related problems in a computer system.

13. _____

14. Some vacuum leaks can upset the operation of a(n) _____ system and cause a wide range of symptoms.

14. _____

15. A trouble code indicates a MAP sensor problem. Technician A checks the vacuum lines leading to the sensor. Technician B checks the intake manifold gasket area for leaks. Who is right?
    (A) A only.
    (B) B only.
    (C) Both A and B.
    (D) Neither A nor B.

15. _____

16. Describe how to test a *variable resistance sensor* with an ohmmeter. _____

_____

_____

_____

_____

_____

_____

17. Explain how to test a *variable resistance sensor* with a voltmeter. _____

_____

_____

_____

_____

_____

_____

_____

18. What is the typical reference voltage for a passive sensor?

18. _____

19. Explain how to measure reference voltage to a passive sensor.

_____

_____

_____

_____

_____

_____

_____

_____

20. What should be done if a passive sensor's reference voltage is low? _____

_____

_____

21. Describe how to test an active sensor with a digital voltmeter. _____

22. List eight rules to follow when replacing a sensor.

_____

_____

_____

_____

_____

_____

_____

_____

_____

_____

_____

23. What does *actuator service* involve? _____

_____

_____

_____

24. Why are *relays* a common source of computer system problems? _____

_____

_____

25. List at least three of the rules to follow when replacing an actuator.

_____

_____

_____

_____

_____

_____

Computer Service

26. What does *computer service* consist of? _____

_____

_____

_____

_____

27. Describe the problems that can upset the operation of an automotive computer.

_____

_____

_____

_____

_____

28. The _____ will tell you which computer or electronic control unit is having a problem.

28. _____

29. Most computers produce a reference voltage of about _____ volts.

29. _____

30. _____ identify the location and purpose of each terminal in a computer wiring harness connector.

30. _____

31. What should you do if it is necessary to use an ohmmeter to check the continuity of a wire or circuit in the computer harness?

_____

_____

_____

_____

32. Why must the ignition key be off and the vehicle's negative battery cable disconnected before removing the computer?

_____

_____

_____

_____

_____

33. When handling computers, keep one _____ on chassis ground and use the other to remove the component.

33. _____

34. Most PROMs have a(n) _____ surrounding the outside of the integrated circuit chip.

34. _____

35. Why should you avoid touching the PROM terminals with your fingers? _____

_____

_____

_____

_____

36. Describe the procedures to follow before installing the PROM in the new computer.

_____

_____

_____

37. Explain how to install a PROM._____

_____

_____

_____

_____

_____

_____

_____

38. Why is it important to make aure no trouble codes are set after PROM and computer installation have been completed?

_____

_____

_____

39. Identify the operations, components, and tool used for PROM installation.

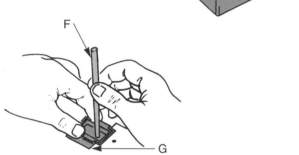

(A) _____

(B) _____

(C) _____

(D) _____

(E) _____

(F) _____

(G) _____

Chapter 20

Automotive Fuels, Gasoline and Diesel Combustion

Name: _____ Date: _____

Instructor: _____ Score: _____ Textbook pages 291–304

Objective: After studying this chapter, you will be able to describe the byproducts of crude oil and will learn about the different aspects of gasoline and diesel fuel combustion.

Petroleum (Crude Oil)

1. Define *petroleum.* _____

_____

_____

_____

2. _____ is a mixture of semisolids, liquids, and gases.   2._____

3. What are *hydrocarbons?* _____

_____

_____

_____

4. A(n) _____ converts crude oil into more useful substances.   4._____

5. _____ is the first crude oil conversion process.   5._____

6. Define *fractionating tower.*_____

_____

_____

_____

_____

Gasoline

7. Gasoline is the most common type of _____.   7._____

8. _____ slow down the burning of gasoline.   8._____

9. Define *octane rating.* _____

_____

_____

_____

_____

10. Octane numbers _____.   10._____
   (A) give the antiknock value of gasoline
   (B) are given on the side of the gas station pump
   (C) represent the fuel's ability to resist ping
   (D) All of the above.

11. Describe the purpose of *octane enhancers.* _____

_____

_____

_____

12. In order for gasoline to burn properly, it must be mixed with the right   12._____
   amount of _____.

13. When does *normal* gasoline combustion occur? _____

_____

_____

_____

14. Describe the stages of normal combustion and draw spark flame travel in the chambers. Use arrows to show piston
   movement.

(A) _____

_____

(B) _____

_____

(C) _____

_____

(D) _____

_____

A

B   C   D

15. Define *stoichiometric fuel mixture.* _____

_____

_____

16. What is the stoichiometric fuel mixture for gasoline?   16._____

17. A lean air-fuel mixture contains a large amount of _____ compared to   17._____
_____.
_____

18. A(n) _____ air-fuel mixture is the opposite of a lean mixture.   18._____

19. A slightly lean mixture is desirable for _____ gas mileage and _____   19._____
exhaust emissions.
_____

20. A(n) _____ mixture will reduce engine power, foul spark plugs, and cause   20._____
incomplete burning.

21. When does *abnormal* combustion occur? _____

_____

_____

_____

22. What is *detonation?* _____

_____

_____

_____

23. Identify the four stages of detonation.

(A) _____

_____

(B) _____

_____

(C) _____

_____

(D) _____

_____

24. Describe how *detonation* can damage an engine. _____

_____

_____

_____

25. _____ results when an overheated surface in the combustion chamber   25._____
ignites the air-fuel mixture.

26. Define *dieseling.* _____
    _____
    _____
    _____

27. _____ is an engine combustion problem caused by the spark plug firing too   27._____
    soon in relation to the position of the piston.

Diesel Fuel

28. Diesel fuel can produce more cylinder _____ and vehicle _____ than an   28._____
    equal amount of gasoline.
                                                                                     _____

29. Diesel fuel will not _____ as easily as gasoline.   29._____

30. Diesel engines inject the diesel fuel directly into the _____.   30._____

31. Diesel fuel grades ensure that diesel fuel sold all over the country has   31._____
    _____.

32. What diesel fuel grade is normally recommended for use in diesel auto-   32._____
    motive engines?

33. _____ is the thinner diesel fuel and is sometimes recommended as a winter   33._____
    fuel.

34. _____ temperatures tend to thicken diesel fuel, causing performance   34._____
    problems.

35. At cloud point, the _____ can clog the fuel filters and prevent diesel engine 35._____
    operation.

36. Why is water so damaging to a diesel injection pump?_____
    _____
    _____
    _____
    _____

37. Define *cetane rating.* _____
    _____
    _____
    _____

38. Most automakers recommend a cetane rating of about _____.   38._____

39. What is a *compression-ignition engine?* _____
    _____
    _____
    _____

40. A(n) _____ would not ignite diesel fuel properly.   40._____

41. Identify the actions that occur during *normal diesel combustion.*

(A) _____

(B) _____

(C) _____

(D) _____

_____

42. _____ occurs when too much fuel ignites at one time, producing a loud knocking noise.

42. _____

43. Define *ignition lag.* _____

_____

_____

44. A high cetane fuel with a(n) _____ lag time reduces the chances of diesel knock.

44. _____

45. List four causes of *diesel knock.* _____

_____

_____

_____

_____

_____

Alternative Fuels

46. What types of vehicles commonly use *LPG?* _____

_____

_____

_____

47. What is *ethyl alcohol* made from? _____

_____

_____

_____

_____

48. _____ can be made out of wood chips, petroleum, garbage, and animal manure.

48. _____

49. Why is *gasohol* commonly used as an alternative fuel in motor vehicles? _____

_____

_____

_____

50. _____ percent alcohol can increase 87 octane gasoline to 91 octane.   50. _____
    (A) Five
    (B) Seven
    (C) Ten
    (D) Twelve

51. Synthetic fuels are synthesized from a(n) _____ hydrocarbon state to a(n)   51. _____
_____ state.
_____

52. Why is hydrogen an ideal fuel? _____

_____

_____

_____

_____

53. Give one reason why hydrogen is *not* presently used in vehicles. _____

_____

_____

_____

_____

54. Identify the components and operations of the LPG fuel system illustrated below.

    (A) _____   (E) _____

    (B) _____   (F) _____

    (C) _____   (G) _____

    (D) _____   (H) _____

Chapter 21

Fuel Tanks, Pumps, Lines, and Filters

Name: _____ Date: _____

Instructor: _____ Score: _____ Textbook pages 305–329

Objective: After studying this chapter, you will be able to describe and explain the components, operations, construction, and service procedures of modern automotive fuel supply systems.

Fuel Supply System

1. Name and explain the three subsystems of a modern fuel system.

   (1) _____

   _____

   (2) _____

   _____

   (3) _____

   _____

2. Modern vehicles use _____ fuel pumps.

   2. _____

3. List and explain the basic parts of a fuel supply system.

   _____

   _____

   _____

   _____

   _____

   _____

4. Automotive fuel tanks are normally made of what materials? _____

   _____

   _____

   _____

5. The fuel tank _____ is the extension tube on the tank for filling the tank with fuel.

   5. _____

6. Define *spillback ball*. _____

   _____

   _____

   _____

7. Describe the purpose of *fuel tank baffles.* _____

_____

_____

_____

8. Fuel tank _____ are used to secure the tank to the vehicle. 8. _____

9. Explain the operation of a tank *pickup-sending unit.* _____

_____

_____

_____

_____

10. Explain the function of a fuel tank *pressure sensor.* _____

_____

_____

_____

_____

11. Identify the basic parts of the fuel tank assembly.

(A) _____	(J) _____
(B) _____	(K) _____
(C) _____	(L) _____
(D) _____	(M) _____
(E) _____	(N) _____
(F) _____	(O) _____
(G) _____	(P) _____
(H) _____	(Q) _____
(I) _____	(R) _____

12. Fuel lines are normally made of what materials? _____

_____

_____

_____

_____

13. A fuel _____ is a large diameter fuel line that feeds fuel into multiport gasoline injectors.

13. _____

14. Fuel _____ are needed where severe movement occurs between fuel system parts.

14. _____

15. Hose _____ secure fuel hoses to fuel lines or metal fittings.

15. _____

16. Describe the function of a *fuel return system.* _____

_____

_____

_____

_____

17. Explain the purpose of *fuel filters.* _____

_____

_____

_____

_____

18. Where are fuel filters normally located in an automotive fuel system? _____

_____

_____

_____

_____

19. Most fuel filters use _____ to trap contaminants present in the fuel.

20. Describe the function of a *fuel pump.* _____

_____

_____

_____

_____

21. A mechanical fuel pump is usually powered by a(n) _____ on the engine camshaft.

21. _____

22. Mechanical fuel pumps are commonly used with _____ fuel systems.

22. _____

23. The fuel pump _____ keeps the rocker arm pressed against the eccentric.

23. _____

24. A mechanical fuel pump's _____ is a synthetic rubber disc clamped between the halves of the pump body.

24. _____

25. Fuel can flow in either direction through a mechanical fuel pump's _____.

25. _____

26. During an engine's _____ stroke, a mechanical fuel pump's eccentric lobe pushes on the rocker arm.

26. _____

27. Why is a mechanical fuel pump made to idle? _____

_____

_____

_____

28. Define *vapor lock*. _____

_____

_____

_____

29. Where is an electric fuel pump normally located? _____

_____

_____

_____

30. Name some of the advantages an *electric fuel pump* has over a *mechanical pump.*

_____

_____

_____

_____

_____

_____

_____

31. Identify the components and operations of the following roller vane electric fuel pump.

(A) _____

(B) _____

(C) _____

(D) _____

(E) _____

(F) _____

(G) _____

(H) _____

(I) _____

(J) _____

32. The _____ in a rotary electric fuel pump keep fuel from draining out of the fuel line when the pump is not running.

32. _____

33. What limits maximum output pressure in a rotary electric fuel pump?

33. _____

34. A(n) _____ electric fuel pump has the same basic action as a mechanical fuel pump.

34. _____

35. Identify the components and testing operations in this electric fuel pump circuit equipped with an oil pressure safety switch.

(A) _____   (G) _____

(B) _____   (H) _____

(C) _____   (I) _____

(D) _____   (J) _____

(E) _____   (K) _____

(F) _____

Fuel Supply System Service

36. Why is a scan tool helpful when servicing a fuel supply system? _____

_____

_____

_____

_____

37. Name some typical fuel tank problems. _____

_____

_____

_____

_____

_____

38. Describe the procedures used to remove an automotive fuel tank. _____

_____

_____

_____

_____

_____

_____

39. What normally is the cause of a faulty fuel tank sending unit?_____

_____

_____

_____

40. Explain how to remove a fuel tank sending unit._____

_____

_____

_____

_____

_____

41. List and explain at least three of the rules you should remember when working with fuel lines and hoses.

(1) _____

_____

_____

(2) _____

_____

_____

(3) _____

_____

_____

42. Some late-model fuel lines have a(n) _____ -type fitting.   42._____

43. How can a clogged fuel filter affect engine operation? _____

_____

_____

_____

_____

_____

_____

44. Some fuel filters have a(n) _____ that opens when the filter becomes   44._____
    clogged.

45. _____ fuel pump pressure, more frequent with electric pumps, indicates an   45._____
    inoperative pressure relief valve.

46. What are the usual causes of mechanical fuel pump noise? _____

_____

_____

_____

_____

47. What normally causes fuel pump leaks? _____

_____

_____

_____

_____

48. Describe how to measure fuel pump pressure. _____

_____

_____

_____

_____

49. What should be the fuel pressure for a diesel supply pump?   49. _____

50. Describe how to check fuel pump volume. _____

_____

_____

_____

_____

_____

51. Fuel pump _____ should be checked when a fuel pump fails pressure and   51. _____
    volume tests.

52. Explain how to measure fuel pump vacuum. _____

_____

_____

_____

_____

53. Name some problems that can affect electric fuel pump operation.

_____

_____

_____

_____

54. Label the components and testing instruments in the following illustration depicting a fuel pump voltage supply test.

(A) _____

(B) _____

(C) _____

(D) _____

(E) _____

(F) _____

55. A(n) _____ can be used to block current flow to the electrical fuel pump after a severe impact or collision.

55. _____

56. A(n) _____ switch can be used to shut off the electric fuel pump if engine oil pressure drops too low.

56. _____

57. Describe how to remove a *mechanical* fuel pump. _____

_____

_____

_____

_____

58. Explain how to remove an *inline* electric fuel pump. _____

_____

_____

_____

59. Explain the procedure to follow when either a mechanical or electric fuel pump is bad.

_____

_____

_____

_____

60. What is the function of an *engine air filter?* _____

_____

_____

_____

_____

_____

_____

Gasoline Injection
Fundamentals

Name: _____ Date: _____

Instructor: _____ Score: _____ Textbook pages 330–359

Objective: After studying this chapter, you will be able to explain the construction, operation, and classifications of modern gasoline injection systems.

Gasoline Injection Fundamentals

1. A gasoline injection system uses _____ from an electric fuel pump to spray fuel into the engine's intake manifold.

    1._____

2. What are three of the advantages a gasoline injection system has over a carburetor-type fuel system?

_____

_____

_____

_____

_____

3. Any space with less than _____ psi of pressure at sea level has a vacuum.

    3._____

4. What is the function of the engine *throttle valve?*_____

_____

_____

_____

_____

5. When the engine throttle valve is _____, airflow, fuel flow, and engine power increase.

    5._____

Throttle Body and Multiport Injection

6. Explain the term *throttle body injection system.* _____

_____

_____

_____

_____

7. Define *multiport injection system.* _____

_____

_____

_____

8. A(n) _____ injection system sprays fuel into the engine intake manifold.   8. _____

9. A(n) _____ injection system forces fuel into the engine combustion chambers.   9. _____

Gasoline Injection Controls

10. Name and explain the three common methods used to control the amount of gasoline injected into an engine.

_____

_____

_____

_____

_____

_____

_____

11. The timing of a gasoline injection system links the engine valve action to the time when fuel is sprayed into the _____.   11. _____

12. List and describe the three basic classifications of gasoline injection timing.

(1) _____

_____

_____

(2) _____

_____

_____

(3) _____

_____

_____

Electronic Fuel Injection

13. What components does the fuel delivery system of an EFI system normally include? _____

_____

_____

_____

14. The _____ draws gasoline out of the tank and forces it into the pressure regulator.   14. _____

Name _____

15. What is the function of an EFI system's *fuel pressure regulator?* _____

_____

_____

_____

_____

16. Describe how a *fuel injector* operates. _____

_____

_____

_____

_____

17. Identify the parts of the fuel delivery system.

(A) _____

(B) _____

(C) _____

(D) _____

(E) _____

(F) _____

(G) _____

(H) _____

(I) _____

(J) _____

18. Name the typical components of an *air induction system.* _____

_____

_____

_____

_____

_____

19. The EFI _____ system monitors engine operating conditions and reports this information to the control module.

19. _____

20. The _____ system uses electrical data from the sensors to control the operation of the fuel injectors.

20. _____

Engine Sensors

21. What is the function of an EFI *oxygen sensor?* _____

_____

_____

_____

_____

22. Why do vehicles with OBD II use two oxygen sensors for each catalytic converter? _____

_____

_____

_____

23. The voltage output of an oxygen sensor varies with changes in the oxygen content of the _____.

23. _____

24. When in _____ loop, the electronic injection system does *not* use engine exhaust gas content as a main indicator of the air-fuel mixture.

24. _____

25. A(n) _____ sensor measures the pressure, or vacuum, inside the engine intake manifold.

25. _____

26. Explain how a *throttle position sensor* operates. _____

_____

_____

_____

27. A(n) _____ sensor monitors the operating temperature of the engine.

27. _____

28. A(n) _____ sensor is used in many EFI systems to measure the amount of outside air entering the engine.

28. _____

29. Explain the purpose of an *inlet air temperature sensor.* _____

_____

_____

_____

_____

_____

Injector Pulse Width

30. Identify the operations and components of the illustration showing how pulse width controls injector output.

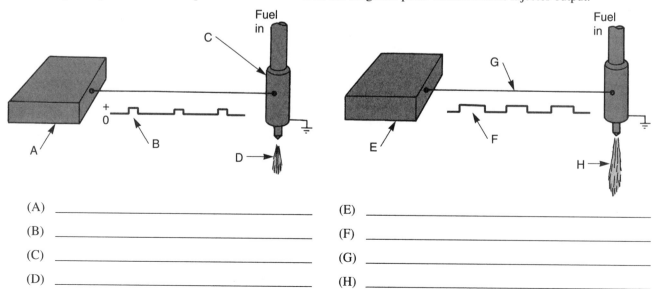

(A) _____   (E) _____

(B) _____   (F) _____

(C) _____   (G) _____

(D) _____   (H) _____

31. Explain the term *injector pulse width.* _____

_____

_____

_____

_____

Throttle Body Injection

32. Describe the operation of a *throttle body injection system.* _____

_____

_____

_____

_____

_____

33. Label the parts and operations of the following throttle body. Also, use arrows to show airflow.

(A) _____

(B) _____

(C) _____

(D) _____

(E) _____

(F) _____

34. Explain how a *throttle body injector* operates. _____

_____

_____

_____

_____

35. The TBI throttle body bolts to the pad on the _____.   35. _____

36. What components does a throttle body pressure regulator include? _____

_____

_____

_____

Engine Idle Speed Control

37. A(n) _____ valve opens to increase idle speed when the engine is cold.   37. _____

38. Describe how a throttle body assembly's throttle positioner operates. _____

_____

_____

_____

_____

_____

Continuous Throttle Body Injection

39. How does a continuous throttle body injection system increase or decrease fuel flow? _____

_____

_____

_____

_____

40. Where is the computer located on a continuous throttle body injection system? _____

_____

_____

Electronic Multiport Injection

41. Electronic multiport injection systems use a computer, engine sensors, and   41. _____
one solenoid injector for each _____.

42. What components does a multiport throttle body assembly include? _____

_____

_____

_____

43. Label the parts of the following multipoint injection system.

(A) _____

(B) _____

(C) _____

(D) _____

(E) _____

(F) _____

(G) _____

(H) _____

(I) _____

(J) _____

44. A(n) _____ is a tubing assembly that connects the main fuel line to the inlet of each injector.

44. _____

45. A multiport injector valve is aimed to spray toward an engine _____.

45. _____

46. What components does an EFI multiport injector typically include? _____

_____

_____

_____

_____

_____

Unitized Multiport Injection

47. Define *unitized multiport injection.* _____

_____

_____

_____

_____

48. Describe the difference between a *unitized fuel injector* and an *electronic multiport injector.*

_____

_____

_____

_____

49. Identify the parts of this unitized fuel injector.

(A) _____

(B) _____

(C) _____

(D) _____

(E) _____

(F) _____

Injector Resistor Pack

50. Explain the term *injector resistor pack.* _____

_____

_____

_____

51. What is the function of an injector resistor pack? _____

_____

_____

_____

Airflow Sensing Multiport EFI

52. An airflow sensing multiport EFI uses a(n) _____ as a main control of the   52._____
system.

53. Describe how an *airflow sensing multiport EFI* operates._____

_____

_____

_____

_____

_____

Pressure-Sensing Multiport EFI

54. In pressure-sensing multiport injection, a pressure sensor is connected to a   54._____
passage going into the _____.

55. What is the purpose of the *pressure sensor* in pressure-sensing multiport injection?_____

_____

_____

_____

Hydraulic-Mechanical Continuous Injection System

56. A fuel _____ is a hydraulically-operated valve mechanism that controls   56._____
fuel flow or pressure to each CIS injector.

57. A(n) _____ injector is an additional fuel injector valve used to supply extra   57._____
fuel for cold engine starting.

58. Name two functions of a *fuel accumulator.* _____

_____

_____

_____

_____

Chapter 23

Gasoline Injection Diagnosis and Repair

Name: _____ Date: _____

Instructor: _____ Score: _____ Textbook pages 360–384

Objective: After studying this chapter, you will be able to troubleshoot and repair common problems associated with gasoline injection systems.

Gasoline Injection Problem Diagnosis

1. What must a technician use in order to diagnose problems in a gasoline injection system?

   _____

   _____

   _____

2. Why should a technician check all possible sources *before* starting a repair of a gasoline injection system?

   _____

   _____

   _____

   _____

   _____

3. What should you look for when inspecting a gasoline injection system for problems?

   _____

   _____

   _____

   _____

   _____

4. Why shouldn't you disconnect an EFI harness terminal when the ignition switch is in the *on* position?

   _____

   _____

5. What is the purpose of a *malfunction indicator light?* _____

   _____

   _____

   _____

6. Vehicles equipped with OBD II systems can set _____ that pinpoint injector problems.

6._____

7. Explain the term *fuel system monitoring.*_____

_____

_____

_____

_____

8. What is normally used to determine fuel mixture content in a gasoline injection system?

_____

_____

9. _____ fuel trim refers to the temporary adjustment of injector pulse width to correct the fuel mixture.

9._____

10. Define *long-term fuel trim.*_____

_____

_____

_____

_____

11. Minor fuel _____ adjustments are normal with part wear.

11._____

12. What is the purpose of *oxygen sensor monitoring?*_____

_____

_____

_____

_____

_____

13. Why are oxygen sensors in OBD II systems heated? _____

_____

_____

_____

14. An oxygen sensor _____ checks the action of the heating element in the sensor.

14._____

EFI Testers

15. When is an EFI tester normally used on an EFI system? _____

_____

_____

16. An EFI tester uses _____ and sometimes a digital meter to check system operation.

16._____

17. A(n) _____ can sometimes be used to test or view the electrical waveforms at the EFI injectors.

17._____

Fuel Pressure Regulator Service

18. How can a faulty fuel pressure regulator affect engine operation? _____
_____
_____
_____

19. Why should you always relieve fuel pressure before disconnecting any EFI fuel line?
_____
_____
_____
_____
_____

20. A(n) _____ can be used to test a fuel pressure regulator and fuel pump   20. _____
    pressure.

21. Describe how to test fuel pressure regulator operation. _____
_____
_____
_____
_____

22. What should be done if a fuel pressure regulator test indicates low fuel pressure?
_____
_____

23. Identify the components and test equipment in the drawing below depicting a fuel pressure, pump, and filter test.

(A) _____

(B) _____

(C) _____

Injector Problems

24. How can a bad injector affect engine performance? _____
_____
_____

25. What are some of the possible causes of a leaking injector? _____

_____

_____

_____

26. An inoperative EFI injector normally has _____ or opened coil windings.   26._____

Throttle Body Injector Service

27. How can you quickly check the operation of a throttle body injection system?_____

_____

_____

_____

28. What procedures should be followed if the TBI injector does not spray fuel?_____

_____

_____

_____

29. What is indicated if there is no power to a TBI injector? _____

_____

_____

30. A TBI injector has power but does not produce a spray pattern. Explain the possible problem.

_____

_____

_____

31. Name the rules to follow when replacing a TBI injector. _____

_____

_____

_____

_____

_____

32. What does a throttle body rebuild involve?_____

_____

_____

_____

Servicing EFI Multiport Injectors

33. How do you quickly check to make sure each EFI injector is opening and closing?

_____

34. A(n) _____ sound means the injector is opening and closing.   34._____

35. Describe how to check the condition of the coils on an inoperative EFI injector.

_____

_____

_____

_____

_____

36. Identify the components and testing instruments in the injector test illustration.

(A) _____

(B) _____

(C) _____

(D) _____

37. What is indicated if there is a high resistance in the circuit between the injector solenoid and the control module?

_____

_____

_____

38. Define *noid light.* _____

_____

_____

39. An injector _____ uses a fuel injector tester to measure the amount of fuel   39. _____
flowing through each injector.

40. Describe how to replace an *EFI multiport injector.* _____

_____

_____

_____

_____

Engine Sensor Service

41. Most EFI engine sensors can be checked with a(n) _____.   41. _____

42. When a service manual directs you to measure voltage or resistance in an   42. _____
EFI sensor, use a(n) _____ impedance meter or a digital meter.

43. A throttle position sensor should produce a given amount of _____ for dif-   43. _____
ferent throttle openings.

44. Many manuals recommend checking the resistance of the throttle position   44. _____
sensor at different _____.

45. Describe how to test a manifold pressure sensor. _____

_____

_____

_____

_____

46. How can a bad oxygen sensor affect engine performance? _____

_____

_____

_____

47. Name some of the causes of oxygen sensor contamination. _____

_____

_____

48. How can a digital voltmeter be used to test the output of an oxygen sensor? _____

_____

_____

_____

_____

49. Describe a quick test used to see if an oxygen sensor reacts to a change in air-fuel mixture.

_____

_____

_____

_____

_____

_____

50. How do you test an oxygen sensor circuit? _____

_____

_____

_____

51. List nine rules to follow when installing an oxygen sensor.

(1) _____

_____

_____

(2) _____

_____

_____

(3) _____

_____

(4) _____

_____

_____

(5) _____

_____

_____

(6) _____

_____

_____

(7) _____

_____

_____

(8) _____

_____

_____

(9) _____

_____

_____

52. How does a bad coolant sensor affect engine operation? _____

_____

_____

_____

_____

53. Explain how to replace a coolant sensor. _____

_____

_____

_____

_____

Control Module Service

54. Define *PROM*. _____

_____

_____

_____

55. When a control module tests faulty in a pre-OBD II vehicle, you must   55. _____
normally reuse the old _____ in the new control module.

56. Why is an EFI control module normally mounted under the dash? _____

_____

_____

Gasoline Injection Adjustments

57. Name four gasoline injection system tune-up adjustments._____

_____

_____

_____

58. Why do some automakers warn against making large mixture adjustments?_____

_____

_____

59. A bad idle _____ may not be able to maintain the correct engine idle speed.   59._____

Multiport Throttle Body Service

60. What does multiport throttle body service normally include?_____

_____

_____

61. What is normally the first procedure to follow during multiport throttle body service?

_____

_____

62. Identify the multiport throttle body parts.

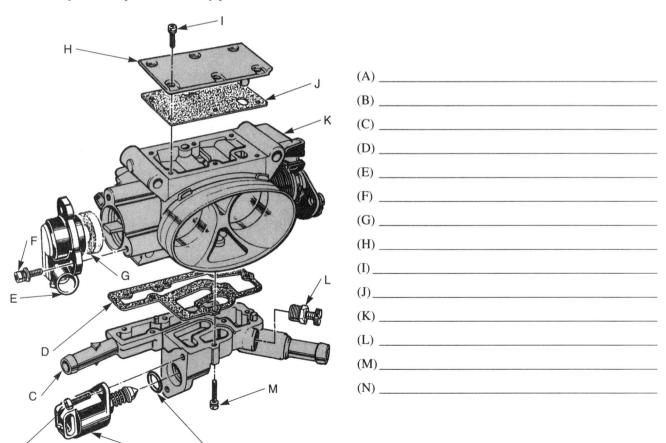

(A) _____

(B) _____

(C) _____

(D) _____

(E) _____

(F) _____

(G) _____

(H) _____

(I) _____

(J) _____

(K) _____

(L) _____

(M) _____

(N) _____

Chapter 24

Carburetor Fundamentals

Name: _____ Date: _____

Instructor: _____ Score: _____ Textbook pages 385–402

Objective: After studying this chapter, you will be able to describe the various designs, parts, and operating systems of modern carburetors.

Basic Carburetor

1. What is a *carburetor?* _____

    _____

    _____

    _____

2. When the engine is running, downward-moving pistons on their _____ strokes produce a suction in the manifold.

    2. _____

3. Identify the basic parts and operations of the carburetor fuel system illustrated below.

    (A) _____

    (B) _____

    (C) _____

    (D) _____

    (E) _____

Basic Carburetor Parts

4. Many carburetor parts perform the same functions as corresponding _____ system parts.

    4. _____

5. The carburetor _____ routes outside air into the engine intake manifold.

    5. _____

6. The _____ controls the power output of a gasoline engine.

6._____

7. A(n) _____ produces sufficient suction to pull fuel out of the main discharge tube.

7._____

8. Define *main discharge tube.*_____

_____

_____

_____

_____

Basic Carburetor Systems

9. What is a *carburetor system?*_____

_____

_____

_____

_____

10. List five of the various air-fuel ratios produced by a carburetor.

_____

_____

_____

_____

_____

_____

11. The _____ keeps the fuel pump from forcing too much gasoline into the carburetor bowl.

11._____

12. The _____ in the top of the fuel bowl regulates the amount of fuel passing through the fuel inlet and needle seat.

12._____

13. Describe the function of a carburetor's *idle system.* _____

_____

_____

_____

_____

_____

14. The _____ is a restriction in the idle passage that limits maximum fuel flow in the idle circuit.

14._____

15. What is the function of a carburetor's *idle passage?*_____

_____

_____

_____

_____

16. Explain the purpose of *idle mixture screw limiter caps.* _____

_____

_____

_____

17. For the idle system to function, the throttle plate must be _____ (open/closed).

17. _____

18. The _____ system feeds more fuel into the air horn when the throttle plates are partially open.

18. _____

19. Explain the purpose of a carburetor's *acceleration system.* _____

_____

_____

_____

_____

20. Without the acceleration system, too much _____ would rush into the engine as the throttle is quickly opened.

20. _____

21. Describe the function of an *accelerator pump.* _____

_____

_____

_____

_____

22. The pump _____ prevents fuel from being pulled into the air horn by venturi vacuum.

22. _____

23. Identify the parts and operations of the accelerator pump system illustrated below.

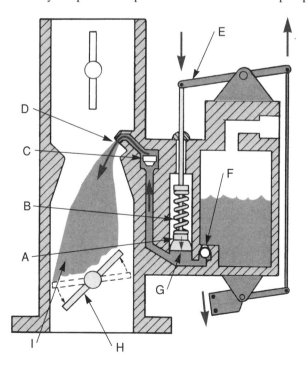

(A) _____

(B) _____

(C) _____

(D) _____

(E) _____

(F) _____

(G) _____

(H) _____

(I) _____

24. Describe the purpose of the carburetor's *high-speed system.* _____

_____

_____

_____

25. What does the number stamped on the high-speed jet normally represent? _____

_____

_____

_____

26. The _____ venturi is the venturi formed in the side of the carburetor air   26. _____
horn.

27. What is the function of the carburetor's *full-power system?* _____

_____

_____

_____

_____

28. A(n) _____ rod is a stepped rod that moves in and out of the main jet to   28. _____
alter fuel flow.

29. Explain how a *power valve* operates. _____

_____

_____

_____

_____

_____

_____

30. Explain how the choke system operates. _____

_____

_____

_____

_____

_____

_____

_____

31. _____ chokes open and close the choke plate with changes in temperature.   31. _____

32. What is the function of a *choke break?* _____

_____

_____

_____

_____

Carburetor Devices

33. A fast idle _____ increases engine idle speed when the choke is closed.

33. _____

34. A fast idle _____ opens the carburetor throttle plates during engine operation but allows the throttle plates to close as soon as the engine shuts off.

34. _____

35. Explain the purpose of a *throttle return dashpot.* _____

_____

_____

_____

_____

_____

36. Why is a throttle return dashpot commonly used on carburetors for cars equipped with automatic transmission?

_____

_____

_____

_____

_____

37. A(n) _____ compensator is a carburetor device that prevents engine stalling or a rough idle under high engine temperature conditions.

37. _____

38. A(n) _____ compensator can be used to change the carburetor's air-fuel mixture with changes in the vehicle's altitude.

38. _____

Carburetor Barrels

39. What does the *primary* of a carburetor include? _____

_____

_____

_____

40. What does the *secondary* of a carburetor include? _____

_____

_____

_____

Carburetor Size

41. What is *CFM?* _____

_____

42. A _____ (smaller/larger) CFM rating would be desirable for high engine power output.

42. _____

Computer-Controlled Carburetors

43. How does a computer-controlled carburetor system send information to the computer? _____
_____
_____

44. Define *electromechanical carburetor.* _____
_____
_____
_____

45. Explain how a computer-controlled carburetor operates. _____
_____
_____
_____
_____
_____
_____
_____
_____

46. Identify the parts of the computer-controlled carburetor system illustrated below.

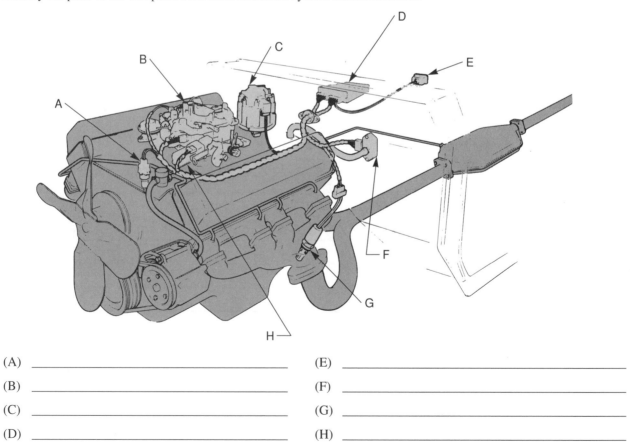

(A) _____   (E) _____

(B) _____   (F) _____

(C) _____   (G) _____

(D) _____   (H) _____

Chapter 25

Carburetor Diagnosis, Service, and Repair

Name: _____ Date: _____

Instructor: _____ Score: _____ Textbook pages 403–419

Objective: After studying this chapter, you will be able to troubleshoot and repair common carburetor problems. Also, you will be able to remove and install modern carburetors and perform minor setup adjustments.

Carburetor Problem Diagnosis

1. Explain what a visual service inspection of a carburetor should include. _____
   _____
   _____
   _____

2. An exhaust gas _____ is a testing device that measures the chemical con-   2. _____
   tent of the engine exhaust gases.

3. Describe the problems that can result from carburetor float system problems. _____
   _____
   _____
   _____
   _____

4. Explain the cause of carburetor *flooding.* _____
   _____
   _____
   _____
   _____

5. What service procedures should be followed to correct carburetor flooding?
   _____
   _____
   _____
   _____
   _____
   _____
   _____
   _____

6. Name some of the causes of engine flooding. _____

_____

_____

_____

_____

_____

7. A high float level _____ the air-fuel mixture.   7._____

8. A low float level normally produces a(n) _____ air-fuel mixture.   8._____

9. Describe the symptoms of carburetor idle system problems. _____

_____

_____

_____

10. A clogged idle _____ can restrict fuel flow to the idle port.   10._____

11. A clogged idle _____ can enrich the mixture by obstructing the premixing 11._____
of air, upsetting engine operation at idle.

12. How do carburetor acceleration system problems affect engine operation? _____

_____

_____

_____

13. Identify some of the problems that can affect acceleration system operation.

(A) _____

(B) _____

(C) _____

(D) _____

(E) _____

(F) _____

(G) _____

(H) _____

(I) _____

14. Explain how to check accelerator pump operation. _____

_____

_____

_____

_____

_____

_____

15. Engine _____ is a condition in which engine power at cruising speeds   15._____
seems to alternately increase and decrease.

16. How does full-power system problems affect engine performance?_____
_____
_____
_____

17. A faulty metering rod mechanism will generally upset only _____ engine operation.

17._____

18. Carburetor choke system problems will usually make the engine perform poorly when _____ or right after warm-up.

18._____

19. How does a *rich* choke setting affect engine operation? _____
_____
_____
_____

20. What are the symptoms of fast idle cam problems? _____
_____
_____
_____
_____

Carburetor Removal

21. Why should a shop rag be wrapped around the fitting when removing a fuel line?_____
_____
_____
_____

22. Describe how to remove a carburetor from an engine. _____
_____
_____
_____

Carburetor Body Sections

23. A carburetor's _____ fits on the top of the main body and serves as a lid for the fuel bowl.

23._____

24. What is the largest section of a carburetor?

24._____

25. The _____ body is the lower section of the carburetor and contains the throttle valves.

25._____

Carburetor Rebuild

26. When is a carburetor rebuild necessary? _____
_____
_____
_____

27. What does a carburetor rebuild normally involve? _____

_____

_____

_____

_____

_____

_____

28. Describe the proper procedures to follow when using decarbonizing cleaner to clean carburetor parts.

_____

_____

_____

_____

_____

_____

_____

29. Why must carburetor jets be reinstalled in the same location? _____

_____

30. What should you look for when checking carburetor parts after they have been cleaned?

_____

_____

_____

_____

_____

_____

31. Describe the typical adjustments that should be made during carburetor reassembly.

_____

_____

_____

_____

_____

_____

Carburetor Installation

32. Explain how to install a carburetor. _____

_____

_____

_____

_____

_____

_____

_____

_____

_____

33. Describe how to set the carburetor's fast idle cam. _____

_____

_____

_____

_____

_____

_____

_____

_____

34. Typically, hot idle speed is from about _____ rpm.   34. _____

35. What is the lowest idle speed setting?   35. _____

36. Explain how to adjust curb idle. _____

_____

_____

_____

_____

_____

37. Identify the following carburetor adjustment procedure and parts.

(A) _____

(B) _____

38. Describe how to adjust the carburetor idle mixture. _____

_____

_____

_____

_____

_____

_____

_____

_____

_____

_____

39. How is propane used to set idle mixture adjustment? _____

_____

_____

_____

_____

_____

_____

40. Most carburetors on late-model vehicles have _____ idle mixture screws   40._____
    that are preset at the factory.

Computer-Controlled Carburetor Service

41. When using a dwell meter to check certain computer-controlled carburetor   41._____
    systems, a high dwell signal would indicate a(n) _____ command from the
    computer.

42. Under certain operating conditions, such as wide-open throttle, the   42._____
    vehicle's computer may produce a(n) _____ during dwell meter testing.

43. Identify the parts and instruments used in the following computer-controlled carburetor test procedure.

(A) _____

(B) _____

(C) _____

(D) _____

(E) _____

(F) _____

(G) _____

Chapter 26

Diesel Injection Fundamentals

Name: _____ Date: _____

Instructor: _____ Score: _____ Textbook pages 420–438

Objective: After studying this chapter, you will be able to explain the operating principles of diesel injection systems.

Basic Diesel Injection

1. How does a *diesel fuel injection system* work? _____

    _____

    _____

    _____

    _____

2. A diesel engine uses a compression ratio of approximately _____.   2._____
    - (A) 8:1 to 9:1
    - (B) 10:1 to 15:1
    - (C) 17:1 to 25:1
    - (D) 30:1 to 35:1

3. *True or False?* A diesel engine has a lower compression ratio than a   3._____
   gasoline engine.

4. A diesel engine compresses _____ on its compression stroke.   4._____

5. Explain the four major parts of a diesel injection system.

    Injection pump: _____

    _____

    Injection lines: _____

    _____

    Injector nozzles: _____

    _____

    Glow plugs: _____

    _____

6. The diesel fuel supply system feeds fuel to the injection pump normally   6._____
   using a(n) _____ pump.

7. A(n) _____ injection pump controls when and how much fuel is forced to   7._____
   the injector nozzles.

8. What determines *airflow* in a diesel engine?   8._____

9. Identify the parts of the diesel injection system illustrated below.

(A) _____

(B) _____

(C) _____

(D) _____

(E) _____

(F) _____

(G) _____

(H) _____

(I) _____

(J) _____

Diesel Injection Pumps

10. List and explain eight functions of a diesel injection pump.

(1) _____

_____

_____

(2) _____

_____

(3) _____

_____

(4) _____

_____

_____

(5) _____

_____

(6) _____

_____

(7) _____

_____

_____

(8) _____

_____

11. A(n) _____ diesel injection pump has one plunger for each engine cylinder.   11._____

12. A distributor injection pump normally uses _____ or _____ plungers to supply fuel for all of the engine cylinders.   12._____

_____

13. Identify the parts of the diesel injection pump illustrated below.

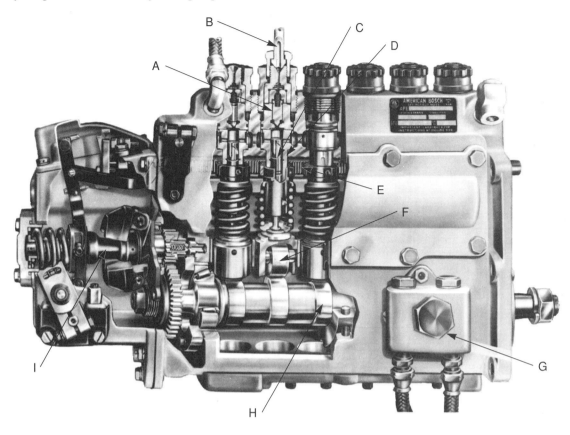

(A) _____   (F) _____

(B) _____   (G) _____

(C) _____   (H) _____

(D) _____   (I) _____

(E) _____

14. The _____ are the small cylinders in an injection pump that hold the pumping plungers.

14. _____

15. How do the *control sleeves* work in an in-line injection pump? _____

_____

_____

_____

16. How does a *governor* control speed? _____

_____

_____

_____

17. Define *injection timing*. _____

_____

_____

_____

18. What is a *transfer pump?* _____

_____

_____

_____

19. The _____ is the housing that contains passages for filling the plunger   19._____
barrel with fuel and for injecting fuel into the delivery valves.

20. Why is an electric *fuel shut-off* needed? _____

_____

_____

_____

Diesel Injector Nozzles

21. Diesel injector nozzles are _____ valves that spray fuel directly into the   21._____
engine.

22. Explain the five parts of a diesel injector.

Injector pressure chamber: _____

_____

_____

_____

Heat shield: _____

_____

_____

_____

Needle valve: _____

_____

_____

_____

Injector body: _____

_____

_____

_____

Injector spring: _____

_____

_____

_____

23. An inward opening, _____ injector is commonly used in automotive diesel   23._____
engines.

24. Identify the parts of the diesel injection nozzle.

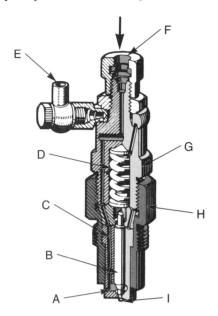

(A) _____

(B) _____

(C) _____

(D) _____

(E) _____

(F) _____

(G) _____

(H) _____

(I) _____

Glow Plugs

25. Glow plugs are _____ used to help start a cold diesel engine.

25. _____

26. A glow plug control _____ automatically disconnects the glow plugs when the appropriate temperature has been reached.

26. _____

27. Identify the parts of the glow plug circuit and draw the missing wires.

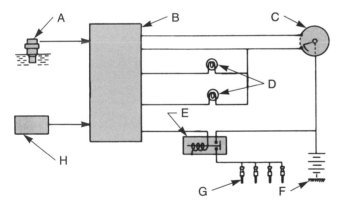

(A) _____

(B) _____

(C) _____

(D) _____

(E) _____

(F) _____

(G) _____

(H) _____

28. Glow plugs are threaded into holes in the _____.

28. _____

29. Glow plugs normally stay on for _____.
    (A) a few seconds
    (B) a minute
    (C) an hour
    (D) None of the above.

29. _____

Diesel Injection System Accessories

30. A(n) _____ may be used to warn the driver of moisture in the diesel fuel.

30. _____

31. When water mixes with the diesel fuel, it can cause _____ of the precision parts of the system.

31. _____

32. Define *fuel jelling*. _____

_____   _____

_____

_____

33. What device is used to prevent fuel jelling and how does it work? _____

_____

_____

_____

_____

34. A(n) _____ may be used to warm the engine in cold weather, also aiding   34. _____
    starting.

35. Why is a *vacuum pump* commonly needed on a diesel? _____

_____

_____

_____

36. Name two types of diesel engine vacuum pumps.   36. _____

    _____

Computer-Controlled Diesel System

37. A computer-controlled diesel system uses _____ to increase the efficiency   37. _____
    of mechanical diesel injection.
    - (A) sensors
    - (B) a computer
    - (C) actuators
    - (D) All of the above.

38. How do *solenoids* help control injection pump operation? _____

_____

_____

_____

_____

_____

_____

39. How do *sensors* affect diesel injection?_____

_____

_____

_____

_____

_____

Diesel Injection Diagnosis, Service, and Repair

Name: _____ Date: _____

Instructor: _____ Score: _____ Textbook pages 439–458

Objective: After studying this chapter, you will be able to summarize the most common methods of diagnosing and repairing diesel injection system problems.

Diesel Injection Diagnosis

1. Begin diesel injection diagnosis by checking for these six problems.

_____

_____

_____

_____

_____

_____

2. Excess diesel exhaust smoke is normally due to _____.   2._____
   (A) injection system troubles
   (B) engine troubles
   (C) incomplete combustion
   (D) Any of the above.

3. Which of the following is *not* a normal cause of abnormal knock?   3._____
   (A) Low engine operating temperature.
   (B) Early ignition timing.
   (C) High engine compression.
   (D) Oil consumption.

4. How do you measure diesel exhaust smoke?_____

_____

_____

_____

5. Define *ignition lag.*_____

_____

_____

_____

_____

■ What are probable causes of the following?

6. *Diesel engine miss:* _____

_____

_____

7. *No-start condition:* _____

_____

_____

8. *Lack of power:* _____

_____

_____

9. *Poor fuel mileage:* _____

_____

_____

10. *Excessive knock:* _____

_____

_____

Testing Diesel Injection Operation

11. What is a diesel *cylinder balance test* and how is it performed? _____

_____

_____

_____

12. A diesel compression gauge should read to approximately _____.   12. _____

13. When a cylinder is firing, it will raise the internal resistance of the _____   13. _____
    in that cylinder.

14. How is a *digital pyrometer* used to check diesel engine operation? _____

_____

_____

_____

Injector Nozzle Service

15. A bad injector in a diesel usually causes _____.   15. _____
    (A) engine miss
    (B) smoking and knocking
    (C) engine power reduction
    (D) All of the above.

16. An easy way to verify an injector problem is to _____ a good injector for   16. _____
    the one being tested.

17. What does a *pop tester* do? _____
_____
_____
_____
_____

18. Typical injector nozzle opening pressure is about _____ (12 000–15 000 kPa).

18. _____

19. How do you check a diesel injector spray pattern? _____
_____
_____
_____
_____

20. When installing a new injector, coat the threads with _____. Use a new _____ and torque the injector to specifications.

20. _____
_____

21. Identify the parts of the diesel injector nozzle.

(A) _____

(B) _____

(C) _____

(D) _____

(E) _____

(F) _____

(G) _____

(H) _____

(I) _____

Injection Pump Service

22. Most garages remove and install a(n) _____ injection pump when internal parts are faulty.

22. _____

23. An injection pump _____ is used to check pump performance.

23. _____

24. How do you remove and replace an injection pump? _____
_____
_____
_____
_____
_____

25. Diesel injection pump timing is adjusted by _____ the injection pump on its mounting.

25. _____

26. Identify the parts that allow external repairs on a diesel injection pump.

(A) _____

(B) _____

(C) _____

(D) _____

(E) _____

(F) _____

(G) _____

(H) _____

(I) _____

(J) _____

(K) _____

(L) _____

(M) _____

(N) _____

27. Identify the parts that must be disconnected to remove an injection pump.

(A) _____

(B) _____

(C) _____

(D) _____

(E) _____

(F) _____

(G) _____

(H) _____

(I) _____

Diesel Idle Speed Adjustment

28. What are the three speed adjustments commonly used on a diesel injection pump?

_____

_____

_____

Exhaust Systems, Turbochargers, and Superchargers

Name: _____ Date: _____

Instructor: _____ Score: _____ Textbook pages 459–481

Objective: After studying this chapter, you will be able to summarize the construction, operation, and service of exhaust and turbocharging systems.

Exhaust Systems

1. Describe the basic parts of a typical exhaust system.

   Exhaust manifold: _____

   _____

   Header pipe: _____

   _____

   Catalytic converter: _____

   _____

   Intermediate pipe: _____

   _____

   Muffler: _____

   _____

   Tailpipe: _____

   _____

   Hangers: _____

   _____

   Heat shields: _____

   _____

   Muffler clamps: _____

   _____

2. *True or False?* A single exhaust system is used on *only* the smallest four-cylinder engines.

   2. _____

3. A dual exhaust system has two separate exhaust paths to reduce _____.

   3. _____

4. What purpose does a *crossover pipe* serve?_____

_____

_____

5. *True or False?* The exhaust pipes include the header pipe, just ahead of the   5._____
catalytic converter.

6. An exhaust manifold heat valve forces hot exhaust to flow into the _____   6._____
to aid cold weather starting.

7. What is a *heat shield?* _____

_____

_____

8. Identify the parts of the muffler illustrated below.

(A) _____

(B) _____

(C) _____

(D) _____

(E) _____

(F) _____

(G) _____

(H) _____

Exhaust System Service

9. Exhaust system service is usually needed when a component in the system   9._____
_____ and begins to _____.   _____

10. Why is a leaking exhaust system dangerous? _____

_____

_____

_____

11. It is especially important to use rust _____ on the exhaust manifold flange   11._____
nuts or bolts.

12. A(n) _____ socket is recommended for faster removal without rounding   12._____
off the fastener heads.

13. You should always wear _____ to keep rust and dirt from entering your   13._____
eyes.

14. A pipe _____ should be used to enlarge pipe ends as needed.   14._____

15. A pipe _____ can be used to straighten dented pipe ends.

15. _____

16. Check _____ operation using the information in a service manual.

16. _____

17. When replacing exhaust system pipes, you must make sure that all pipes are fully _____ and that all _____ are positioned properly.

17. _____

_____

18. You should always maintain adequate _____ between the exhaust system and the car body and chassis.

18. _____

19. When doing service work on stainless steel exhaust systems, use heavy-duty _____ designed for this type of system to prevent dangerous exhaust gas leakage.

19. _____

20. *True or False?* Stainless steel will not rust and will provide much longer service life.

20. _____

Superchargers and Turbochargers

21. *True or False?* Superchargers depend on exhaust gases for their operation.

21. _____

22. What is a *turbocharger?*_____

_____

_____

_____

_____

_____

23. Explain the six major parts of a turbocharger.

Turbine wheel: _____

_____

_____

*Turbine housing:*_____

_____

_____

Turbo shaft: _____

_____

_____

Compressor wheel: _____

_____

_____

Compressor housing: _____

_____

_____

Bearing housing: _____

_____

_____

24. Identify the parts of the turbocharger illustrated below.

(A) _____

_____

(B) _____

(C) _____

(D) _____

(E) _____

(F) _____

(G) _____

(H) _____

(I) _____

(J) _____

(K) _____

25. A turbocharger can operate at speeds up to _____ rpm.

25. _____

26. What is *turbo lag?* _____

_____

_____

_____

27. A(n) _____ limits the amount of boost pressure developed to prevent detonation.

27. _____

28. With computer control of the turbocharging system, the ECM uses _____ to determine if boost pressure or ignition timing should be altered.

28. _____

29. What turbo related sensors will most late-model OBD II systems check when using a scan tool?

_____

_____

_____

_____

30. What type of supercharger is illustrated below? Identify the parts as indicated.

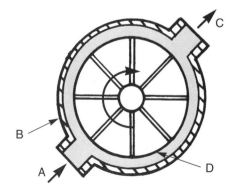

Type: _____

(A) _____

(B) _____

(C) _____

(D) _____

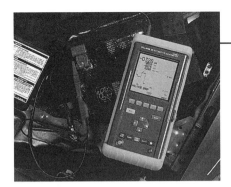

Chapter 29

Automotive Batteries

Name: _____Date: _____

Instructor: _____Score: _____Textbook pages 483–492

Objective: After studying this chapter, you will be able to explain the construction and operation of automotive batteries.

Battery Principles

1. What is an automotive *battery?* _____

_____

_____

2. When _____ (charging/discharging), the battery changes chemical energy into electrical energy.

2._____

3. During _____ (charging/discharging), electrical energy is converted into chemical energy.

3._____

4. What does a simple battery *cell* consist of?_____

_____

_____

5. Define the term *load.* _____

_____

_____

6. List the five functions of a battery.

   (1) _Operate starting motor, ign. system, ect._

   (2) _Supply electrical power_

   (3) _help charging system_

   (4) _act as a Capacitor_

   (5) _store energy_

7. Identify the parts of this battery.

(A) _____

(B) _____

(C) _____

(D) _____

(E) _____

(F) _____

Battery Construction

8. Define *battery element*. _____

_____

9. What are *battery plates?* _____

_____

_____

10. *True or False?* Batteries can have either side terminals or top posts.

10._____

11. What are *separators?* _____

_____

_____

_____

12. How can battery hydrogen gas be dangerous?_____

_____

_____

13. _____ is a mixture of sulfuric acid and distilled water.

13._____

14. The battery _____ shows the general charge condition of the battery.

14._____

15. A 12-volt battery has six cells that produce an open circuit voltage of _____ volts.

15._____

16. What happens to voltage and current if you connect two 12-volt batteries in parallel?

_____

_____

_____

Name _____

17. What is the *body ground wire* for?_____

_____

_____

_____

18. What is a battery *heat shield?* _____

_____

_____

_____

19. How can you tell if a battery is *maintenance-free?* _____

_____

_____

_____

Battery Ratings

20. What does battery *cold cranking rating* indicate? _____

_____

_____

_____

_____

_____

21. What is *reserve capacity rating?* _____

_____

_____

_____

_____

Battery Temperature and Efficiency

22. As battery temperature drops, battery power is _____.   22._____
    (A) increased
    (B) reduced
    (C) unaffected
    (D) fluctuates up and down

23. What is a *parasitic load* on a battery? _____

_____

_____

_____

_____

_____

Notes

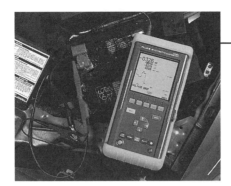

Chapter 30

Battery Testing and Service

Name: _____ Date: _____

Instructor: _____ Score: _____ Textbook pages 493–507

Objective: After studying this chapter, you will be able to summarize the most common methods for testing and servicing batteries.

Battery Maintenance

1. What five steps are done during battery maintenance?

   (1) _____

   _____

   (2) _____

   _____

   (3) _____

   _____

   (4) _____

   _____

   (5) _____

   _____

2. Technician A says you should wear eye protection when working around batteries. Technician B says even the film buildup on a battery can contain acid. Who is right?
   - (A) A only.
   - (B) B only.
   - (C) Both A and B.
   - (D) Neither A nor B.

   2. _____

3. Technician A says you should wash the top of a battery with a detergent solution. Technician B says you should wash the top of a battery with baking soda and water. Who is right?
   - (A) A only.
   - (B) B only.
   - (C) Both A and B.
   - (D) Neither A nor B.

   3. _____

4. What is a *battery terminal test?* _____

   _____

   _____

5. All of the following are procedures to perform a battery terminal test,   5._____
   except:
      (A) crank the engine while watching the voltmeter reading.
      (B) connect an ammeter to the appropriate cable ends.
      (C) disable the ignition or injection system.
      (D) connect a voltmeter to the appropriate cable ends.

6. What should you use to keep battery terminals from corroding? _____
   _____

7. What is a *memory saver?* _____
   _____
   _____

8. Technician A says the invisible hydrogen gas is not flammable. Technician   8._____
   B says that batteries can explode. Who is right?
      (A) A only.
      (B) B only.
      (C) Both A and B.
      (D) Neither A nor B.

9. If a battery is low, fill the cells to the correct level with _____.   9._____

10. A battery _____ measures the specific gravity (and the state of charge) for   10._____
    battery electrolyte.

11. A discharged battery will have _____.   11._____
       (A) lower specific gravity than a fully charged battery
       (B) higher specific gravity than a fully charged battery
       (C) lower specific gravity than water
       (D) the same specific gravity as water

12. A hydrometer test indicates a battery's electrolyte has a specific gravity of   12._____
    1.269 at 90°F (32.5°C). Technician A says the battery is fully charged.
    Technician B says the battery may be defective or in need of recharging.
    Who is right?
       (A) A only.
       (B) B only.
       (C) Both A and B.
       (D) Neither A nor B.

13. What should happen if the specific gravity in any cell varies 25–50 points from the other cells?
    _____
    _____

14. How do you check battery state of charge with a voltmeter? _____
    _____
    _____
    _____
    _____

15. What is the purpose of a *cell voltage test?* _____
    _____
    _____
    _____

16. What is a *battery drain test?* _____

_____

_____

_____

17. A battery drain test indicates a drain of .75 amps. Technician A says this is   17. _____
an acceptable drain. Technician B says this is a normal parasitic drain
caused by the clock and computer. Who is right?
  - (A) A only.
  - (B) B only.
  - (C) Both A and B.
  - (D) Neither A nor B.

18. A battery charger is a(n) _____ that changes wall outlet voltage to slightly   18. _____
above battery voltage.

19. Technician A says charging a frozen battery can cause the case to rupture   19. _____
and may cause an explosion. Technician B says you should allow a frozen
battery to thaw before charging. Who is right?
  - (A) A only.
  - (B) B only.
  - (C) Both A and B.
  - (D) Neither A nor B.

Jump Starting

20. When jump starting, connect the two batteries in order, _____.   20. _____
  - (A) positive to negative and negative to positive
  - (B) negative to negative and positive to positive
  - (C) negative to positive and positive to positive
  - (D) positive to positive and negative to negative

21. Technician A says you can short jumper cables together and connect them   21. _____
backward. Technician B says by connecting the last negative jumper cable
away from the battery, the battery gas will explode. Who is right?
  - (A) A only.
  - (B) B only.
  - (C) Both A and B.
  - (D) Neither A nor B.

Battery Load Test

22. A(n) _____ tests the battery under full load conditions.   22. _____

23. Most load testers have a(n) _____ type ammeter lead.   23. _____

24. During a load test, if the amp-hour rating is given, you should load the   24. _____
battery to _____ its rating.
  - (A) two times
  - (B) three times
  - (C) four times
  - (D) five times

25. If a battery is rated at 90 amp-hours, what amperage should be used for a   25. _____
load test?

26. Many batteries are ranked in SAE _____, rather than amp-hours.   26. _____

27. To determine the load test for a battery rated in cold crank amps, divide the cold crank rating by _____.
    - (A) two
    - (B) twenty
    - (C) three
    - (D) two hundred

27. _____

28. During a load test, if the 12V battery reads _____ volts or more, the battery is good.

28. _____

29. A(n) _____ test will determine if the battery is sulfated and the plates ruined.

29. _____

30. If a battery passes all tests, what are some other problems to check? _____

_____

_____

_____

_____

Activating Dry-Charged Battery

31. A new dry-charged battery must be _____ before installation.

31. _____

32. Technician A says you should use a metal funnel when pouring electrolyte into a dry-charged battery. Technician B says you should use a plastic funnel. Who is right?
    - (A) A only.
    - (B) B only.
    - (C) Both A and B.
    - (D) Neither A nor B.

32. _____

Removing and Replacing a Battery

33. Which of the following is the correct order for removing a battery?
    - (A) Loosen the battery hold-down, use a battery strap to remove the battery, disconnect the cables.
    - (B) Use a battery strap to remove the battery, loosen the battery hold-down, disconnect the cables.
    - (C) Disconnect the cables, use a battery strap to remove the battery, loosen the battery hold-down.
    - (D) Disconnect the cables, loosen the battery hold-down, use a battery strap to remove the battery.

33. _____

34. Technician A says you should always wear safety glasses when carrying a battery. Technician B says you should use a battery strap or tool to carry a battery. Who is right?
    - (A) A only.
    - (B) B only.
    - (C) Both A and B.
    - (D) Neither A nor B.

34. _____

35. All of the following criteria must be used when selecting a replacement battery, *except:*
    - (A) battery must fit properly.
    - (B) power rating must be equal to factory recommendations.
    - (C) the tray edge must not cut through the plastic case.
    - (D) power rating must be less than factory recommendations.

35. _____

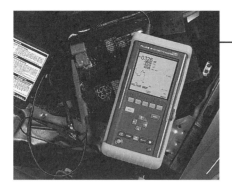

Chapter 31

Starting System Fundamentals

Name: _____ Date: _____

Instructor: _____ Score: _____ Textbook pages 508–519

Objective: After studying this chapter, you will be able to explain the operation and construction of modern starting systems.

Starting System Principles

1. The _____ uses battery power and an electric motor to turn the engine crankshaft.

   1. _____

2. Briefly describe what occurs in the starting system when the ignition is turned to the start position.

   _____

   _____

   _____

3. Describe a *commutator.* _____

   _____

   _____

4. Technician A says some late-model starting systems are programmed to open the circuit between the ignition key and the starter solenoid when the engine is running. Technician B says this prevents the driver from accidentally engaging the starting motor while the engine is running. Who is right?

   4. _____

   (A) A only.
   (B) B only.
   (C) Both A and B.
   (D) Neither A nor B.

5. A(n) _____ is made up of invisible magnetic lines of force.

   5. _____

6. What is another name for the *pole pieces?*

   6. _____

7. Identify the parts in this basic starting system.

   (A) _____

   (B) _____

   (C) _____

   (D) _____

   (E) _____

   (F) _____

   (G) _____

8. The _____ ride on top of the commutator.

8._____

9. All of the following are used to increase starter motor power and smoothness, *except:*
    (A) several loops of wire.
    (B) a commutator with no segments.
    (C) a commutator with many segments.
    (D) connecting each winding to its own segment on the commutator.

9._____

10. A starter armature consists of four components. Name them._____

    _____

    _____

    _____

11. A(n) _____ is a stationary insulated wire wrapped in a circular shape.
    (A) field winding
    (B) armature
    (C) commutator
    (D) pinion

11._____

12. The magnetic field developed between the pole shoes can be _____ times larger than that of a permanent magnet.

12._____

13. The starter pinion gear is the small gear on the _____ that engages the large gear on the _____.

13._____

14. List the parts of this overrunning clutch.

    (A) _____
    (B) _____
    (C) _____
    (D) _____
    (E) _____
    (F) _____
    (G) _____
    (H) _____
    (I) _____

15. Why is an overrunning clutch needed? _____

    _____

    _____

16. List the seven parts of a starter solenoid._____

    _____

    _____

    _____

    _____

17. Summarize starter solenoid operation. _____
  _____
  _____
  _____
  _____

18. The starter solenoid is located _____.　　　　　　　　　　　18. _____
  (A) on the starter motor
  (B) on a body panel away from the starter motor
  (C) in the starter motor itself
  (D) Both A and B.

Starting Motor Construction

19. What components are included in the *pinion drive assembly?* _____
  _____
  _____

20. What components are included in the *commutator end frame?* _____
  _____
  _____

21. All of the following are parts of the field frame, *except:* 　　　21. _____
  (A) field coils.
  (B) center housing.
  (C) commutator.
  (D) shoes.

22. What is the *drive end frame?* _____
  _____
  _____

23. Technician A says a movable pole shoe starter uses a yoke lever to move 　　23. _____
  the pinion gear. Technician B says a movable pole shoe starter has a
  plunger that moves a shift lever to engage the pinion gear. Who is right?
  (A) A only.
  (B) B only.
  (C) Both A and B.
  (D) Neither A nor B.

24. Summarize the operation of the movable pole shoe starter. _____
  _____
  _____
  _____
  _____
  _____
  _____
  _____

25. A permanent magnet starter uses special _____ in place of conventional 　25. _____
  field windings.

26. A(n) _____ is sometimes used to increase the rotating force applied to the engine flywheel.

26._____

27. List three types of dc motor circuits. _____

_____

_____

28. What prevents the engine from starting unless the shift selector is in neutral or park?

28._____

29. Where is the neutral safety switch mounted on cars with automatic transmissions?
    (A) On the shift lever.
    (B) On the transmission.
    (C) On a body panel.
    (D) Both A and B.

29._____

30. The neutral safety switch is wired into the circuit going into the _____.
    (A) starter motor
    (B) starter solenoid
    (C) starter relay
    (D) None of the above.

30._____

31. In most late-model cars, the _____ is wired into the same control circuit as the neutral safety switch.

31._____

32. A _____ uses a small current from the ignition switch to control a slightly higher current to the starter solenoid.
    (A) transistor
    (B) diode
    (C) starter relay
    (D) neutral safety switch

32._____

33. Summarize starter relay operation. _____

_____

_____

_____

_____

_____

_____

_____

_____

_____

_____

_____

_____

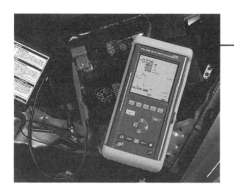

Starting System Testing and Repair

Name: _____ Date: _____

Instructor: _____ Score: _____ Textbook pages 520–537

Objective: After studying this chapter, you will be able to test and repair common starting system troubles.

Starting System Diagnosis

1. Define a *no-crank* problem. _____

_____

_____

2. Technician A says poor electrical connections can cause a no-crank problem. Technician B says that broken flywheel teeth can cause a no-crank problem. Who is right?
   (A) A only.
   (B) B only.
   (C) Both A and B.
   (D) Neither A nor B.

2. _____

3. A single click sound, without cranking, may be due to all of the following, *except:*
   (A) burned solenoid contacts.
   (B) engine mechanical problems.
   (C) weak overrunning clutch.
   (D) bad starter motor.

3. _____

4. List the causes of a humming sound after momentary engine cranking. _____

_____

_____

5. Technician A says normal cranking without starting is caused by the starter system. Technician B says normal engine cranking without starting is caused by worn pinion gear teeth. Who is right?
   (A) A only.
   (B) B only.
   (C) Both A and B.
   (D) Neither A nor B.

5. _____

6. A *start/die* symptom is an indication of what conditions? _____

_____

_____

7. What is a *starting headlight test?* _____

_____

_____

8. List eight problems that can develop in a starting system.

_____

_____

_____

_____

9. A vehicle's lights stay bright with no cranking. What might be the problem?

_____

_____

_____

_____

10. Technician A says a discharged or poorly connected battery can operate the
lights, but may *not* have enough power to operate the starting motor.
Technician B says a discharged or poorly connected battery will *not*
operate the lights or the starting motor. Who is right?
    (A) A only.
    (B) B only.
    (C) Both A and B.
    (D) Neither A nor B.

10. _____

11. Describe the procedure for performing a *starter current draw test.* _____

_____

_____

_____

_____

_____

_____

_____

12. When performing a starter current draw test, you should crank the engine
for no longer than _____ seconds.

12. _____

13. List the typical starter current draw values for the following engines.

    (A) Engine with 4 or 6 cylinders = __?__ amps.

    (B) Engine under 300 CID = __?__ amps.

13. (A) _____

     (B) _____

14. _____ tests will quickly locate a part with higher-than-normal resistance.

14. _____

15. During an insulated circuit resistance test on the starter solenoid, the voltmeter reads a 3.2 volt drop. Technician A says this could be caused by
burned solenoid contacts. Technician B says this could be caused by pitted
solenoid contacts. Who is right?
    (A) A only.
    (B) B only.
    (C) Both A and B.
    (D) Neither A nor B.

15. _____

16. Describe a *starter ground circuit test.* _____

_____

_____

_____

_____

Battery Cable Service

17. Technician A says you can remove starting system parts without disconnecting the battery. Technician B says if you do not disconnect the battery before removing starting system parts, an electrical fire could result. Who is right?

    (A) A only.
    (B) B only.
    (C) Both A and B.
    (D) Neither A nor B.

17. _____

18. How do you do a battery cable connection test with a voltmeter? _____

_____

_____

_____

_____

_____

_____

_____

19. All of the following should be taken into consideration when replacing battery cables, *except:*

    (A) cable length.
    (B) cable diameter.
    (C) using aluminum terminals.
    (D) using lead terminals.

19. _____

20. Technician A says when tightening the connections on the end of battery or starter cables, only snug down the fasteners. Technician B says many of the threaded studs, bolts, and nuts are made of soft lead and can strip and break easily. Who is right?

    (A) A only.
    (B) B only.
    (C) Both A and B.
    (D) Neither A nor B.

20. _____

Starter Solenoid Service

21. Which of the following is the *most likely* symptom of a bad starter solenoid?

    (A) Slow cranking.
    (B) Starter engages, but does not turn the engine.
    (C) Grinding noise when cranking.
    (D) Fast cranking.

21. _____

22. Describe how a starter solenoid can become defective. _____

_____

_____

_____

_____

23. A suspect starter solenoid has a voltage drop of 0.1 volt. Technician A says   23. _____
    the starter solenoid is defective. Technician B says the cable connections
    are loose. Who is right?
    (A) A only.
    (B) B only.
    (C) Both A and B.
    (D) Neither A nor B.

24. Briefly describe the procedure for replacing a solenoid that is mounted on the starter.

_____

_____

_____

Ignition Switch Service

25. What can happen if an ignition switch is defective? _____

_____

_____

26. What should happen when you touch a test light to the starter solenoid start   26. _____
    (S) terminal?
    (A) The test light will remain out when the key is turned to start the
        engine.
    (B) The test light will glow when the key is turned to start the engine.
    (C) The test light will glow all the time.
    (D) The test light will remain out all the time.

Starter Relay Service

27. How can you tell if you have a faulty starting motor relay? _____

_____

_____

_____

28. What tool should you use to test a starter relay?   28. _____

Neutral Safety Switch Service

29. A car will not start in park, but will start in neutral. Technician A says this   29. _____
    is caused by a misadjusted neutral safety switch. Technician B says this is
    caused by a defective ignition switch. Who is right?
    (A) A only.
    (B) B only.
    (C) Both A and B.
    (D) Neither A nor B.

30. All of the following are locations for the neutral safety switch, *except:*   30._____
    (A) transmission.
    (B) steering column.
    (C) shift lever.
    (D) brake pedal.

31. Describe how to test a neutral safety switch._____

_____

_____

_____

_____

_____

Starter Service

32. All of the following are symptoms of a faulty starter motor, *except:*   32._____
    (A) fast cranking.
    (B) no cranking.
    (C) starter cable overheating.
    (D) abnormal noises while cranking.

33. List the five major steps for a *starting motor rebuild.*

_____

_____

_____

_____

_____

34. Technician A says many shops do not rebuild starter motors. Technician B   34._____
    says the cost of labor is too high to make in-shop starter rebuilding
    economical. Who is right?
    (A) A only.
    (B) B only.
    (C) Both A and B.
    (D) Neither A nor B.

35. Which of the following is *false* about starter repairs?   35._____
    (A) The pinion gear can be replaced without complete starting motor
        disassembly.
    (B) When the starter must be repaired, it has to be completely
        disassembled.
    (C) When the starter must be repaired, you may only need to disas-
        semble a section of the starter.
    (D) By removing only the drive and C-lock, the brushes are not
        removed.

36. List, in order, the procedure for starter removal.

_____

_____

_____

_____

_____

37. Identify the parts and problems common to a starting motor.

(A) _____

(B) _____

(C) _____

(D) _____

(E) _____

(F) _____

(G) _____

(H) _____

(I) _____

(J) _____

38. What should you check for whenever you remove a starter?

38._____

39. Technician A says if the shims are not replaced, the pinion and flywheel gears will not mesh properly. Technician B says the shims have no effect on pinion and flywheel gear alignment. Who is right?

    (A) A only.

    (B) B only.

    (C) Both A and B.

    (D) Neither A nor B.

39._____

40. Some late-model engines place the starting motor under the engine _____.

40._____

41. List the six steps for starter disassembly.

(1) _____

_____

(2) _____

_____

(3) _____

_____

(4) _____

_____

(5) _____

_____

(6) _____

_____

42. After the starter has been disassembled, blow all the parts clean with _____.

42._____

43. All of the following parts *cannot* be cleaned with solvent, *except:*   43._____
    - (A) armature.
    - (B) overrunning clutch.
    - (C) brushes.
    - (D) drive end housing.

44. Worn starter brushes can cause _____.   44._____
    - (A) reduced starter torque
    - (B) excessive starter current draw
    - (C) noisy starter operation
    - (D) Both A and B.

45. How are the brush wire leads attached?_____
    _____

46. Technician A says you should inspect the armature windings and commu-   46._____
    tator for signs of burning or overheating. Technician B says if the armature
    has been rubbing on a field pole shoe, the shaft may be bent. Who is right?
    - (A) A only.
    - (B) B only.
    - (C) Both A and B.
    - (D) Neither A nor B.

47. Describe how to use a *growler* properly. _____
    _____
    _____
    _____
    _____

48. What test do you use to check armature continuity?   48._____

49. If the armature windings are in good condition, the commutator should be   49._____
    cleaned using _____.
    - (A) solvent
    - (B) a fine chamois
    - (C) very fine sandpaper
    - (D) emery cloth

50. After machining, the _____ between each commutator may need to be   50._____
    undercut.

51. A field coil is being tested for an open. Technician A says you can use a   51._____
    battery-powered test light. Technician B says you can use a voltmeter. Who
    is right?
    - (A) A only.
    - (B) B only.
    - (C) Both A and B.
    - (D) Neither A nor B.

52. What should happen if ohmmeter leads are touched across the field coil and ground?
    _____
    _____
    _____

53. When should the overrunning clutch be replaced? _____
    _____
    _____

54. Technician A says you should replace the pinion gear during starter service. Technician B says if the pinion is to be reused, you should check the gear teeth for wear. Who is right?
    (A) A only.
    (B) B only.
    (C) Both A and B.
    (D) Neither A nor B.

54._____

55. All the following should be lubricated when reassembling the starter, *except:*
    (A) brushes.
    (B) armature shaft bushings.
    (C) pinion gear splines.
    (D) starter drive yoke.

55._____

56. How can brushes be locked out of the way during starter reassembly? _____
_____
_____
_____
_____

57. What should be done to the starter *before* it is mounted on the engine?_____
_____
_____
_____
_____

58. Define *starter pinion gear clearance.* _____
_____
_____
_____
_____
_____

59. What would happen if the shims are left out during starter installation? _____
_____
_____
_____
_____

60. Technician A says if the starter has a solenoid on it, you should connect the wires on the solenoid before bolting the starter to the engine. Technician B says you should connect the wires to the solenoid after the starter is bolted to the engine. Who is right?
    (A) A only.
    (B) B only.
    (C) Both A and B.
    (D) Neither A nor B.

60._____

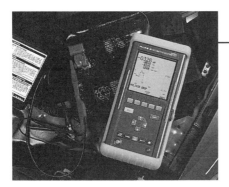

Chapter 33

Charging System Fundamentals

Name: _____Date: _____

Instructor: _____Score: _____Textbook pages 538–552

Objective: After studying this chapter, you will be able to explain charging system operation.

Basic Charging System Parts

1. Identify the parts of this charging system.

(A) _____   (F) _____

(B) _____   (G) _____

(C) _____   (H) _____

(D) _____   (I) _____

(E) _____

2. What is an *alternator?* _____

_____

_____

3. What does the *voltage regulator* do? _____

_____

4. What purpose does the *alternator belt* serve? _____

_____

5. The _____ is an ammeter, voltmeter, or warning light that informs the   5._____
driver of charging system condition.

6. The charging system _____ is the wiring that connects parts of the system.   6._____

7. How does the battery serve the charging system?

_____

_____

8. Technician A says the voltage regulator keeps alternator output at a preset   8._____
charging voltage. Technician B says the precharging voltage is 13–15 volts.
Who is right?
    (A) A only.
    (B) B only.
    (C) Both A and B.
    (D) Neither A nor B.

Charging System Functions

9. List four purposes of the charging system.

_____

_____

_____

_____

Types of Charging Systems

10. All of the following are advantages of the alternator, *except:*   10._____
    (A) smaller than a dc generator.
    (B) heavier than a dc generator.
    (C) more dependable than a dc generator.
    (D) has higher output than a dc generator.

11. In a way, alternator construction is the _____ of dc generator construction.   11._____

Alternator Operation

12. The alternator current must be _____ into direct current before entering the   12._____
vehicle's electrical system.
    (A) forward biased
    (B) rectified
    (C) reverse biased
    (D) None of the above.

13. What is a *diode?* _____

_____

_____

14. Technician A says an alternator uses several diodes. Technician B says using several diodes results in smooth current flow. Who is right?
    14._____
    - (A) A only.
    - (B) B only.
    - (C) Both A and B.
    - (D) Neither A nor B.

Alternator Construction

15. All of the following are main components in a typical alternator, *except:*
    15._____
    - (A) rotor assembly.
    - (B) brush assembly.
    - (C) charge indicator.
    - (D) housing.

16. Describe the makeup of the *alternator rotor.* _____

    _____

    _____

    _____

17. Describe *slip rings* and state their purpose. _____

    _____

    _____

    _____

18. Technician A says alternator bearings are usually roller bearings. Technician B says alternator front bearings are usually press-fit. Who is right?
    18._____
    - (A) A only.
    - (B) B only.
    - (C) Both A and B.
    - (D) Neither A nor B.

19. Small _____ hold the brushes in contact with the slip rings.
    19._____

20. List and describe parts of an *alternator rectifier assembly.* _____

    _____

    _____

    _____

21. A _____ may be used to supply current to the rotor field windings.
    21._____

22. Describe the construction of an *alternator stator.* _____

    _____

    _____

    _____

23. A(n) _____ has the wire ends from the stator windings connected to a neutral junction.
    23 ._____

24. Explain the differences between the *rotor* and *stator* in an alternator. _____

    _____

    _____

    _____

25. What is the job of the alternator fan?_____

_____

26. An alternator uses all of the following for power, *except:*   26 ._____
    (A) V-belt.
    (B) chain.
    (C) cogged V-belt.
    (D) ribbed belt.

27. Identify the parts of this alternator.

(A) _____

(B) _____

(C) _____

(D) _____

(E) _____

(F) _____

(G) _____

(H) _____

(I) _____

(J) _____

(K) _____

(L) _____

(M) _____

28. Describe the operation of a *voltage regulator.* _____

_____

_____

_____

_____

29. There are three basic types of conventional voltage regulators. Name them.

_____

_____

_____

30. Explain the construction and elements of an electronic voltage regulator. _____

_____

_____

_____

_____

_____

Name _____

31. Technician A says an electronic voltage regulator is a sealed unit and cannot be repaired. Technician B says the circuits of an electronic voltage regulator are surrounded by a rubber-like gel. Who is right?
    (A) A only.
    (B) B only.
    (C) Both A and B.
    (D) Neither A nor B.

31. _____

32. What is an *integral voltage regulator?*_____

_____

_____

33. Explain how the *electronic voltage regulator* works. _____

_____

_____

_____

_____

34. Technician A says alternator speed determines whether the regulator increases or decreases charging output. Technician B says alternator temperature determines whether the regulator increases or decreases charging output. Who is right?
    (A) A only.
    (B) B only.
    (C) Both A and B.
    (D) Neither A nor B.

34. _____

35. The _____ is sometimes used to supplement or replace the conventional voltage regulator to more precisely control the charging circuit.

35. _____

36. With computer control of the charging system, there is more computer logic to react to the vehicle conditions. Explain what this means.

_____

_____

_____

_____

_____

37. Voltage regulator switching is very fast, about _____ cycles per second to help prevent radio noise.
    (A) 40
    (B) 60
    (C) 200
    (D) 400

37. _____

38. Why do some modern electronic voltage regulators progressively switch on charging voltage?

_____

_____

_____

_____

_____

39. What is an alternator *failsafe circuit?* _____

_____

_____

_____

_____

_____

Charge Indicators

40. All of the following are charge indicators, *except:*   40. _____
    (A) MIL light.
    (B) warning light.
    (C) voltmeter indicator.
    (D) ammeter indicator.

41. Describe the operation of an alternator *warning light.* _____

_____

_____

_____

_____

_____

42. The voltmeter simply shows _____.   42. _____

43. What is *overcharging?* _____

_____

_____

_____

44. Technician A says some overcharging is okay. Technician B says over-   44. _____
    charging can result in battery overheating. Who is right?
    (A) A only.
    (B) B only.
    (C) Both A and B.
    (D) Neither A nor B.

45. What happens if an ammeter reads to the right side of the scale (positive dial mark)?

_____

_____

_____

_____

_____

_____

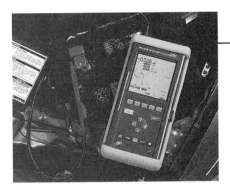

Charging System Diagnosis, Testing, and Repair

Name: _____ Date: _____

Instructor: _____ Score: _____ Textbook pages 553–571

Objective: After studying this chapter, you will be able to summarize the testing and service of modern charging systems.

Charging System Diagnosis

1. Technician A says a charging system problem will have little effect on other vehicle systems. Technician B says that sometimes, another system fault will appear to be caused by charging system problems. Who is right?
   (A) A only.
   (B) B only.
   (C) Both A and B.
   (D) Neither A nor B.

1._____

2. A problem described as a no-charge condition may be caused by a _____.
   (A) shorted starting motor
   (B) battery drain
   (C) worn starter pinion
   (D) Both A and B.

2._____

3. Describe three or more things you would check during an inspection of a charging system.

_____

_____

_____

_____

_____

4. Two technicians are discussing the adjustment of an alternator belt. Technician A says you should tighten an alternator belt only enough to prevent belt slippage or flap. Technician B says overtightening can quickly ruin alternator bearings. Who is right?
   (A) A only.
   (B) B only.
   (C) Both A and B.
   (D) Neither A nor B.

4._____

5. How do you check for abnormal noise from an alternator? _____

_____

_____

6. On most vehicles with self-diagnostic systems, you can connect a(n) _____ to the vehicle to aid in troubleshooting.

6. _____

Charging System Precautions

7. List five precautions to follow when working on a charging system.

(1) _____

_____

(2) _____

_____

(3) _____

_____

(4) _____

_____

(5) _____

_____

8. Technician A says you should disconnect the battery before connecting it to a battery charger. Technician B says electronic components have internal protection from the high voltages of the battery charger. Who is right?
   (A) A only.
   (B) B only.
   (C) Both A and B.
   (D) Neither A nor B.

8. _____

9. All of the following will occur if battery polarity is reversed, *except:*
   (A) damage to the diodes in the alternator.
   (B) the battery will recharge faster.
   (C) damage to the voltage regulator circuits.
   (D) damage to electronic components in computer systems.

9. _____

10. Should you operate the alternator with the output disconnected? _____ Explain your answer.

_____

_____

_____

_____

11. Technician A says you must polarize an alternator after repairs. Technician B says you must *not* polarize a dc generator. Who is right?
    (A) A only.
    (B) B only.
    (C) Both A and B.
    (D) Neither A nor B.

11. _____

Charging System Tests

12. When should a charging system test be performed? _____

_____

_____

_____

13. Explain the following common charging system tests.

Charging system output test: _____

_____

Regulator voltage test: _____

_____

Regulator bypass test: _____

_____

Scope testing: _____

_____

Circuit resistance tests: _____

_____

14. All of the following test equipment can be used to perform a charging system test, *except:*
    (A) dwell-tach.
    (B) load tester.
    (C) scope tool.
    (D) common VOM.

14._____

15. A(n) _____ test measures system current and voltage under maximum load.

15._____

16. Why do you bypass the regulator when testing system output? _____

_____

_____

_____

17. An alternator rated at 80 amps has steady voltage but is only producing 22 amps. Technician A says the voltage regulator is defective. Technician B says the voltage regulator may need adjustment. Who is right?
    (A) A only.
    (B) B only.
    (C) Both A and B.
    (D) Neither A nor B.

17._____

18. An alternator rated at 75 amps is not charging. The alternator begins to charge normally when a regulator bypass test is performed. Which of the following is the *most likely* cause of the no-charge condition?
    (A) Defective stator.
    (B) Defective diodes.
    (C) Defective rotor.
    (D) Defective voltage regulator.

18._____

19. A charging system _____ test involves analyzing the alternator voltage waveform for signs of abnormal ripple.

19._____

20. Two technicians are discussing scope meter usage. Technician A says you should connect both scope leads to the alternator output terminal. Technician B says you should connect one lead to the alternator output terminal and the other to ground. Who is right?
    (A) A only.
    (B) B only.
    (C) Both A and B.
    (D) Neither A nor B.

20._____

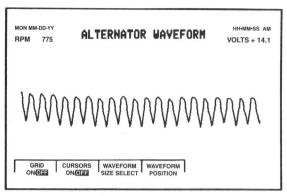

21. An alternator scope test produces the waveform pattern shown above.   21._____
    Which of the following is the *most likely* cause of this waveform?
    (A) One open diode.
    (B) No alternator output.
    (C) Shorted stator windings.
    (D) Possible dead battery.

22. What is the purpose of a *circuit resistance test?* _____

    _____

    _____

23. List three wiring problems a circuit resistance test can locate. _____

    _____

    _____

    _____

24. An insulated-circuit resistance test indicates a portion of the charging system circuit has a voltage drop of 1.9 volts.
    What does this indicate?

    _____

    _____

    _____

25. List the four steps involved in performing a voltmeter test of the charging system.

    _____

    _____

    _____

    _____

26. What is the base voltage reading of a fully charged battery?   26._____

27. Technician A says a no-load voltage reading of 0.5–2 volts higher than the   27._____
    base voltage is normal. Technician B says if the no-load voltage is more
    than 2–3 volts higher than base voltage, the alternator is overcharging the
    battery. Who is right?
    (A) A only.
    (B) B only.
    (C) Both A and B.
    (D) Neither A nor B.

28. During a load voltage test, the voltmeter should read at least _____ higher   28._____
    than the base voltage.

Alternator Service

29. When removing an alternator, what should be done *first?* _____

_____

_____

30. Most alternators are attached to the engine block with _____ bolts.   30. _____

31. Technician A says, depending on vehicle design, the alternator can come out from the top. Technician B says, depending on vehicle design, the alternator can come out from the bottom. Who is right?   31. _____
    (A) A only.
    (B) B only.
    (C) Both A and B.
    (D) Neither A nor B.

32. What tools may be needed to remove a drive pulley? _____

_____

33. Technician A says, depending on the type of repair, you may *not* need to completely disassemble the alternator. Technician B says the alternator must be completely disassembled for any repair. Who is right?   33. _____
    (A) A only
    (B) B only.
    (C) Both A and B.
    (D) Neither A nor B.

34. List four indications of a bad alternator rotor. _____

_____

_____

35. A rotor winding short-to-ground test measures the _____ between the shaft and windings.   35. _____

36. In a rotor winding open circuit test, the meter should read _____ resistance.   36. _____
    (A) 10–20
    (B) 1000–2000
    (C) 2–4
    (D) 100–1000

37. A(n) _____ test checks the windings for internal shorts.   37. _____

38. Besides an oscilloscope, three methods of checking diodes include using: _____

_____

_____

39. Technician A says a shorted diode will have low resistance in both directions. Technician B says an open diode will have high resistance in both directions. Who is right?   39. _____
    (A) A only.
    (B) B only.
    (C) Both A and B.
    (D) Neither A nor B.

40. Why should you heat wires quickly when replacing diodes? _____

_____

_____

41. If bad, the _____ produce a rumbling or grinding sound from inside the alternator.

41._____

42. All of the following are reasons for alternator bearing replacement, *except:*
    (A) the bearings are dry.
    (B) abnormal alternator waveform.
    (C) bearings are worn.
    (D) alternator is being rebuilt.

42._____

43. How do you check the front bearings on an alternator?
    (A) Load test.
    (B) Rotate it with your fingers.
    (C) Using a dial indicator.
    (D) Bearing cannot be tested.

43._____

44. When assembling an alternator, how do you *normally* hold the brushes in place?

_____

_____

_____

45. When assembling the alternator, Technician A says you should check the alignment marks after fitting the front end frame into position. Technician B says this is *not* necessary. Who is right?
    (A) A only.
    (B) B only.
    (C) Both A and B.
    (D) Neither A nor B.

45._____

46. All of the following are alternator assembly steps, *except:*
    (A) install all the components in the rear end frame.
    (B) pull the piece of wire.
    (C) polarize the alternator.
    (D) install the fan, front pulley, and nut.

46._____

47. Test alternator output on a(n) _____ before installation.

47._____

Regulator Service

48. Where is the electronic voltage regulator normally located?_____

_____

49. Technician A says contact point regulators were used on dc generator and early alternator charging systems. Technician B says, due to point wear and pitting, the voltage regulator is a common cause of problems. Who is right?
    (A) A only.
    (B) B only.
    (C) Both A and B.
    (D) Neither A nor B.

49._____

50. What tool should you use and which properties should be checked when testing computer voltage regulators?

_____

_____

_____

51. With computer control of the alternator, charging voltage can be slightly _____ than normal.

51._____

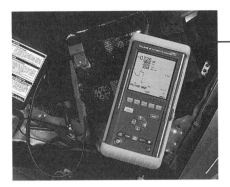

Chapter 35

Ignition System Fundamentals

Name: _____ Date: _____

Instructor: _____ Score: _____ Textbook pages 572–598

Objective: After studying this chapter, you will be able to explain the operating principles of modern ignition systems.

Functions of an Ignition System

1. In your own words, explain the basic purpose of an engine's ignition system.

   _____

   _____

   _____

   _____

   _____

2. Explain the six major parts of an ignition system.

   Battery: _____

   _____

   Ignition switch: _____

   _____

   Ignition coil: _____

   _____

   Switching device: _____

   _____

   Spark plug: _____

   _____

   Ignition system wires: _____

   _____

Ignition System Supply Voltage

3. The ignition system supply voltage is fed to the ignition system by the battery and _____.

   3. _____

4. A key-operated switch in the driver's compartment is the _____ switch.

   4. _____

5. Explain the purpose and operation of the following ignition system components.

   Bypass circuit: _____

   _____

   _____

   Resistor circuit: _____

   _____

   _____

6. Which ignition systems do *not* use bypass or resistance circuits? _____

   _____

Primary and Secondary Circuits

7. What parts of the ignition system are included in the *primary circuit?* _____

   _____

   _____

8. What parts of the ignition system are included in the *secondary circuit?* _____

   _____

   _____

Ignition Coil

9. An ignition coil is a(n) _____ transformer capable of producing short   9. _____
   bursts of high voltage to start combustion.

10. Explain the normal operating voltages of an ignition coil with older and newer systems.

    _____

    _____

    _____

11. Why is more voltage needed in today's vehicles to make the electricity surge through all the parts of the ignition system?

    _____

    _____

12. During ignition coil operation, when the current flowing through the coil   12. _____
    is interrupted, the magnetic field _____ across the secondary windings.

13. Identify the two methods used to break current flow and fire the coil. _____

    _____

14. What is a *coil pack*? _____

    _____

    _____

15. What is a *wasted spark ignition coil*? _____

    _____

    _____

    _____

Ignition Distributors

16. All of the following are functions of an ignition distributor, *except:*
    (A) it actuates on/off cycles for ignition coil.
    (B) it times spark.
    (C) it drives oil pump.
    (D) All of the above are correct.

17. List the four types of ignition distributors. _____

    _____

    _____

18. The method used to rotate the distributor shaft to match engine rpm is the   18. _____
    _____ method.

Contact Point Ignition System

19. Name the three major parts of a contact point distributor. _____

    _____

20. In your own words, explain the operation of a *contact point-type ignition.* _____

    _____

    _____

    _____

21. The amount of time, given in degrees of distributor rotation, that the points   21. _____
    remain closed between each opening is point dwell, or _____.

Electronic Ignition System

22. What does an electronic ignition system use to operate the ignition coil? _____

    _____

23. How do the trigger wheel and pickup coil produce a signal for the ECU?_____

    _____

    _____

    _____

    _____

24. What is a *Hall-effect pickup?* How does it work? _____

    _____

    _____

    _____

    _____

    _____

    _____

25. What does an optical pickup use to produce an engine speed signal for the ignition system?

    _____

    _____

26. Identify the parts of the electronic ignition control module.

(A) _____

(B) _____

(C) _____

(D) _____

(E) _____

(F) _____

Distributor Cap and Rotor

27. The distributor cap's center terminal transfers voltage from the coil wire to the _____.

27. _____

28. The rotor transfers voltage from the distributor cap center terminal to the distributor cap _____.

28. _____

29. About _____ to _____ volts is needed for the spark to jump the rotor-to-cap gap in today's ignition systems.

29. _____

    _____

Secondary Wires

■ *Items 30 through 32.* Match the following terms to their definitions.

30. Carries voltage from the high voltage (high tension) terminal of the ignition coil to the distributor cap.

    (A) Spark plug wires

    (B) Secondary wires

    (C) Coil wire

30. _____

31. Carry the high voltage produced by the ignition coil.

31. _____

32. Carry coil voltage from the side terminals of the distributor cap to the spark plugs.

32. _____

Spark Plugs

33. Somewhere between _____ and _____ volts are needed to make current jump the gap at the spark plug electrodes.

33. _____

    _____

34. Explain the basic parts of a spark plug.

    Ceramic insulator: _____

    _____

    Grounded side electrode: _____

    _____

    Steel shell: _____

    _____

    Center terminal: _____

    _____

35. Why are *resistor spark plugs* used? _____

_____

_____

36. Normal gap specifications range from _____ to _____.   36._____

_____

37. Define *spark plug heat range*. _____

_____

_____

38. A(n) _____ spark plug is self-cleaning due to its long insulator tip which   38._____
burns off deposits.

39. A(n) _____ spark plug has a shorter insulator tip which operates at a cooler   39._____
temperature.

Ignition Timing

40. Timing advance occurs when the spark plugs fire _____ (sooner/later) on   40._____
the engine compression stroke.

41. Explain when timing advance is needed. _____

_____

_____

42. Explain when timing retard is needed._____

_____

_____

43. A method of matching ignition timing to engine load is the distributor _____.   43._____

44. What is a *dual-diaphragm vacuum advance?* _____

_____

_____

45. Name and describe *three* sensors that influence ignition timing.

(1) _____

_____

(2) _____

_____

(3) _____

_____

Crankshaft-Triggered Ignition

46. What is a *crankshaft trigger wheel?* _____

_____

_____

_____

47. The _____ sensor monitors preignition or knock so the computer can retard   47._____
    timing or reduce turbocharger boost pressure as necessary.

Distributorless Ignition System

48. What components does an electronic coil module include? _____

    _____

    _____

    _____

49. A(n) _____ sensor is commonly installed in place of the ignition distributor.   49._____

50. What are the advantages of a *distributorless ignition?* _____

    _____

    _____

    _____

    _____

    _____

    _____

Direct Ignition System

51. A direct ignition system has an ignition coil mounted _____ each spark plug.   51._____
    (A) on the sides of
    (B) over the top of
    (C) under
    (D) in the middle of

52. Explain a difference between a *distributorless ignition* and *direct ignition system.*

    _____

    _____

    _____

53. In some cases, what is detected by an *ionization knock sensing system?* _____

    _____

    _____

    _____

54. Define *engine firing order.*_____

    _____

    _____

    _____

55. What is the reason for the cylinders being marked 1-2-3-4, starting at the front of the engine?

    _____

    _____

    _____

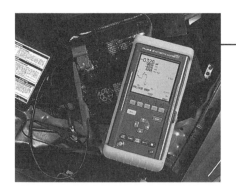

Chapter 36

Ignition System Problems, Testing, and Repair

Name: _____ Date: _____

Instructor: _____ Score: _____ Textbook pages 599–632

Objective: After studying this chapter, you will be able to troubleshoot and repair common ignition system troubles.

Ignition System Problem Diagnosis

1. How has *computer networking* affected ignition system diagnosis? _____

   _____

   _____

   _____

2. An inoperative gasoline injector and a fouled spark plug could cause a(n) _____.   2. _____

Preliminary Checks of Ignition System

3. Name three obvious problems to look for when visually inspecting the ignition system.

   (1) _____

   _____

   (2) _____

   _____

   (3) _____

   _____

4. With late-model OBD II vehicles, what ignition system circuits and components can a scan tool be used to check?

   _____

   _____

   _____

5. What does it mean if your scan tool reads engine misfire? _____

   _____

   _____

6. Which test is a quick and easy way of checking the general operation of the ignition system?   6. _____

7. Why should the engine only be run for a short period of time with a spark plug wire off?

_____

_____

8. What qualities indicate a strong spark? _____

_____

9. If a strong spark is present, the engine no-start problem may be due to   9._____
_____.
    (A) engine trouble
    (B) fouled spark plugs
    (C) fuel system problems
    (D) All of the above.

10. A weak spark or no spark indicates that something is wrong in the _____   10._____
system.

11. What are the symptoms of a *dead cylinder?* _____

_____

_____

12. How do you check for a dead cylinder?_____

_____

_____

_____

_____

Evaluating the Symptoms

13. How is a *hand-held* scope sometimes used to analyze the operation of an ignition system?

_____

_____

_____

14. What test equipment makes up an *engine analyzer?*_____

_____

_____

15. Describe an *electronic ignition tester.* _____

_____

_____

_____

Spark Plug Service

16. List some of the problems caused by bad spark plugs. _____

_____

_____

_____

17. Why must you *never* remove a spark plug wire by pulling on the wire itself?_____

_____

_____

18. When is it necessary to remove all of the ignition coils to replace spark plugs?

_____

19. How do you "read" spark plugs? _____

_____

_____

20. Spark plug cleaning is _____.   20._____
    (A) preferred over replacement with new plugs
    (B) highly recommended by most manufacturers
    (C) accomplished by blasting
    (D) accomplished with a spark plug cleaner

21. Read the spark plugs and describe their indications.

A   B

(A) _____

(B) _____

22. In your own words, how do you *gap* spark plugs? _____

_____

_____

_____

_____

_____

23. Why is it incorrect to use the ratchet to start spark plug threads?_____

_____

_____

Secondary Wire Service

24. Why is secondary wire leakage a problem?_____

_____

25. When an oscilloscope is not available, a(n) _____ test can be used to check   25._____
    for a bad wire.

26. Explain spark plug wire resistance readings when testing with an ohmmeter.

_____

_____

_____

27. How do you check for secondary wire insulation leakage?_____

_____

_____

28. All of the following are true about installing new spark plug wires, *except:*   28._____
    (A) compare the old wire's length with the new wire's length.
    (B) use the engine firing order if all the wires are removed at once.
    (C) replace each wire with one of a longer or shorter length.
    (D) make sure the new wire is fully attached on the plug.

Distributor Service

29. Explain why a distributor is critical to the proper operation of an ignition system.

_____

_____

30. How can *carbon trace* affect engine operation? _____

_____

31. A(n) _____ is used to check the inside of the cap for cracks and carbon   31._____
traces.

32. For what should the rotor tip be checked?_____

_____

33. What can be used to secure the distributor caps? _____

_____

34. What can be used to hold distributor rotors? _____

_____

35. How should a rotor be installed? _____

_____

_____

_____

36. What ensures that a distributor cap is correctly aligned with the rotor? _____

_____

_____

37. What could happen if a distributor cap is *not* installed correctly? _____

_____

_____

38. Why does an electronic ignition distributor use a pickup coil?_____

_____

_____

Pickup Coil Service

39. A(n) _____ test compares actual sensor coil resistance or voltage output   39. _____
    with specifications.

40. Magnetic pickup or sensor coil resistance will usually vary between _____   40. _____
    and _____ ohms, but always refer to service manual specifications.
                                                                                _____

41. The space between the pickup coil and a trigger wheel tooth is the pickup   41. _____
    coil _____.

42. In your own words, how do you replace a crankshaft sensor? _____

    _____

    _____

    _____

    _____

Contact Point Distributor Service

43. How do you measure contact point resistance? _____

    _____

    _____

44. Explain how an ohmmeter can be used to test a condenser. _____

    _____

    _____

    _____

45. What does the tach-dwell meter include? _____

    _____

46. What does the dwell meter portion of the tach-dwell meter measure? _____

    _____

    _____

Dwell

47. An 8-cylinder engine with contact points will usually require _____   47. _____
    degrees of dwell.

▓ *Items 48 through 50.* Match the following terms to their definitions.

48. Means the dwell time should remain the same at   (A) Variable dwell   48. _____
    all engine speeds.
                                                      (B) Fixed dwell

49. Means the engine control module sends high   49. _____
    current through the ignition coil windings until a   (C) Current limiting dwell
    strong magnetic field is developed around the
    coil windings.

50. Means the engine control module alters ignition   50. _____
    coil dwell time with engine speed.

Ignition Timing Adjustment

51. What are the symptoms of an ignition timing that is too advanced?_____

_____

52. The engine will be sluggish during acceleration, and the engine will have poor fuel economy if the ignition timing is too _____.

52. _____

53. Ignition timing without computer-controlled advance is called _____.

53. _____

54. A(n) _____ is sometimes used to measure ignition timing.

54. _____

55. Explain how to adjust timing in systems that require rotating the distributor.

_____

_____

_____

_____

Testing Centrifugal and Vacuum Distributor Advance Systems

56. A distributor _____ may be used to check distributor operation.

56. _____

57. Label the illustration showing timing light use and timing advance.

(A) _____   (D) _____

(B) _____   (E) _____

(C) _____

Removing the Ignition Distributor

58. What must be performed before removing a distributor? _____

_____

_____

_____

59. Explain how to remove the distributor. _____

_____

_____

_____

60. Name the five steps in a distributor rebuild. _____

_____

_____

_____

_____

_____

Ignition Supply Voltage Test

61. Where can an ignition supply voltage test help locate troubles?_____

_____

_____

62. In what way does a resistance wire perform the same basic function as a ballast resistor?

_____

_____

Ignition Coil (Coil Pack) Service

63. Normally, a bad coil pack winding will show _____.   63. _____

64. Why should reverse polarity be avoided during coil replacement?_____

_____

Ignition Switch Service

65. What problems could a bad ignition switch cause?_____

_____

_____

66. When testing an ignition switch, a test light should glow when the key has   66. _____
been turned to _____.

67. How do you remove a steering column-mounted ignition switch? _____

_____

_____

Ignition Control Module Service

68. What problems will a faulty ignition control module produce? _____

_____

_____

69. When do ignition control unit problems typically occur and why? _____

_____

_____

_____

70. The electronic control unit is one of the _____ (first/last) components to test when problems occur.

70._____

71. Why do many technicians use a heat gun or lightbulb to warm the ignition control module?

_____

_____

_____

72. Why is special grease commonly needed under a control unit mounted inside the distributor?

_____

_____

_____

Distributorless Ignition System Service

73. When can a computerized ignition system be seriously damaged?_____

_____

_____

_____

_____

74. How do you check a knock sensor?_____

_____

_____

_____

_____

Direct Ignition System Service

75. Explain the differences in testing a direct ignition system. _____

_____

_____

_____

_____

_____

76. When working on a direct ignition system, why would you remove the coil cover and connect conventional spark plug wires between the coil output terminals and the spark plugs?

_____

_____

_____

_____

_____

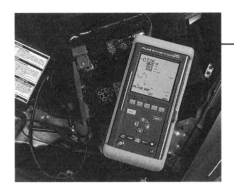

Chapter 37

Lights, Instrumentation, Wipers, and Horns— Operation and Service

Name: _____Date:_____

Instructor: _____Score: _____Textbook pages 633–668

Objective: After studying this chapter, you will be able to explain the operation and service of light, wiper, and horn systems.

Lighting Systems

1. Name four components in the lighting system that operate the interior and exterior lights on a vehicle.

   _____

   _____

2. Which components are included in the headlamp system? _____

   _____

   _____

   _____

   _____

   _____

3. What does the headlamp switch control?_____

   _____

4. A headlamp switch may contain a(n) _____ for adjusting the brightness of   4._____
   the instrument panel lights.

5. Define *multifunction switch.*_____

   _____

   _____

   _____

6. What is the purpose of a *flash-to-pass* feature?_____

   _____

   _____

7. When are low beams used? _____

   _____

8. When are high beams used?_____

   _____

9. What are the two different types of sealed-beam headlamp bulbs? _____
_____

10. A halogen headlamp increases light output by about _____ without increasing current draw.

10. _____

11. The maximum brightness for low beams, according to federal regulations, is _____ candle power.

11. _____

12. A glass or plastic _____ disperses the light beam in front of the vehicle and protects the bulb.

12. _____

13. A lamp number is generally stamped on the _____.

13. _____

14. Explain what happens when the driver activates the dimmer switch. _____
_____
_____
_____

15. How does an *automatic headlight dimmer system* function?_____
_____
_____
_____

16. Where can a turn signal switch be mounted? _____
_____

17. Explain how a turn signal flasher works._____
_____
_____
_____
_____

18. What components are included in the emergency light system?_____
_____
_____

19. The _____ closes the light circuit when the transmission is shifted into reverse.

19. _____

20. Identify the types of switches.

A

B

C

D

(A) _____   (C) _____

(B) _____   (D) _____

Light System Service

21. Why must you *not* touch the surface of a headlight bulb insert? _____
_____
_____

22. What is indicated if all or several of the lights flicker?_____
_____
_____

23. All of the following are ways to test a light switch, *except:*   23._____
    (A) check the fuse unit.
    (B) use a test light.
    (C) check with a voltmeter.
    (D) test with an ohmmeter.

24. What is a *headlight aiming screen?* _____
_____
_____

Items 25 through 27. Match the following terms to their definitions.

25. Built into late-model headlight assemblies to simplify headlight aiming.

    (A) Headlight aimers

    (B) Headlight leveling bubbles

26. Alter the direction of the headlamp beams.

    (C) Headlight adjusting screws

27. Point the car's headlamps in a specified position.

25._____

26._____

27._____

Instrumentation

28. What is the purpose of *instrumentation?* _____
_____
_____

Items 29 through 32. Match the following terms to their definitions.

29. Small glass tubes filled with neon or argon gas.

    (A) Digital instruments

30. Use various types of lights and electronic displays to show operating conditions.

    (B) Vacuum fluorescent displays

    (C) Liquid crystal displays

31. Use rotating needles or dials to indicate operating conditions.

    (D) Analog instruments

32. Semiconductor panels that will pass light when electrically energized and block light when not energized.

29._____

30._____

31._____

32._____

33. Define *sending units.* _____
_____
_____

34. If a gauge is not working, what should you do first? _____
_____
_____

35. Information displayed onto the windshield or a plastic dash panel for easier viewing is reflected by a(n) _____.

35._____

Windshield Wipers

36. What protects a windshield wiper system? _____

_____

37. Name the two common types of pumps used with windshield washer systems.

_____

38. How does a *rain-sensing wiper system* detect water? _____

_____

_____

_____

39. What should be checked if the windshield washer does *not* work? _____

_____

_____

Horns

40. What should be done to adjust horn current? _____

_____

_____

41. How can meter damage be prevented?_____

_____

_____

Finding Common Electrical Problems

42. What could cause an *open circuit?* _____

_____

_____

_____

43. What should you do to find a *high resistance?* _____

_____

_____

_____

44. A voltage drop across an electrical conductor should not exceed _____ volts.

44._____

45. How do you test a relay? _____

_____

_____

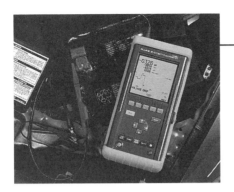

Chapter 38

Sound Systems and Power Accessories

Name: _____Date:_____

Instructor: _____Score: _____Textbook pages 669–695

Objective: After studying this chapter, you will be able to summarize the operation and general service of optional devices.

Sound Systems

1. What components are included in a basic radio system? _____

   _____

   _____

2. The radio station sends out a(n) _____ from a large broadcasting tower.　　2._____

3. A radio speaker's diaphragm moves back and forth, producing _____.　　3._____

Radio

4. Name and explain the differences between the two types of radio signals. _____

   _____

   _____

   _____

   _____

5. If a radio fails to work, what should you do? _____

   _____

   _____

6. Often two power leads feed the radio, one for the circuitry and the other for　　6._____
   the _____.

7. A speaker's permanent magnet and coil of wire mounted on a flexible diaphragm converts electricity into what?

   _____

Items 8-10. Match each term to its correct definition.

8. Internal problems require a specialized electronic technician; incorporated into the radio.

9. Increases volume without sound distortion.

10. Stores and plays music digitally.

(A) CD player

(B) Tape player

(C) Power booster

8. _____

9. _____

10. _____

11. When a transistor is driven too hard, sometimes to failure, _____ occurs.   11._____

12. Diagnose the following radio noise sounds:

    (A) *Low-pitched clicking that changes with engine speed:* _____

    _____

    _____

    (B) *High-pitched whirring sound that also changes with engine speed:* _____

    _____

    _____

Power Seats

13. What operates power seats? _____

_____

14. Explain the use of a *memory seat.* _____

_____

15. For a seat to return to a desired position for different drivers, it can be   15._____
    programmed with a(n) _____.

16. When the power seat only fails in one mode (up and down, for example), what should you do first?

_____

_____

17. Identify the most common reasons for power seat problems. _____

_____

Power Windows

18. Identify what a power window system uses to operate the door windows._____

_____

_____

19. The up-down mechanism for the glass is known as the _____.   19._____

20. Explain how a window motor is protected from overheating damage. _____

_____

_____

21. What might you suspect if you hear a humming sound when a window switch is pressed? _____

_____

22. Why must a technician avoid wearing a wristwatch or rings when servicing inside a door?_____

_____

_____

Power Door Locks

23. What do power door locks usually use to operate the door lock mechanisms?

_____

24. Explain the basic procedure for removing a door panel. _____

_____

_____

_____

_____

25. What is a leading reason why wiring going through the body and into the door can break internally?

_____

_____

Power Trunk Release

26. What happens when you close the trunk release switch? _____

_____

_____

27. What does a power steering wheel use to automatically tilt and telescope the steering wheel?_____

_____

_____

Rear Window Defogger

28. How does a rear window defogger function? _____

_____

_____

_____

29. If a window has _____, one area is heated and cleared before another.   29._____

30. What procedure should be followed when the grid-type rear window defogger does not work?

_____

_____

_____

_____

Heated Windshield

31. When _____ to _____ volts pass through the invisible film in a heated   31._____
    windshield system, the glass heats up and melts ice or snow.
    _____

32. Why must caution be taken when working on heated windshield systems?_____

_____

_____

33. Under what conditions does a reminder system make an audible signal?_____

_____

_____

Cruise Control Systems

34. Briefly explain the major parts of a modern cruise control system.

    Power switches: _____

    _____

    Neutral safety switch: _____

    _____

    Throttle actuator: _____

    _____

    Vehicle speed sensor: _____

    _____

    Cruise computer: _____

    _____

    Clutch switch: _____

    _____

35. Cruise control senses engine speed and controls the _____ opening on the   35. _____
    engine.

Power Mirrors

36. Power mirrors usually use tiny reversible _____ to tilt the sideview mirror   36. _____
    glass into different positions.

37. What should be done to service power mirrors? _____

    _____

    _____

38. Rearview mirror glass is often removed with a(n) _____ if cracked.   38. _____

Cellular Mobile Telephone

39. Explain how a cellular mobile telephone uses a transceiver. _____

    _____

    _____

40. Identify the parts of the cellular phone system.

(A) _____

(B) _____

(C) _____

(D) _____

(E) _____

(F) _____

Chapter 39

Cooling System Fundamentals

Name: _____ Date: _____

Instructor: _____ Score: _____ Textbook pages 697–715

Objective: After studying this chapter, you will be able to describe the operation of modern automotive cooling systems.

1. Explain the general purpose and importance of a cooling system. _____

_____

_____

_____

_____

Cooling System Functions

2. All of the following are functions of a cooling system, *except:*   2._____
   (A) providing a means for warming the passenger compartment.
   (B) causing the engine to seize.
   (C) removing excess heat from the engine.
   (D) maintaining a constant engine operating temperature.

3. A combustion flame temperature of _____°F is enough heat to melt metal   3._____
   parts.

4. What can happen if excess heat is *not* removed from the engine? _____

_____

5. A usual engine operating temperature is between _____°F and _____°F.   5._____

6. Why is it important for an engine to warm up rapidly?_____

_____

_____

Cooling System Types

7. What is an *air cooling system?* _____

_____

_____

8. Air can be routed over the cylinder fins by plastic or sheet metal ducts and   8._____
   ____.

9. What advantages does a liquid cooling system have over an air cooling system? _____

_____ _____

_____

_____

10. What is *reverse flow cooling?* _____

_____

_____

Basic Cooling System

11. Briefly explain the basic parts of a cooling system.

Water pump: _____

_____

Thermostat: _____

_____

Radiator: _____

_____

Radiator hoses: _____

_____

12. What kind of impellers are sometimes used to reduce engine power   12. _____
consumption?

13. Identify the parts of the water pump.

(A) _____

(B) _____

(C) _____

(D) _____

(E) _____

(F) _____

(G) _____

14. A crossflow radiator has its tanks on the ____ of the core.   14. _____

15. Why is a transmission oil cooler often placed in the radiator of cars with automatic transmissions or transaxles?

_____

_____

Name _____

■ *Items 16 through 22.* Match the following parts of a typical water pump to the correct description.

16. Fits between the engine and pump housing to prevent coolant leakage.

17. Steel shaft that transfers turning force from the hub to the impeller.

18. Provides mounting place for belt pulley and fan.

19. Iron or aluminum casting that forms the main body of pump.

20. Disk with fan-like blades, the impeller spins and produces pressure and flow.

21. Prevents coolant leakage between pump shaft and pump housing.

22. Plain or ball bearings that allow the pump shaft to spin freely in housing.

(A) Water pump shaft

(B) Water pump bearings

(C) Water pump housing

(D) Water pump impeller

(E) Water pump gasket

(F) Water pump seal

(G) Water pump hub

16._____

17._____

18._____

19._____

20._____

21._____

22._____

■ *Items 23 through 29.* Match the following terms to their correct definition.

23. Hold the radiator hoses and heater hoses on their fittings.

24. Frequently used in the lower radiator hose to prevent its collapse.

25. Carry coolant between the engine water jackets and the radiator.

26. Has an accordion shape and can be bent to different angles.

27. Uses a worm gear that engages slots in the clamp strap to allow tightening around the hose.

28. Small-diameter hoses that carry coolant to the heater core.

29. Manufactured in a special shape, with bends to clear the cooling fan and other parts.

(A) Radiator hoses

(B) Molded hose

(C) Flexible hose

(D) Hose spring

(E) Heater hoses

(F) Hose clamps

(G) Worm drive hose clamp

23._____

24._____

25._____

26._____

27._____

28._____

29._____

30. Explain the principle by which a radiator cap works. _____

_____

_____

31. Typical radiator cap pressure is _____ psi.

31._____

32. What could occur without a cap vacuum valve? _____

_____

_____

Closed and Open Cooling Systems

33. Explain the operation of a closed cooling system._____

_____

_____

_____

■ *Items 34 through 39*. Match the following fan terms to their correct descriptions.

34. Provides cooling action with an electric motor and a thermostatic switch.

(A) Fluid coupling fan clutch

34._____

(B) Thermostatic fan clutch

35. Designed to slip at higher engine speeds.

(C) Flex fan

35._____

36. Bolts to the water pump hub and pulley.

(D) Engine-powered fan

36._____

37. A small direct current motor.

(E) Electric cooling fan

37._____

38. Has a temperature-sensitive, bimetal spring that controls fan action.

(F) Fan motor

38._____

39. Has thin, flexible blades that alter airflow with engine speed.

39._____

40. How does a *coolant sensor* work? _____

41. How does a radiator shroud keep the engine from overheating?_____

42. Why are high thermostat heating ranges used in modern automobiles? _____

43. When the engine is cold, the thermostat will be _____ and coolant cannot circulate through the radiator.

43._____

44. A(n) _____ valve permits coolant circulation through the engine when the thermostat is closed.

44._____

45. A(n) _____ valve helps prevent air pockets from forming in the housing.

45._____

46. How does the engine temperature warning light work on many late-model vehicles?

Cooling System Instrumentation

47. What does antifreeze prevent? _____

48. Why does antifreeze cool the engine better than water? _____

49. Ideal cooling and protection from freeze-up is a _____ mixture of water and antifreeze.

49._____

50. A 120-volt heating element mounted in the block water jacket that can be used to aid engine starting in cold weather is a(n) _____.

50._____

Chapter 40

Cooling System Testing, Maintenance, and Repair

Name: _____ Date: _____

Instructor: _____ Score: _____ Textbook pages 716–738

Objective: After studying this chapter, you will be able to explain common service tasks performed on engine cooling systems.

Cooling System Problem Diagnosis

1. Many on-board diagnostic systems will trip a(n) _____ when certain cooling related circuits are operating or seem to be operating out of range.

   1. _____

2. Name at least four cooling system functions that are often monitored by an OBD II system.

   _____

   _____

   _____

   _____

   _____

3. A cooling system _____ should be used when problems are difficult to locate and correct.

   3. _____

4. What troubles should be checked for in a visual inspection of a cooling system? _____

   _____

   _____

   _____

Cooling System Problems

5. How can a coolant leak problem be recognized? _____

   _____

   _____

6. Why is it unsafe to remove a radiator cap when the engine is hot? _____

   _____

   _____

7. How does a cooling system pressure test work? _____

_____

_____

_____

8. A(n) _____ is one of the most commonly used and important cooling   8._____
   system testing devices.

9. Label the parts and tool being used to check for combustion gas in the cooling system.

(A) _____

(B) _____

(C) _____

(D) _____

(E) _____

(F) _____

10. What could happen if too much pressure is pumped into the cooling system? _____

_____

11. A(n) _____ test should be performed when signs point to a blown head   11._____
    gasket, cracked block, or cracked cylinder head.

12. What does a milky white solution found in the engine oil or in valve covers indicate?_____

_____

13. Rust or scale, loose fan belt, collapsed lower hose, and ice in coolant are   13._____
    four causes of _____.

14. What indicates *overcooling*? _____

_____

_____

Water Pump Service

15. A bad water pump may _____.   15._____
    (A) fail to circulate coolant
    (B) produce a grinding sound
    (C) leak coolant
    (D) All of the above.

16. What are two common reasons for pump failure?_____

_____

_____

17. How should you check for worn water pump bearings? _____

_____

_____

_____

18. A(n) _____ can be used to listen for worn, noisy water pump bearings.   18. _____

19. Why should you *never* use excess force to try to remove an old water pump? _____

_____

_____

_____

20. Why are few water pumps rebuilt? _____

_____

21. When installing a water pump gasket, use an approved _____ to adhere the   21. _____
new gasket to the pump.

Thermostat Service

22. A stuck thermostat can cause engine _____.   22. _____
    (A) overcooling
    (B) overheating
    (C) Both A and B.
    (D) Neither A nor B.

23. How can you use a digital thermometer to check part temperatures and cooling system operation?

_____

_____

_____

_____

24. Label the parts relating to thermostat replacement.

(A) _____

(B) _____

(C) _____

(D) _____

(E) _____

(F) _____

(G) _____

(H) _____

(I) _____

25. Why is it easy to damage the thermostat housing? _____

_____

26. With some engine designs, a rubber _____ seal is used instead of a gasket.   26. _____

27. An area in the engine suffering from a buildup of combustion heat is a(n) _____.

27._____

28. A(n) _____ is sometimes provided to help remove trapped air when refilling the cooling system.
    (A) bleed valve
    (B) freeze plug
    (C) refractometer
    (D) flushing

28._____

Cooling System Hose Service

29. An old radiator hose may _____.
    (A) become soft and mushy
    (B) cause cooling system problems
    (C) become hard and brittle
    (D) All of the above.

29._____

30. What steps help in removing a hose?_____
_____
_____

Radiator and Pressure Cap Service

31. What problems can limit air circulation through the core of the radiator? _____
_____
_____

32. A radiator _____ test measures the cap opening pressure and checks the condition of the sealing washer.

32._____

33. How do you remove a radiator? _____
_____
_____
_____
_____

Fan Belt Service

34. What is a problem with an overtightened belt? _____
_____

35. What happens with a loose belt? _____
_____

Engine Fan Service

36. What problems can a faulty engine fan cause? _____
_____
_____

37. How should you test a thermostatic fan clutch? _____

_____

_____

_____

38. Most electric cooling fans are controlled by a heat sensitive switch located   38. _____
somewhere in the _____.
    (A) engine block
    (B) thermostat housing
    (C) radiator
    (D) Any of the above.

39. How do you test an electric cooling fan? _____

_____

_____

_____

40. Check the operation of an electric cooling fan using a(n) _____ or high   40. _____
impedance _____.

Freeze Plug Service

41. Engine freeze plugs are _____ than the metal in the engine block and will   41. _____
rust through before the other engine part.

42. List the steps (in order) for replacing a freeze plug.

    (1) _____

    _____

    (2) _____

    _____

    (3) _____

    _____

    (4) _____

    _____

    (5) _____

    _____

Coolant Service

43. What tool can be used to measure how acidic antifreeze solution is?   43. _____

44. When should coolant be changed? _____

_____

45. To measure the freezing point of the cooling system antifreeze solution,   45. _____
use a cooling system _____.

46. What is the most common reason for cracked blocks and cylinder heads? _____

_____

_____

47. How is a refractometer used as a coolant strength measuring device? _____

_____

_____

_____

48. If the lowest normal temperature for the area is 10°F, the coolant should   48. _____
    test to _____.
    (A) −10°F
    (B) −20°F
    (C) −30°F
    (D) −40°F

Flushing a Cooling System

49. What effect does flushing have on a cooling system? _____

_____

50. Why is rust bad for a cooling system? _____

_____

_____

51. The thermostat does not have to be _____ from the engine when fast   51. _____
    flushing cleaning is performed.

52. Describe the process of *reverse flushing*. _____

_____

_____

_____

Temperature Gauge Service

53. What indicates a defective temperature gauge? _____

_____

_____

54. What should happen when the temperature gauge sending unit wire is grounded? _____

_____

_____

55. A gauge tester is a special testing device with a(n) _____.   55. _____

56. How do you test a temperature indicating light? _____

_____

_____

57. Summarize how you would remove a radiator for service. _____

_____

_____

_____

_____

Lubrication System Fundamentals

Name: _____ Date: _____

Instructor: _____ Score: _____ Textbook pages 739–755

Objective: After studying this chapter, you will be able to describe the operation of an engine lubrication system.

Lubrication System Basics

1. The lubrication system forces oil to high _____ in the engine to protect moving parts from friction, wear, and damage.

   1. _____

2. What would happen to an engine without a lubrication system? _____

   _____

   _____

   _____

   _____

   _____

   _____

Lubrication System Operation

3. Engine oil is commonly refined from _____, which is extracted from deep within the earth.

   3. _____

Items 4 through 9. Match the lubrication system parts to their correct definitions.

4. Strains out impurities in the oil.	(A) Engine oil	4. _____
5. Forces oil throughout the inside of the engine.	(B) Oil pump	5. _____
6. Lubricant for moving parts in engine.	(C) Pressure relief valve	6. _____
7. Limits maximum oil pump pressure.	(D) Oil pan	7. _____
8. Reservoir or storage area for engine oil.	(E) Oil filter	8. _____
9. Oil passages through the engine.	(F) Oil galleries	9. _____

10. A(n) _____ separates engine parts to prevent metal-on-metal contact.

    10. _____

11. The small space between moving engine parts for the lubricating oil film is called _____.

    11. _____

12. A rod bearing clearance is normally around _____ of an inch.

    12. _____

13. Name the locations where friction type bearings are used in an engine. _____
_____
_____

14. Describe *high viscosity oil.* _____
_____

15. Describe *low viscosity oil.* _____
_____

16. What problems can cold motor oil cause? _____
_____
_____
_____
_____

17. Fill in the information on oil viscosity and temperature.

Look for this label

API SERVICE SJ
SAE
5W-30
ENERGY CONSERVING II

Hot weather

F   C
+100 +38
+60   -16
+40   +4
+32   0
+20   -7
+10   -12
0   -18
-20   -29

A   B   C   D   E

Cold weather   SAE viscosity grade

(A) _____

(B) _____

(C) _____

(D) _____

(E) _____

18. _____ oil seems to seal rings and provide better bearing protection.   18._____

19. _____ can prevent oil oxidation, engine deposits, breakdown, foaming, and   19._____
other problems.

20. Explain the *pressure-fed oiling* method. _____
_____
_____
_____

21. Explain the *splash oiling* method. _____
_____
_____
_____

Name _____

22. What are the two types of full-pressure lubrication systems? _____
_____
_____

23. Which type of full-pressure lubrication system is the more common type?   23. _____

■ *Items 24 through 30.* Match the following terms to their correct definitions.

24. Lowest area in the oil pan.

25. Designed to add strength to the engine bottom end and cylinder block.

26. Secure the pan to the engine block.

27. Bolts to the bottom of the engine block.

28. Prevents oil leakage between the engine block and pan.

29. May be used to keep the oil from splashing up on the spinning crankshaft.

30. Allows removal of the old oil during oil changes.

(A) Oil pan drain plug

(B) Oil pan gasket

(C) Sump

(D) Structural oil pan

(E) Oil pan

(F) Oil pan bolts

(G) Oil pan baffle

24. _____

25. _____

26. _____

27. _____

28. _____

29. _____

30. _____

31. Describe the function of the *pickup screen.* _____
_____
_____
_____
_____

32. The heart of the engine lubrication system is the _____.   32. _____

33. All of the following are methods used to drive an oil pump, *except:*   33. _____
   (A) rotary oil pump.
   (B) crankshaft-driven oil pump.
   (C) shaft-driven oil pump.
   (D) gear-driven oil pump.

34. A(n) _____ valve limits maximum oil pressure.   34. _____

35. Describe the function of a *filter element.* _____
_____
_____

36. A(n) _____ valve is commonly used to protect the engine from oil starvation if the filter element becomes clogged.   36. _____

37. What is the number one reason for premature engine wear? _____
_____

38. A heat exchanger that may be used to help lower and control the operating temperature of the engine oil is a(n) _____.   38. _____

39. Oil coolers are frequently used on _____.   39. _____

40. The _____ are the small passages for oil through the engine block and head.   40. _____
   (A) valleys
   (B) tubes
   (C) galleries
   (D) None are correct.

41. Identify the parts of the oil cooler and filter housing.

(A) _____

(B) _____

(C) _____

(D) _____

(E) _____

42. How are oil spray nozzles used? _____

_____

_____

_____

43. A positive crankcase ventilation (PCV) system draws fumes out of the engine crankcase and ____ them inside the engine.

43. _____

44. A PCV system helps prevent engine _____, which could restrict oil circulation.

44. _____

Oil Pressure Indicator

45. How does an oil pressure indicator operate? _____

_____

_____

_____

_____

_____

46. What could occur before the warning light is energized?
    (A) Low oil pressure
    (B) Hearing light engine bearing knock
    (C) Hearing lifter noise
    (D) All of the above.

46. _____

47. What is an *oil pressure sending unit?* _____

_____

_____

_____

48. If oil pressure drops too low, a low pressure _____ can be used to shut off the engine.

48. _____

49. An oil level sensor is usually mounted in the _____.

49. _____

Chapter 42

Lubrication System Testing, Service, and Repair

Name: _____ Date: _____

Instructor: _____ Score: _____ Textbook pages 756–771

Objective: After studying this chapter, you will be able to summarize lubrication system testing, service, and repair techniques.

Lubrication System Problem Diagnosis

1. Name and explain the limited number of problems found in a lubrication system. _____
_____
_____
_____
_____

2. In a visual inspection to diagnose lubrication system problems, what should be checked? _____
_____
_____
_____
_____
_____

3. What is a clue to the vehicle owner that a problem with high oil consumption exists? _____
_____
_____

4. External oil leakage is easily detected as _____, oil-wet areas around or on   4._____
the engine.

5. What is usually the source of external oil leakage?_____
_____

6. What method can be used to clean parts around the point of oil leakage? _____
_____

7. Explain how oil dye works to help check for external oil leaks._____
_____
_____

8. Internal engine oil leakage shows up as _____ smoke in the exhaust.   8._____

9. How is *low* oil pressure indicated? _____

_____

_____

10. Name and briefly describe three causes of low oil pressure._____

_____

_____

_____

_____

_____

_____

11. High oil pressure causes the gauge to read higher than normal and can   11._____
cause the _____ to rupture.

12. Name and explain the four common causes of high oil pressure.

_____

_____

_____

_____

_____

_____

_____

13. An oil pressure test uses a test gauge to measure actual lubrication system   13._____
_____.

14. Depending upon the type of engine and number of miles of use, oil   14._____
pressure should be at least _____ to _____ psi at idle.

_____

15. Why should safety glasses be worn when checking engine oil pressure?_____

_____

_____

Engine Oil and Filter Service

16. Why is it critical for an engine's oil and oil filter to be serviced regularly?_____

_____

_____

_____

17. New vehicles can go _____ miles between oil changes.   17._____
   (A) 1000–5500
   (B) 2000–6500
   (C) 3000–7500
   (D) 4000–8500

18. Which engines usually require more frequent oil and filter service than naturally aspirated engines? _____

_____

19. Explain the basic steps for changing engine oil and the oil filter.

(A)_____

_____

(B)_____

_____

(C)_____

_____

(D)_____

_____

(E) _____

_____

(F) _____

_____

Oil Pan Service

20. All of the following are steps to removing an oil pan, *except:*   20._____
    (A) drain motor oil.
    (B) unscrew the bolts around the outside of the pan flange.
    (C) pound hard on the pan with a rubber hammer to free it from the
        cylinder block.
    (D) remove all old gasket or silicone material from the pan and
        engine block.

21. After removing the oil pan, check it for _____.   21._____

22. Define the term *prelubricator* and explain its purpose. _____

_____

_____

_____

_____

_____

23. How do you use silicone sealer to install an oil pan? _____

_____

_____

_____

_____

_____

_____

24. What can occur if the oil pan bolts are overtightened? _____

_____

_____

_____

Oil Pump Service

25. What does a bad oil pump cause? _____

_____

_____

26. What procedures are followed for oil pump installation? _____

_____

_____

_____

_____

_____

Pressure Relief Valve Service

27. _____ can be used to increase spring tension.   27._____

28. Use a(n) _____ and small hole gauge to check valve and valve bore wear.   28._____

29. Identify the parts of the engine oil pump that mounts on the front of the engine.

(A) _____

(B) _____

(C) _____

(D) _____

(E) _____

(F) _____

(G) _____

(H) _____

(I) _____

Oil Pressure Indicator and Gauge Service

30. A faulty oil _____ can make the indicator light glow or gauge read low   30._____
when oil pressure is normal.

31. Describe how to check the action of the indicator or gauge._____

_____

_____

_____

_____

_____

32. Typically, minimum oil pressure at idle is _____ to _____ psi.   32._____

_____

Chapter 43

Emission Control Systems

Name: _____ Date: _____

Instructor: _____ Score: _____ Textbook pages 773–799

Objective: After studying this chapter, you will be able to explain the operation of emission control systems.

Air Pollution

1. Why are *emission control systems* used on cars and trucks? _____
   _____
   _____
   _____

2. What is *carbon monoxide?* What produces it? _____
   _____
   _____
   _____
   _____
   _____
   _____

3. What are *oxides of nitrogen?* _____
   _____
   _____
   _____
   _____
   _____
   _____

4. What are *particulates?* What causes their formation? _____
   _____
   _____
   _____
   _____
   _____

5. What percentage of all particulate emissions float in the air for extended periods of time?

5. _____

6. List and explain *two* engine modifications designed to reduce exhaust emissions.

(1) _____

_____

_____

_____

(2) _____

_____

_____

_____

Vehicle Emission Control Systems

■ Match the emission control systems below with the statement that best describes its function.

7. Forces outside air into the exhaust system to help burn unburned fuel.

8. Keeps engine crankcase fumes out of atmosphere.

9. Chemically changes exhaust byproducts into harmless substances.

10. Injects burned exhaust gases into engine to lower combustion temperature and prevent formation of No_x.

11. Uses natural pressure pulses in the exhaust system to operate aspirator valves.

12. Closed vent system that prevents fuel vapors from entering atmosphere.

13. Electronic controls are used to monitor and interface various systems to increase efficiency and reduce emissions.

14. Maintains a constant temperature of the air entering the engine for improved combustion and performance in cold weather.

(A) Positive crankcase ventilation system (PCV)

(B) Evaporative emissions control system (EVAP)

(C) Exhaust gas recirculation system (EGR)

(D) Air injection system

(E) Thermostatic air cleaner system

(F) Catalytic converter

(G) Computer control system

(H) Pulse air system

7. _____

8. _____

9. _____

10. _____

11. _____

12. _____

13. _____

14. _____

Positive Crankcase Ventilation

15. Engine blowby gases contain _____.
    - (A) unburned fuel (HC)
    - (B) water, sulfur, and acid
    - (C) particulates
    - (D) All of the above.

15. _____

16. Name four undesirable conditions caused by engine blowby gases.

_____

_____

_____

_____

17. The PCV _____ is used to control the flow of air through the system.

17._____

18. Identify the parts of the PCV system illustrated below.

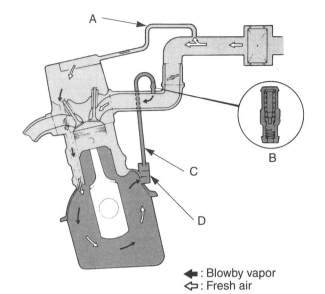

◀ : Blowby vapor
⇦ : Fresh air

(A) _____

(B) _____

(C) _____

(D) _____

Evaporative Emissions Control Systems

19. The EVAP system uses a(n) _____ fuel tank cap to prevent fuel vapors from entering the atmosphere.

19._____

20. The _____ allows for fuel expansion and tank filling without spillage.

20._____

21. What type of component can be used to keep liquid fuel from entering the evaporative emission system?

21._____

22. What function does a *rollover valve* serve? _____

_____

_____

23. Identify the parts of the evaporative emissions control system illustrated below.

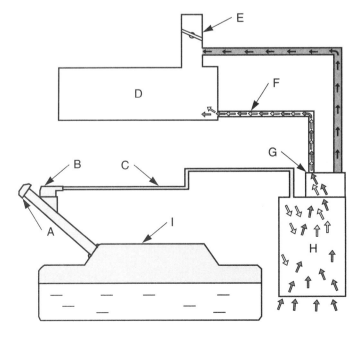

(A) _____

(B) _____

(C) _____

(D) _____

(E) _____

(F) _____

(G) _____

(H) _____

(I) _____

24. What is the purpose of the *charcoal canister?* _____

_____

_____

25. List three additional components found on an *enhanced evaporative emissions control system* and explain their function.

(1) _____

_____

(2) _____

_____

(3) _____

_____

Exhaust Gas Recirculation (EGR)

26. How does an *electronic-vacuum operated EGR valve* work? _____

_____

_____

_____

_____

_____

27. What is an *electronic EGR system* and how does it operate? _____

_____

_____

_____

_____

_____

28. Label the components of the EGR valve illustrated below.

(A) _____

(B) _____

(C) _____

(D) _____

(E) _____

(F) _____

(G) _____

(H) _____

(I) _____

(J) _____

Air Injection System

29. The _____ of an air injection system keeps air from entering the exhaust
    system during acceleration.
    - (A) vacuum valve
    - (B) diverter valve
    - (C) air injection pump
    - (D) None of the above.

29. _____

30. How is *backfiring* prevented in an air injection system? _____

_____

_____

_____

Thermostatic Air Cleaner System

31. The thermostatic air cleaner system _____.
    - (A) cools the air entering the engine
    - (B) is used with fuel injection systems
    - (C) speeds engine warmup
    - (D) All of the above.

31. _____

32. A(n) _____ is used to control the vacuum motor and heat control door.

32. _____

33. The heat control door in the air cleaner inlet is operated by the _____.

33. _____

34. A(n) _____ is used to block or pass airflow in a vacuum line with changes
    in temperature.

34. _____

Pulse Air System

35. The _____ valves in a pulse air system block airflow in one direction and
    allow airflow in the other direction.

35. _____

36. How does a pulse air system operate? _____

_____

_____

_____

_____

Catalytic Converter

▉ Match the catalytic converter listed below with the statement that best describes its operation.

37. Can only reduce two types of exhaust emissions.

38. Uses a ceramic honeycomb catalyst.

39. Can reduce HC, CO, and No_x exhaust emissions.

40. A very small converter placed close to the engine
    exhaust manifold.

41. Uses small ceramic beads.

42. Contains separate catalyst units enclosed in a
    single housing.

- (A) Reduction type converter
- (B) Oxidation converter
- (C) Mini catalytic converter
- (D) Dual-bed catalytic converter
- (E) Monolithic converter
- (F) Pellet catalytic converter

37. _____

38. _____

39. _____

40. _____

41. _____

42. _____

Computerized Emission Control Systems

43. An increase in oxygen indicates a lean mixture which would make the oxygen sensor output voltage _____ (increase/decrease).

43._____

44. The _____ oxygen sensor is mounted downstream in the exhaust system and can be used to check the exhaust gas for oxygen content before it enters the catalytic converter.

44._____

45. The _____ oxygen sensor is used to monitor the oxygen in the exhaust gases as it leaves the engine.

45._____

46. How are oxygen sensor positions numbered? _____

_____

_____

_____

_____

47. What benefit do *heated oxygen sensors* provide? _____

_____

_____

_____

_____

48. A(n) _____ oxygen sensor has the advantage of an almost instant oxygen content signal upon cold startup.
    (A) zirconia
    (B) heated
    (C) titania
    (D) All of the above.

48._____

OBD II Emission System Monitoring

49. Most OBD II systems will monitor _____.
    (A) EGR valve action
    (B) catalytic converter efficiency
    (C) evaporative emissions system operation
    (D) All of the above.

49._____

50. OBD II _____ monitoring checks components for leakage and restrictions.

50._____

51. OBD II EGR monitoring is done when the computer turns the _____ off while checking O_2 sensor readings.

51._____

52. Air injection system monitoring uses data from the _____ to determine if the right amount of air is being injected into the engine's exhaust system.

52._____

Chapter 44

Emission Control System Testing, Service, and Repair

Name: _____ Date: _____

Instructor: _____ Score: _____ Textbook pages 800–825

Objective: After studying this chapter, you will be able to service emission control systems.

Computer-Controlled Emission System Service

1. With late-model OBD II, the vehicle's ECM will monitor many functions that affect emissions. Name three emission control devices that are monitored.

   _____

   _____

   _____

2. Name the systems that should be checked before suspecting emissions control devices.

   _____

   _____

   _____

3. How does *OBD II engine misfire monitoring* function? _____

   _____

   _____

4. Summarize *OBD II sensor monitoring.* _____

   _____

   _____

   _____

   _____

5. Explain why actuator monitoring uses the ECM software data. _____

   _____

6. Name two OBD II systems checked by actuator monitoring. _____

   _____

   _____

7. Summarize the operation of *OBD II fuel injector monitoring.* _____

_____

_____

_____

8. Briefly explain the purpose of a scan tool to check emission control systems.

_____

_____

_____

Inspecting Emission Control Systems

9. Using scan tool information, finding the source of the emission control problems should begin with an inspection of what two things?

_____

10. _____ is the ratio of heat actually developed in the combustion process to   10. _____
the heat that would be released if the combustion were perfect.

11. If CO_2 and O_2 are not toxic substances, why are they measured? _____

_____

_____

Exhaust Gas Analyzer

12. Describe what an *exhaust gas analyzer* measures. _____

_____

_____

13. What does a *five-gas exhaust analyzer* measure? _____

_____

_____

_____

14. In your own words, explain an HC reading measured by an exhaust analyzer. _____

_____

_____

_____

_____

_____

15. Explain *CO readings.* _____

_____

_____

_____

16. Explain O_2 *readings.* _____

_____

_____

_____

Emissions Testing Programs

17. What is the *IM 240 test?* _____

_____

_____

18. Summarize how an evaporative system *purge test* is done.

_____

_____

_____

_____

19. Describe an evaporative system *pressure test.* _____

_____

_____

_____

PCV System Service

20. Identify three possible problems created by an inoperative PCV system._____

_____

_____

_____

21. A leaking PCV system can cause a vacuum leak and produce a lean _____   21._____
mixture, causing a rough engine idle.

22. What is one problem with a *restricted* PCV system? _____

_____

_____

_____

Evaporative Emissions Control System Service

23. Maintenance on an evaporative emissions control system usually involves   23._____
cleaning or replacing the _____ in the charcoal canister.

24. What is a good way to inspect the condition of the fuel tank filler cap?

_____

_____

_____

25. What are three possible problems caused by a faulty evaporative emissions control system?

_____

_____

_____

Pulse Air System Service

26. Exhaust analyzer oxygen readings should _____ when the pulse air system is disabled.

26. _____

27. How are the *aspirator valves* of a pulse air system tested? _____

_____

_____

_____

_____

Catalytic Converter Service

28. An exhaust _____ test will check for a clogged catalytic converter and other system parts.

28. _____

29. With OBD II equipped vehicles, how is the catalytic converter's condition monitored?

_____

_____

_____

_____

_____

Oxygen Sensor Service

30. What is a consequence of oxygen sensors becoming coated or fouled with exhaust byproducts?

_____

_____

_____

_____

31. If a scan tool readout shows that the O_2 sensor output voltage is abnormal, a technician might want to measure the sensor's _____ or resistance with a multimeter.

31. _____

OBD II Drive Cycle

32. To begin the drive cycle, coolant temperature should be below _____.

32. _____

33. A typical drive cycle will take from _____ to _____ minutes to complete.

33. _____

_____

34. If the engine is shut off for any reason, the drive cycle must be _____ from the beginning.

34. _____

Chapter 45

Engine Performance and Driveability

Name: _____ Date: _____

Instructor: _____ Score: _____ Textbook pages 827–838

Objective: After studying this chapter, you will be able to explain and locate typical engine performance problems.

Locating Performance Problems

1. Any problem that affects the performance of the vehicle is often referred to as a(n) _____ problem.

1._____

2. Use a(n) _____ approach when trying to locate engine performance problems.

2._____

3. _____ diagnostics involves using your knowledge of automotive systems and a logical process of elimination.

3._____

4. The actual cause of a problem is also known as the _____ of failure.

4._____

5. A service manual troubleshooting chart provides all of the following, *except:*
   (A) accurate information.
   (B) lists problems and corrections.
   (C) information for all makes and models of vehicles.
   (D) step-by-step diagnostics.

5._____

6. _____ explain problems that frequently occur in one make or model vehicle.

6._____

7. If you have _____ access, you can search for service information and review problems encountered by other technicians.

7._____

Typical Performance Problems

8. Technician A says a no-crank problem occurs when the starter fails to turn the crankshaft. Technician B says a no-crank problem occurs if there is an engine mechanical problem. Who is right?
   (A) A only.
   (B) B only.
   (C) Both A and B.
   (D) Neither A nor B.

8._____

9. An engine turns with great difficulty. What is the *most likely* cause?_____

_____

_____

10. When diagnosing a no-start problem, you should check for spark by pulling a secondary wire and attaching a _____.
    (A) spark tester
    (B) screwdriver
    (C) paper clip
    (D) noid light

10. _____

11. When diagnosing a no-start problem, how do you check for fuel? _____

_____

_____

_____

_____

12. By checking for the presence of fuel and spark, you have narrowed down the cause of a no-start condition to one of the following systems, *except:*
    (A) computer.
    (B) ignition.
    (C) fuel.
    (D) compression.

12. _____

13. All of the following conditions can keep an engine from starting, *except:*
    (A) jumped timing chain or belt.
    (B) carbon build-up.
    (C) excessively low compression.
    (D) slow cranking speed.

13. _____

14. Which of the following can cause hard starting?
    (A) Engine mechanical problem.
    (B) Vacuum leak.
    (C) Sensor problem.
    (D) All of the above.

14. _____

15. Define *stalling.* _____

_____

_____

16. An engine _____ occurs when the engine fails to ignite and burn the fuel mixture in the combustion chamber.

16. _____

17. Which of the following is the *least likely* cause of misfiring in a fuel injected engine?
    (A) Idle circuit is clogged with debris.
    (B) An injector is not opening.
    (C) Vacuum leak.
    (D) Open plug wire.

17. _____

18. Technician A says an engine misfire can damage the catalytic converter and pollute the environment. Technician B says if an engine only misfires at idle, no catalytic converter damage will result. Who is right?
    (A) A only.
    (B) B only.
    (C) Both A and B.
    (D) Neither A nor B.

18. _____

19. What is *OBD II engine misfire monitoring?* _____

_____

_____

_____

20. A misfire rate no higher than _____ is acceptable because the catalytic converter can easily handle this amount of pollutants.

20. _____

21. What is the purpose of keeping a *misfire history?* _____

_____

_____

22. What is the difference between misfire *passes* and misfire *failures?* _____

_____

_____

_____

23. Summarize what a scan tool readout of misfire data values may tell you.

_____

_____

_____

_____

24. An OBD II compliant scan tool can provide you with which of the following misfire data values?
    (A) Misfiring cylinder.
    (B) RPM at misfire.
    (C) Load at misfire.
    (D) All of the above.

24. _____

Waveform 1

Waveform 2

25. Two technicians are looking at the misfire waveforms shown above. Technician A says that waveform 1 shows normal crankshaft acceleration. Technician B says waveform 2 shows a misfire. Who is right?
    (A) A only.
    (B) B only.
    (C) Both A and B.
    (D) Neither A nor B.

25. _____

26. A popping noise from the exhaust is an indication of a(n) _____ condition.
    (A) surging
    (B) no-start
    (C) hard start
    (D) rough idle

26. _____

27. List common causes of *rough idle.* _____
    _____
    _____

28. A vacuum leak will usually produce a(n) _____ sound and engine rough-   28. _____
    ness will usually _____ when engine rpm is increased.   _____

29. All of the following can be the cause of hesitation, *except:*   29. _____
    (A) a temporary lean air-fuel mixture.
    (B) a defective throttle position sensor.
    (C) a defective carburetor accelerator pump.
    (D) a weak battery.

30. _____ is a condition where engine power fluctuates up and down.   30. _____

31. Technician A says that incorrect ignition timing can cause backfiring.   31. _____
    Technician B says that exhaust system leakage can cause backfiring. Who
    is right?
    (A) A only.
    (B) B only.
    (C) Both A and B.
    (D) Neither A nor B.

32. Technician A says dieseling can be caused by high idle speed. Technician B   32. _____
    says dieseling can be caused by high octane fuel. Who is right?
    (A) A only.
    (B) B only.
    (C) Both A and B.
    (D) Neither A nor B.

33. Define the term *pinging.* _____
    _____
    _____
    _____
    _____
    _____

34. Which of the following is the *most likely* cause of pinging?   34. _____
    (A) Engine undercooling.
    (B) Low octane fuel.
    (C) Low speed idle.
    (D) High octane fuel.

35. _____ occurs when the fuel is overheated, forming air bubbles.   35. _____

36. Technician A says that fuel line freeze is caused by the use of alcohol and   36. _____
    other fuel additives. Technician B says that fuel line freeze is caused when
    moisture in the fuel turns to ice. Who is right?
    (A) A only.
    (B) B only.
    (C) Both A and B.
    (D) Neither A nor B.

37. Which of the following would be the *least likely* cause of poor fuel   37. _____
    economy?
    (A) Lean air-fuel mixture.
    (B) Incorrect ignition timing.
    (C) Engine miss.
    (D) Fuel system leak.

Chapter 46

Advanced Diagnostics

Name: _____ Date: _____

Instructor: _____ Score: _____ Textbook pages 839–867

Objective: After studying this chapter, you will be able to summarize the use of advanced diagnostic techniques.

Advanced Diagnostics

1. Technician A says that an intermittent electrical problem can be found by spraying the suspect circuit with a mist sprayer. Technician B says an intermittent problem inside the ECM can be found by spraying the ECM with a mist sprayer. Who is right?
   - (A) A only.
   - (B) B only.
   - (C) Both A and B.
   - (D) Neither A nor B.

1._____

2. The vacuum gauge shown on the right is normal at idle but fluctuates excessively at higher speeds. Which of the following is the *most likely* cause?
   - (A) Sticking valve.
   - (B) Burned valve.
   - (C) Weak valve spring.
   - (D) Worn valve guides.

2._____

Vacuum and Pressure Gauge Tests

3. A vacuum gauge that slowly drops to zero when engine speed is high indicates a(n) _____.

3._____

4. Two technicians are looking at the vacuum gauge shown on the right. The gauge is 3″–9″ from normal at idle. Technician A says this reading is caused by leaking intake gaskets. Technician B says this is caused by a poor air-fuel mixture. Who is right?
   - (A) A only.
   - (B) B only.
   - (C) Both A and B.
   - (D) Neither A nor B.

4._____

5. A technician uses a hand vacuum pump to test a vacuum diaphragm device. After pumping up the diaphragm, it fails to hold a vacuum. What should the technician do?

    (A) Perform the test again.
    (B) Test the vacuum pump for proper operation.
    (C) Nothing, the vacuum diaphragm device is okay.
    (D) Replace the vacuum diaphragm device.

5._____

Diesel Engine Testers

6. A(n) _____ harness can be used to find the cause of a cold or rough idle problem in a diesel engine.

6._____

7. Technician A says combustion will increase a diesel glow plug's temperature, affecting its resistance. Technician B says an unequal change in diesel glow plug resistance indicates a cylinder is not firing. Who is right?

    (A) A only.
    (B) B only.
    (C) Both A and B.
    (D) Neither A nor B.

7._____

Advanced Scan Tool Tests

8. A scan tool's _____ feature requires the technician to monitor operating conditions and to press a button on the scan tool when the problem occurs.

8._____

9. The data captured in a scan tool snap-shot feature can provide all of the following, *except:*

    (A) the vehicle operating values when the problem occurs.
    (B) any codes that are set when the problem occurs.
    (C) information about the affected circuit(s).
    (D) the actual cause of the problem.

9._____

10. What are scan tool *data stream values?*_____

_____

_____

_____

11. Most scan tools can switch computer-controlled _____ on and off.

11._____

12. All of the following are examples of actuators that can be controlled by using the scan tool, *except:*

    (A) ignition coil.
    (B) throttle plate.
    (C) fuel injector.
    (D) idle speed motor.

12._____

13. A scan tool gives a MAF reading of 0.8 Gms-sec. Using the chart in Figure 46-7 of the text, which of the following conclusions can you make?

    (A) The engine is operating normally at hot idle.
    (B) The MAF sensor is defective.
    (C) The engine is off and the ignition is at cold key on.
    (D) The engine is operating normally at 55 mph cruise.

13._____

Checking Computer Terminal Values

14. A(n) _____ allows you to pinpoint test electrical values at specific pins on the ECM or in the computer system.

14. _____

15. Tests using a breakout box indicate all sensor and actual values are within specifications. Technician A says the problem could be an open ground. Technician B says the problem is in the ECM itself. Who is right?
    (A) A only.
    (B) B only.
    (C) Both A and B.
    (D) Neither A nor B.

15. _____

16. What is *electromagnetic interference (EMI)?* _____
_____
_____
_____
_____

17. All of the following are potential sources of electromagnetic interference, *except:*
    (A) shielded spark plug wires.
    (B) police and CB radios.
    (C) misrouted wiring.
    (D) some aftermarket accessories.

17. _____

18. How can you use a small transistor radio to find electromagnetic interference that could upset computer system operation?
_____
_____
_____
_____

19. What two general repair methods must be used to correct an EMI problem?
_____
_____

20. Name five things a *digital pyrometer* can be used to check during diagnosis.
_____
_____
_____
_____
_____

21. How can you check to see if temperature extremes are affecting ECM operation?
_____
_____
_____
_____
_____

22. A(n) _____ is used to measure an engine's power output and performance.

22. _____

Using an Oscilloscope

23. Oscilloscopes are a piece of test equipment that displays voltages in relation to _____.

23._____

24. The oscilloscope's ability to draw a(n) _____ of circuit voltages for very short time spans makes it very useful for testing ignition and computer system performance.

24._____

25. If the scope is set to read 0–10 volts for checking the ECM, a waveform 5 divisions tall indicates _____ volts peak-to-peak.

25._____

26. Scope sweep rate is the _____ shown on the screen during each test.

26._____

27. What is the advantage of being able to adjust the *scope sweep rate?* _____

_____

_____

_____

_____

28. A shorted component would produce a _____ trace pattern.
    (A) higher than normal
    (B) normal
    (C) lower than normal
    (D) flat

28._____

29. The _____ scope pattern shows the low voltage changes in an ignition system.

29._____

30. A problem in the primary circuit will usually affect the _____.
    (A) primary pattern
    (B) secondary pattern
    (C) secondary circuit
    (D) All of the above.

30._____

31. The _____ is the tall spike or line representing the amount of voltage needed to make the electric arc first jump across the spark plug gap.

31._____

32. Which of the following secondary firing sections shows voltage fluctuations after the plug stops firing?
    (A) Intermediate section.
    (B) Spark line.
    (C) Firing section.
    (D) Dwell section.

32._____

33. The secondary dwell section will indicate all of the following, *except:*
    (A) faulty ignition module.
    (B) burned contact points.
    (C) fouled spark plugs.
    (D) leaking condenser.

33._____

34. Define the term *superimposed* and its significance to scope test patterns.

_____

_____

_____

_____

35. The secondary superimposed pattern will check for _____ in the ignition system.

35._____

Name _____

36. Technician A says a tall firing line indicates high resistance in the ignition secondary. Technician B says a tall firing line may be caused by a burned secondary connection in a distributorless ignition. Who is right?

    (A) A only.
    (B) B only.
    (C) Both A and B.
    (D) Neither A nor B.

36. _____

37. In a raster pattern, the bottom waveform indicates the _____ cylinder.

37. _____

38. What should you look for when you read a scope pattern?

_____

_____

_____

39. A Hall-effect sensor waveform should have a typical voltage output of _____ peak-to-peak.

39. _____

40. Two technicians are inspecting the scope pattern shown on the right. Technician A says this pattern could be caused by an excessively lean air-fuel mixture. Technician B says this could be caused by worn spark plug electrodes. Who is right?

    (A) A only.
    (B) B only.
    (C) Both A and B.
    (D) Neither A nor B.

40. _____

41. A vehicle's electronic ignition system is displaying the scope pattern shown on the right. The same cylinder is consistently high. Which of the following is the *most likely* cause of this pattern?

    (A) Late timing.
    (B) Rich air-fuel mixture.
    (C) Uneven compression.
    (D) Broken spark plug wire.

41. _____

42. A vehicle's ignition system displays the pattern shown on the right. Technician A says this could be caused by a defective coil. Technician B says this could be caused by defective contact points or ignition module. Who is right?

    (A) A only.
    (B) B only.
    (C) Both A and B.
    (D) Neither A nor B.

42. _____

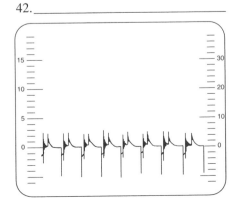

43. What six items should you check when analyzing square waves? _____

_____

_____

_____

_____

_____

_____

44. All of the following can affect a square wave, *except:*   44._____
    (A) low resistance in the circuit.
    (B) faulty circuit.
    (C) amplitude.
    (D) moisture contamination.

45. Which four things should you check with sine wave signals?

_____

_____

_____

_____

46. An optical sensor's waveform should have: 46._____
    (A) straight sides.
    (B) at or near reference voltage output.
    (C) zero voltage output.
    (D) Both A and B.

47. If a crankshaft position sensor's waveform peak-to-peak voltage is short or   47._____
missing, what should you check for?
    (A) Broken tooth on the trigger wheel.
    (B) Debris in the trigger wheel area.
    (C) Defective sensor.
    (D) Unplugged connector.

48. What should you do to probe sealed electrical connectors? _____

_____

_____

_____

49. A typical throttle position sensor (TPS) waveform should show a(n) _____   49._____
curve.

50. How is a scope used to test a knock sensor? _____

_____

_____

_____

_____

51. If alternator diodes are good, the waveform pattern will be _____.   51._____
    (A) wavy, but almost even
    (B) straight across
    (C) wavy and very uneven

52. When tested, a fuel injection system displays the pattern shown on the right. Which of the following is the *most likely* cause?
    - (A) Stuck injector.
    - (B) Open injector.
    - (C) Partially shorted injector.
    - (D) Normally operating injector.

52. _____

53. Since _____ testing varies and is complex, always refer to the service manual for detailed instructions.

53. _____

54. What is a *flight record test?* _____

_____

_____

_____

Engine Analyzer (Computer Analyzer)

55. *True or False?* An engine analyzer will help find problems when a scan tool does not show a trouble code or operating value out of parameter.

55. _____

56. Some analyzers can transmit data over telephone lines using a(n) _____.

56. _____

57. _____ computers are very large computers that can store tremendous amounts of data.

57. _____

58. Name six systems that most analyzers will check. _____

_____

_____

_____

59. Name ten instruments and devices commonly found in a vehicle or electronic analyzer.

_____

_____

_____

_____

_____

60. How can you connect a scope to a direct ignition system?

_____

_____

_____

_____

61. All of the following are precautions you should take when setting up an analyzer, *except:*
    - (A) start the engine first.
    - (B) read the operating manual for the analyzer.
    - (C) make sure all leads are away from hot or moving parts.
    - (D) set the parking brake.

61. _____

62. A scope _____ output test measures the maximum available voltage produced by the ignition coil.

62._____

63. Why is checking the operation of an ignition system *coil pack* different than checking the operation of a regular ignition coil?

_____

_____

_____

_____

_____

64. Coil output voltage should range between _____ volts on older style electronic ignitions. However, some electronic ignition coils are able to produce up to _____ volts.

64._____

_____

65. Explain why ignition coil voltage can still hurt you, despite its low current.

_____

_____

_____

_____

66. A load test is being performed using a scope. Technician A says the highest firing line should not exceed 20 kv in an electronic ignition system. Technician B says if any of the firing lines are high or low, a defect is present. Who is right?
    (A) A only.
    (B) B only.
    (C) Both A and B.
    (D) Neither A nor B.

66._____

67. A percentage within _____ percent of rpm drop is allowable during a cylinder balance test.

67._____

68. Technician A says you should *not* short a cylinder in a catalytic converter-equipped vehicle for more than 15 seconds. Technician B says you should *not* short a cylinder in a catalytic converter-equipped vehicle for more than 30 seconds. Who is right?
    (A) A only.
    (B) B only.
    (C) Both A and B.
    (D) Neither A nor B.

68._____

69. Discuss the purpose for performing a cranking balance test.

_____

_____

_____

_____

_____

_____

_____

Chapter 47

Engine Tune-Up

Name: _____ Date: _____

Instructor: _____ Score: _____ Textbook pages 868–879

Objective: After studying this chapter, you will be able to perform an engine tune-up.

Engine Tune-Up

1. A tune-up is now done as part of _____ rather than to correct a driveability problem.

1._____

2. Many late-model engines do not require spark plug replacement for up to _____.

2._____

3. All of the following are performed during a minor tune-up, *except:*
   (A) throttle body replacement or rebuild.
   (B) replacing spark plugs.
   (C) oil change and chassis lube.
   (D) fuel system adjustments, if available.

3._____

4. Explain the difference between a *minor tune-up* and a *major tune-up.* _____

_____

_____

_____

_____

_____

_____

_____

_____

5. All of the following tools are used to perform a major tune-up, *except:*
   (A) compression gauge.
   (B) vacuum gauge.
   (C) scan tool.
   (D) breakout box.

5._____

6. A tune-up is very important because it can affect _____.
   (A) fuel consumption
   (B) exhaust pollution
   (C) ease of starting
   (D) All of the above.

6._____

7. A computer-controlled vehicle has a rough idle. Technician A says a tune-up will not correct this problem in most cases. Technician B says the rough idle is probably due to a defective sensor, actuator, or ECM. Who is right?
   (A) A only.
   (B) B only.
   (C) Both A and B.
   (D) Neither A nor B.

7. _____

General Tune-Up Rules

8. Why is it important to gather information about the performance of the vehicle and the engine?

   _____

   _____

   _____

9. Why should you warm the engine to full operating temperature?_____

   _____

   _____

10. Technician A says keeping accurate service records is not necessary. Technician B says keeping service records take up too much space, and are therefore, a waste of time. Who is right?
    (A) A only.
    (B) B only.
    (C) Both A and B.
    (D) Neither A nor B.

10. _____

Tune-Up Safety Rules

11. Why do service manuals recommend that you disconnect the battery when performing vehicle maintenance?

    _____

    _____

    _____

12. All of the following are tune-up safety rules you should follow, *except:*
    (A) look into a carburetor or throttle body while the engine is running.
    (B) keep a fire extinguisher handy.
    (C) wear eye protection at all times.
    (D) use an exhaust hose when running an engine in an enclosed shop.

12. _____

Typical Tune-Up Procedures

13. List the six inspections that should be the first steps in any tune-up.

    _____

    _____

    _____

    _____

    _____

    _____

Name _____

14. All of the following are steps in removing a spark plug wire boot, *except:*   14._____
    (A) grasp the boot and pull.
    (B) twist the boot if it sticks.
    (C) grasp the wire and pull.
    (D) check that the wires are located correctly in their clips.

15. Technician A says to make sure the engine is warm before removing spark   15._____
plugs from an aluminum head. Technician B says to make sure the engine
is cold before removing spark plugs from an aluminum head. Who is right?
    (A) A only.
    (B) B only.
    (C) Both A and B.
    (D) Neither A nor B.

16. What tools should you use to remove spark plugs?_____

_____

_____

_____

17. The tip and insulator of a properly burning spark plug should be _____.   17._____
    (A) brown to grayish tan
    (B) wet
    (C) black
    (D) None of the above.

18. What should you do before installing spark plugs in an aluminum head?

_____

_____

_____

19. Spark plugs should be installed _____.   19._____
    (A) by hand
    (B) with a hand ratchet
    (C) with an air impact
    (D) Both A and B.

20. Spark plugs should be tightened _____.   20._____
    (A) one-eighth to one-quarter turn.
    (B) one-third to one-half turn.
    (C) one-half to one-three-quarter turn.
    (D) one full turn.

21. What can happen if you accidentally reroute spark plug wires from their original locations?

_____

_____

_____

_____

_____

22. How often should you replace oxygen sensors? _____

_____

_____

_____

23. Describe how you should remove and install an oxygen sensor._____

_____

_____

_____

_____

_____

24. A(n) _____ test is frequently made during a tune-up to check the engine's
mechanical condition.

24._____

25. Name three tune-up related adjustments._____

_____

_____

_____

Diesel Engine Tune-Up (Maintenance)

26. Technician A says a diesel engine does not have spark plugs to replace or
an ignition system to fail. Technician B says diesel engines do not require
tune-ups like gasoline engines. Who is right?
    (A) A only.
    (B) B only.
    (C) Both A and B.
    (D) Neither A nor B.

26._____

27. What does a diesel engine tune-up or diesel maintenance typically involve?

_____

_____

_____

_____

_____

_____

_____

_____

_____

28. What are *maintenance intervals?*

_____

_____

_____

_____

_____

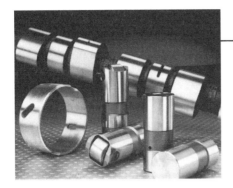

Chapter 48

Engine Mechanical Problems

Name: _____ Date: _____

Instructor: _____ Score: _____ Textbook pages 881–898

Objective: After studying this chapter, you will be able to summarize the cause and correction of typical engine mechanical problems.

Mechanical Problem Diagnosis

1. Explain the causes of engine mechanical problems. _____
   _____
   _____
   _____
   _____
   _____
   _____
   _____
   _____
   _____

2. If a technician does not know how to diagnose problems properly, a great deal of _____, _____, and _____ will be wasted.

   2._____

3. *True or False?* A pre-teardown inspection is made without operating the engine.

   3._____

4. Leaking fluids appear similar. How do you distinguish them? _____
   _____
   _____

5. *True or False?* Black smoke at the tailpipe is commonly caused by worn piston rings.

   5._____

6. If your wet compression test shows a higher reading than the dry test, it indicates the piston rings and _____ may be worn and leaking pressure.

   6._____

7. Why is a wet compression test on a diesel potentially harmful to the engine?_____
   _____
   _____

8. List nine engine problems that could be located during an engine inspection prior to teardown.

(1) _____

(2) _____

(3) _____

(4) _____

(5) _____

(6) _____

(7) _____

(8) _____

(9) _____

9. Describe the symptoms and causes of an engine exhaust leak. _____

_____

_____

_____

_____

_____

_____

_____

10. In your own words, explain how to perform dry and wet compression tests. _____

_____

_____

_____

_____

_____

_____

_____

_____

_____

_____

_____

_____

11. List and describe seven causes of low engine compression.

(1) _____

(2) _____

(3) _____

(4) _____

(5) _____

(6) _____

(7) _____

12. What should be done about the ignition system during a compression test on a gasoline engine?

_____

_____

13. Gasoline engine compression readings should run around _____ (860–1200 kPa).

    (A) 100–125 psi
    (B) 125–175 psi
    (C) 175–200 psi
    (D) 200–225 psi

13. _____

14. Diesel engine compression readings will average _____ psi (_____ kPa).

14. _____

    _____

Evaluating Engine Mechanical Problems

15. A burned valve results when the _____ from combustion blows away a small portion of the valve _____.

15. _____

    _____

16. What might a popping sound at the carburetor or throttle body indicate? At the exhaust system tailpipe?

_____

_____

17. *True or False?* Valve seals can usually be replaced without cylinder head removal.

17. _____

18. Cam lobe wear will reduce valve _____, reducing engine power and causing a(n) _____.

18. _____

    _____

19. What problems can result from a blown head gasket? _____

_____

_____

_____

_____

20. *True or False?* Piston knock or slap is loudest when the engine is warm.

20. _____

21. What is *connecting rod bearing knock?*_____

_____

_____

_____

_____

22. Describe the symptoms of broken engine mounts. _____

_____

_____

_____

_____

23. How do you check for broken engine mounts? _____

_____

_____

_____

_____

_____

24. Label the possible engine mechanical problems.

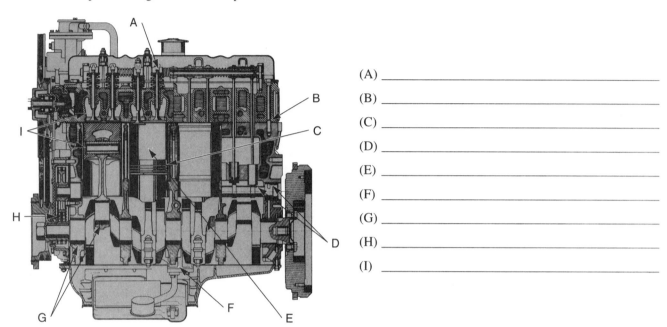

(A) _____

(B) _____

(C) _____

(D) _____

(E) _____

(F) _____

(G) _____

(H) _____

(I) _____

25. Label the engine valve train problems.

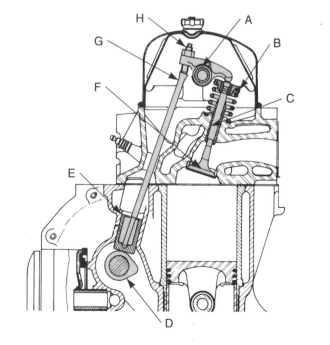

(A) _____

(B) _____

(C) _____

(D) _____

(E) _____

(F) _____

(G) _____

(H) _____

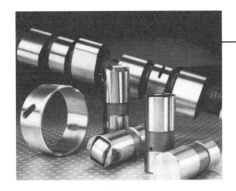

Chapter 49

Engine Removal, Disassembly, and Parts Cleaning

Name: _____ Date: _____

Instructor: _____ Score: _____ Textbook pages 899–915

Objective: After studying this chapter, you will be able to summarize the removal and disassembly of an automotive engine.

Engine Removal

1. Typically, when are engines removed?_____
   _____
   _____

2. If in doubt whether a particular engine needs to be removed for a repair, what should you do?_____
   _____
   _____

3. Position the engine lifting fixture so that it will lift the engine in a _____.   3._____

4. *True or False?* If the engine is properly secured on the lifting crane, it is
   acceptable to reach under the engine.   4._____

5. List the steps to prepare for engine removal.

   (1) _____
   _____

   (2) _____
   _____

   (3) _____
   _____

   (4) _____
   _____

   (5) _____
   _____

   (6) _____
   _____

   (7) _____
   _____

(8) _____

_____

(9) _____

_____

(10) _____

_____

(11) _____

_____

(12) _____

_____

(13) _____

_____

6. Label the actions showing disconnecting or removal of an engine from under a vehicle.

(A) _____   (D) _____

(B) _____   (E) _____

_____   (F) _____

(C) _____

Engine Disassembly

7. During engine disassembly, you should inspect each part for what types of damage?_____

_____

_____

_____

_____

8. If lifters, pushrods, and rocker arms are to be reused, keep them in exact order by using a(n) _____. Wear patterns and _____ parts require reinstallation in the same location.

8. _____

_____

9. Use a valve _____ to remove the valves, keepers, springs, and seals from the cylinder head.

9. _____

10. What must you do if the old valves will not slide easily out of the cylinder head? _____

_____

_____

_____

_____

11. Why must you be careful when turning or rotating a crankshaft in an OHC engine with the timing belt or chain removed?

_____

_____

_____

_____

_____

_____

12. Define *ring ridge.* _____

_____

_____

_____

_____

13. Why are numbers and arrows commonly provided on the cylinder block main caps? _____

_____

_____

_____

_____

_____

Cleaning Engine Parts

14. Begin engine parts cleaning by _____ off all old _____ and other deposits.

14. _____

_____

15. *True or False?* When using a hand scraper, pull it toward your body.

15. _____

16. A(n) _____ is driven by an air or electric drill to remove hard carbon.

16. _____

17. What are *scuff pads,* and when should they be used? _____

_____

_____

_____

_____

_____

18. A ring _____ is used to clean the inside of piston ring grooves.   18._____

19. How do you use a valve guide cleaner?_____

_____

_____

_____

_____

20. Why is an air blow gun the last method used for cleaning parts?_____

_____

_____

_____

_____

21. Label the illustration for removing a cylinder ring ridge.

(A) _____

_____

(B) _____

(C) _____

(D) _____

_____

(E) _____

(F) _____

Chapter 50

Engine Bottom End Service

Name: _____ Date: _____

Instructor: _____ Score: _____ Textbook pages 916–938

Objective: After studying this chapter, you will be able to explain typical methods of service for engine bottom end parts.

Cylinder Block Service

1. List the operations commonly included in cylinder block service.

   (A)_____

   (B)_____

   (C)_____

   (D)_____

   (E)_____

   (F)_____

2. Define *decking the block.* _____

   _____

   _____

   _____

   _____

3. _____ action normally makes the cylinders wear more at right angles to the   3. _____
   centerline of the piston pins.

4. Describe the four types of engine cylinder hones.

   Brush hone: _____

   _____

   Flex hone: _____

   _____

   Ridged or sizing hone: _____

   _____

   Honing machine: _____

   _____

5. Explain how to use different stones when power honing. _____
   _____
   _____

6. Why is *cylinder block boring* needed, and what does it involve? _____
   _____
   _____

7. Normally, a cylinder is bored in increments of _____, and the overbore   7. _____
   limit of most blocks is _____.
   _____

8. What is *overbore limit* and who specifies it? _____
   _____
   _____

9. When should you *sleeve* a cylinder? _____
   _____
   _____

10. Label the major engine bottom end parts that need service.

(A) _____

(B) _____

(C) _____

(D) _____

(E) _____

(F) _____

(G) _____

(H) _____

(I) _____

(J) _____

(K) _____

(L) _____

(M) _____

(N) _____

(O) _____

Piston Service

11. How do you measure *piston size?* _____
    _____
    _____

12. How do you measure *piston taper?* _____
    _____
    _____

13. _____ is frequently used to increase piston diameter.   13._____
    (A) Peening
    (B) Boiling
    (C) Press-fitting
    (D) Knurling

14. To find piston clearance, subtract _____ diameter from _____ diameter.   14._____

    _____

15. When piston-to-cylinder clearance is excessive, you must do one of these four things:

    (1) _____

    (2) _____

    (3) _____

    (4) _____

16. What are *ring spacers?* _____

    _____

    _____

17. Describe how to measure piston ring gap. _____

    _____

    _____

    _____

    _____

Crankshaft Service

18. How do you measure journal *taper* and *out-of-roundness?*_____

    _____

    _____

    _____

19. What does *turning* a crankshaft involve?_____

    _____

    _____

20. _____ are needed after the crankshaft has been turned.   20._____

21. How can you tell if a bearing is undersize?_____

    _____

    _____

22. *True or False?* When installing engine main bearings, oil both the front and   22._____
    back of the bearings.

23. The sealing lip on a rear main oil seal must point toward the _____ of the   23._____
    engine.

24. How do you check *main* and *rod bearing clearance?* _____

    _____

    _____

    _____

25. Label the parts and actions for installing a crankshaft.

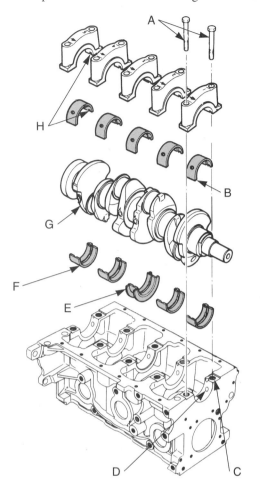

(A) _____

(B) _____

(C) _____

_____

(D) _____

_____

(E) _____

(F) _____

(G) _____

_____

(H) _____

_____

_____

Installing a Piston and Rod Assembly

26. How can you tell if the rod and piston are installed properly in the block? _____

_____

_____

27. Describe how to torque connecting rods. _____

_____

_____

_____

28. When should you balance an engine? _____

_____

_____

29. Define *bob weights* and explain where they are used. _____

_____

_____

30. Why is proper engine balance critical with many of today's cars? _____

_____

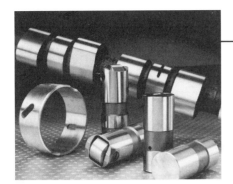

Chapter 51

Engine Top End Service

Name: _____ Date: _____

Instructor: _____ Score: _____ Textbook pages 939–968

Objective: After studying this chapter, you will be able to complete typical service operations on an engine top end.

Cylinder Head Service

1. When inspecting a cylinder head, look closely for problems like _____ between combustion chambers.
    - (A) erosion
    - (B) cracks
    - (C) burning
    - (D) All of the above.

1._____

2. Cylinder head milling is a(n) _____ operation in which a thin layer of metal is removed from the _____ surface of the cylinder head.

2._____

_____

3. How much metal can be removed to mill a warped head so it is once more flat and serviceable?

_____

_____

4. Define *magnafluxing.* _____

_____

_____

5. *True or False?* A cracked cylinder head can be repaired if a replacement is too expensive to purchase.

5._____

Diesel Precombustion Chamber Service

6. *True or False?* Diesel engine precombustion chambers cannot be removed and replaced.

6._____

Valve Grinding

7. What defects does valve grinding correct? _____

_____

_____

_____

8. Explain how to set the chuck angle prior to grinding a valve. _____

_____

_____

_____

_____

9. *True or False?* An interference angle is normally a 1° difference between the two ground surfaces on the face of the valve.

9. _____

10. *True or False?* When grinding a valve, only grind long enough to clean the surface.

10. _____

11. Why would a sharp valve margin cause a valve to burn? _____

_____

_____

_____

_____

_____

Valve Seat Reconditioning

12. Valve seat reconditioning involves grinding (using a _____) or cutting (using a _____) the head seats.

12. _____

_____

13. Replace a valve seat when it is _____ or recessed in the cylinder head.
    (A) pitted
    (B) cracked
    (C) burned
    (D) All of the above.

13. _____

14. To narrow the valve seat contact area and move it inward, use a _____° stone. To move it outward, use a _____° stone.

14. _____

_____

15. _____ is done to check seat location and to smooth the mating surfaces.
    (A) Valve seat runout
    (B) Lapping valves
    (C) Grinding
    (D) None of the above.

15. _____

Testing Valve Springs

16. _____ is pressure measured on a valve spring tester.
    (A) Valve spring tension
    (B) Valve spring free height
    (C) Valve spring squareness
    (D) None of the above.

16. _____

17. When should you shim valve springs? _____

_____

18. Define *valve spring installed height.* _____

_____

_____

Assembling Cylinder Head

19. Before installing the valves in the head, place _____ on the valve stem.

19. _____

20. With umbrella valve seals, simply slide the seals over the _____.

20. _____

21. With O-ring type valve seals, compress the valve spring _____ fitting the seal on the valve stem.

21. _____

22. How can you easily check for valve leakage after head assembly? _____

_____

_____

_____

_____

_____

23. Which of these parts can be replaced without cylinder head removal?
    - (A) Valves
    - (B) Valve seals
    - (C) Valve springs
    - (D) Valve seats

23. _____

24. Summarize *in-car valve seal service.* _____

_____

_____

_____

_____

_____

_____

_____

_____

_____

_____

Camshaft Service

25. Cam lobe wear can be measured with a(n) _____ with the camshaft installed in the engine.

25. _____

26. How do you measure camshaft end play? _____

_____

_____

_____

_____

27. When installing cam bearings, make sure you align the _____.

27. _____

Lifter and Push Rod Service

28. The contact surface between the _____ and a(n) _____ is one of the highest friction and wear points in an engine.

28. _____

_____

29. How do you inspect lifters for wear?_____

_____

_____

_____

_____

30. What will happen if worn lifters are installed on a new camshaft?_____

_____

_____

31. What equipment is needed to make a lifter leak-down test?_____

_____

_____

32. *True or False?* Many auto shops do not rebuild hydraulic lifters; new ones   32._____
    are installed.

33. How do you check for bent push rods? _____

_____

_____

34. A worn rocker shaft will have _____ where the rocker swivels on the shaft.   34._____

Engine Top End Reassembly

35. What components are included in a valve grind gasket set? _____

_____

_____

36. How can you tell if you have installed a head gasket backwards? _____

_____

_____

37. *True or False?* Sealer is not recommended on most modern, permanent   37._____
    torque head gaskets.

38. Why must you request a special gasket when a diesel engine block is bored oversize?

_____

_____

39. In your own words, describe how to torque a cylinder head. _____

_____

_____

_____

_____

_____

_____

_____

_____

Name _____

40. *True or False?* Start all fasteners by hand before tightening.   40. _____

41. Use numbers to label the typical torque sequences for the cylinder head.

(A) _____

(B) _____

(C) _____

(D) _____

(E) _____

(F) _____

(G) _____

(H) _____

(I) _____

(J) _____

Valve Adjustment

42. What can happen if valve clearance is too tight? _____

_____

_____

_____

_____

43. How do you adjust hydraulic lifters with the engine running? _____

_____

_____

_____

_____

_____

_____

_____

44. _____ are commonly used to adjust valve clearance with overhead cams.   44. _____

   (A) Push rods
   (B) Shims
   (C) Adjusting screws
   (D) All of the above are correct.
   (E) None of the above are correct.

45. How do you use shims to adjust the valves on some OHC engines? _____

_____

_____

_____

_____

_____

46. Use numbers to label the typical torque sequences for the intake manifold.

(A) _____

(B) _____

(C) _____

(D) _____

(E) _____

(F) _____

(G) _____

(H) _____

(I) _____

(J) _____

(K) _____

(L) _____

47. Use numbers to label the typical torque sequences for the rocker assembly.

(A) _____

(B) _____

(C) _____

(D) _____

(E) _____

(F) _____

(G) _____

(H) _____

(I) _____

(J) _____

(K) _____

(L) _____

(M) _____

(N) _____

(O) _____

(P) _____

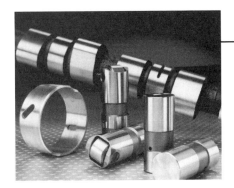

Engine Front End Service and Engine Installation

Name: _____ Date: _____

Instructor: _____ Score: _____ Textbook pages 969–983

Objective: After studying this chapter, you will be able to summarize engine front end service methods.

Timing Chain Service

1. Rather than a timing chain, many modern vehicles use (a) timing _____ to drive a camshaft.
   - (A) belt
   - (B) gears
   - (C) shaft

   1. _____

2. How would you fix excess slack or play in a timing chain? _____

   _____

3. Identify the parts of the engine front end assembly shown in the illustration.

   (A) _____

   (B) _____

   (C) _____

   (D) _____

   (E) _____

   (F) _____

   (G) _____

   (H) _____

   (I) _____

   (J) _____

   (K) _____

   (L) _____

   (M) _____

   (N) _____

   (O) _____

Timing Gears and Chains

4. *True or False?* Timing gears are normally less dependable than timing chains.

   4. _____

5. Timing gear backlash is measured with a(n) _____.

   5. _____

6. Timing gear runout or wobble is measured with a(n) _____.

6. _____

7. Label the illustration to show the use of a wheel puller on the engine.

(A) _____

(B) _____

(C) _____

(D) _____

(E) _____

Front Cover Service

8. The engine front cover is usually made of _____ or _____.

8. _____

_____

9. What is included in a timing cover gasket set and when is it needed? _____

_____

_____

_____

_____

10. *True or False?* Front covers can be installed using gaskets or silicone sealer.

10. _____

11. A tool that may be needed during front cover installation is a _____.

11. _____

    (A) ring compressor
    (B) seal alignment tool
    (C) bearing alignment tool
    (D) sledge hammer

Timing Belt Service

12. Many late-model OHC engines use a(n) _____ belt to operate the engine camshaft.

12. _____

13. Why should you *never* crank an engine with the timing belt removed? _____

_____

_____

_____

_____

_____

14. Identify the parts of the timing belt assembly shown in the illustration.

(A) _____

(B) _____

(C) _____

(D) _____

(E) _____

(F) _____

(G) _____

(H) _____

(I) _____

(J) _____

15. Signs of timing belt deterioration include _____.
    (A) cracks
    (B) hardening or softening
    (C) fraying
    (D) All of the above.

15. _____

16. Most automakers recommend timing belt replacement at periodic intervals of about _____ miles.

16. _____

17. *True or False?* You should never submerse a tensioner wheel in solvent or steam clean it.

17. _____

18. To install a timing belt, align the timing marks on the _____ and _____.

18. _____

_____

19. A simple way to check timing belt tension is to use moderate finger and thumb pressure to _____ the belt _____ turn.

19. _____

_____

20. Identify the parts and methods for aligning timing marks on the OHC engine shown in the illustration.

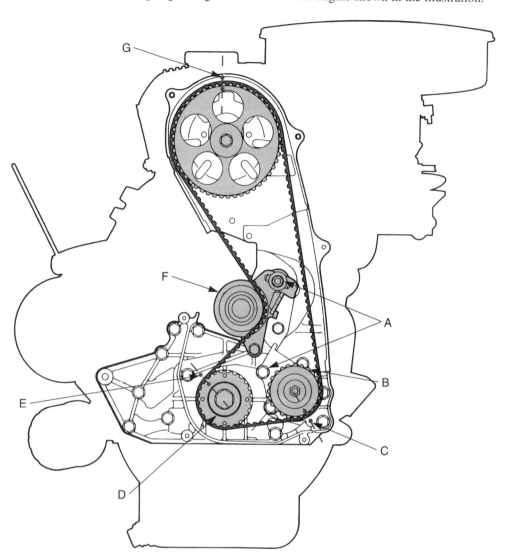

(A) _____   (E) _____

(B) _____   (F) _____

(C) _____   (G) _____

(D) _____

Chapter 53

Clutch Fundamentals

Name: _____ Date: _____

Instructor: _____ Score: _____ Textbook pages 985–998

Objective: After studying this chapter, you will be able to describe basic clutch operating principles.

Clutch Fundamentals

1. Only vehicles with _____ transmissions require a clutch.

2. The _____ is a spring-loaded device that presses the clutch disc against the flywheel.

3. Label the parts of the two manual drive trains shown in the illustration.

1. _____

2. _____

(A) _____

(B) _____

(C) _____

(D) _____

(E) _____

(F) _____

(G) _____

(H) _____

(I) _____

(J) _____

(K) _____

(L) _____

(M) _____

4. The clutch _____ allows the driver to disengage the clutch with a foot pedal.   4. _____

5. What purpose does the *flywheel* serve? _____

_____

_____

_____

_____

_____

6. Label the parts of the clutch mechanism shown in the illustration.

(A) _____

(B) _____

(C) _____

(D) _____

(E) _____

(F) _____

(G) _____

(H) _____

(I) _____

(J) _____

(K) _____

(L) _____

(M) _____

(N) _____

(O) _____

7. Name the parts of a coil spring pressure plate and explain the function of each one.

(1) _____

_____

(2) _____

_____

Name _____

(3) _____

_____

8. Describe coil spring pressure plate action._____

_____

_____

_____

_____

_____

_____

_____

_____

_____

_____

9. What is a *semi-centrifugal pressure plate?* _____

_____

_____

_____

_____

10. The _____ pressure plate uses a single diaphragm spring instead of several
    coil springs.   10. _____

11. Explain the purpose of a *throw-out bearing.* _____

_____

_____

_____

_____

_____

_____

_____

12. What is an *automatic clutch adjuster?*_____

_____

_____

_____

_____

_____

_____

_____

13. What type of fluid do most hydraulic clutch systems use as the medium for
    pressure transfer?   13. _____

14. Label the parts of the hydraulically operated clutch shown in the illustration.

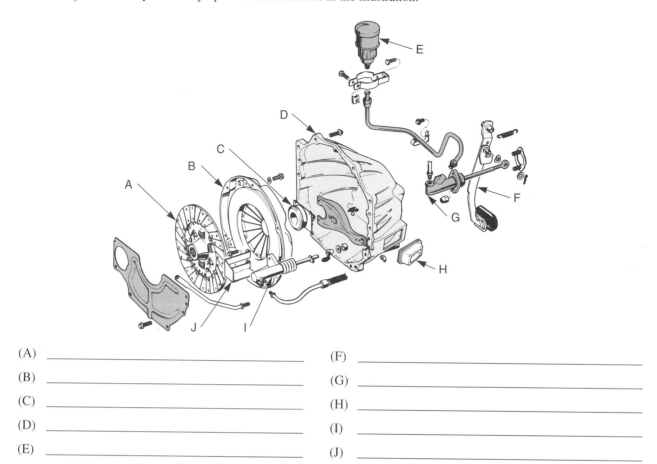

(A) _____   (F) _____

(B) _____   (G) _____

(C) _____   (H) _____

(D) _____   (I) _____

(E) _____   (J) _____

15. Label the parts of the clutch and transaxle shown in the illustration.

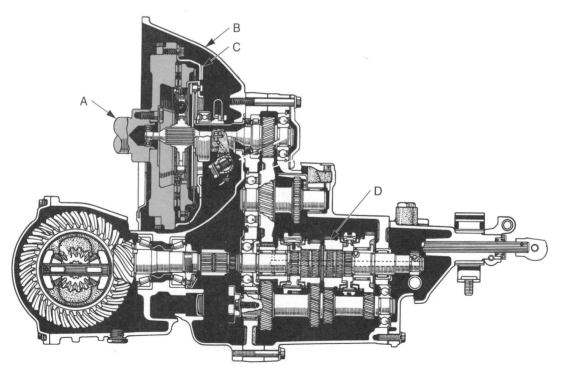

(A) _____   (C) _____

(B) _____   (D) _____

Chapter 54

Clutch Diagnosis and Repair

Name: _____ Date: _____

Instructor: _____ Score: _____ Textbook pages 999–1015

Objective: After studying this chapter, you will be able to explain basic clutch service techniques.

Clutch Diagnosis

1. Why is proper diagnosis so important to clutch repair? _____
   _____
   _____

2. *True or False?* One vehicle's clutch might last 100,000 miles while another   2._____
   might fail in 50,000 miles.

3. Define *riding the clutch.* _____
   _____
   _____
   _____

4. A worn clutch disc will cause clutch _____ and, sometimes, damage to the   4._____
   _____.   _____

5. What type of damage can be caused to a flywheel by overheating?   5._____
   (A) Surface cracks
   (B) Hardened areas
   (C) Warped areas
   (D) All of the above.

6. What clutch problems may result from an overheating of the flywheel? _____
   _____
   _____
   _____

7. Describe some symptoms of a worn pilot bearing. _____
   _____
   _____
   _____
   _____

8. Define clutch *free travel*. _____

_____

_____

_____

9. Clutch slippage is noticed when the engine _____ without an increase in the vehicle's _____.

9. _____

_____

10. Identify the clutch disc problems shown in the illustrations.

A

B

C

(A) _____

_____

(B) _____

_____

(C) _____

_____

11. Identify the problems with the clutch parts shown.

A

B

(A) _____

(B) _____

Name _____

12. Why should you *never* slip a clutch more than a second or two? _____

_____

_____

_____

13. Abnormal sounds from the clutch *only* when the clutch is disengaged may   13. _____
    be from a bad _____.
        (A) throw-out bearing
        (B) disc
        (C) flywheel
        (D) pilot bearing

Clutch Service

14. Why should you disconnect the battery during clutch service? _____

_____

_____

_____

15. _____ or _____ removal is needed to service the clutch.   15. _____

_____

16. In a front-wheel-drive vehicle, what parts may need to be removed for clutch removal? _____

_____

17. When servicing a clutch, always support the weight of the _____.   17. _____
        (A) engine
        (B) transmission
        (C) transaxle
        (D) All of the above.

18. How and why should you mark a clutch during disassembly? _____

_____

_____

_____

_____

_____

19. Tighten each pressure plate bolt a little at a time in a(n) _____ pattern.   19. _____

20. *True or False?* Wash the throw-out bearing in solvent before reassembly.   20. _____

21. How do you lubricate a pilot bushing or bearing? _____

_____

_____

_____

22. Identify the parts of the clutch assembly shown in the illustration. How many can you name before looking in the textbook?

(A) _____

(B) _____

(C) _____

(D) _____

(E) _____

(F) _____

(G) _____

(H) _____

(I) _____

(J) _____

23. Label the illustration showing clutch removal.

(A) _____

(B) _____

(C) _____

(D) _____

24. If a pilot tool is not used during clutch installation, what can result?_____

_____

_____

_____

_____

Chapter 55

Manual Transmission Fundamentals

Name: _____ Date: _____

Instructor: _____ Score: _____ Textbook pages 1016–1037

Objective: After studying this chapter, you will be able to explain the operation of a manual transmission.

Manual Transmission Parts

1. In your own words, describe a *manual transmission.* _____
   _____
   _____
   _____

2. Label the parts of the manual transmission illustrated below.

(A) _____

(B) _____

(C) _____

(D) _____

(E) _____

(F) _____

(G) _____

(H) _____

(I) _____

3. A manual transmission is designed to change the vehicle's _____ and torque in relation to _____ and torque.

   3. _____

4. What should a manual transmission in good condition be able to do?

   (1) _____

   (2) _____

   (3) _____

   (4) _____

   (5) _____

Gear Fundamentals

For Questions 5–7, suppose that a driving gear has 15 teeth and the driven gear has 30 teeth.

5. What is the gear ratio?

5._____

6. Would the arrangement of gears produce *high* or *low* torque?

6._____

7. If the larger gear became the driving gear, and was driven by an engine, would it be like *low gear* or *high gear?*

7._____

8. A(n) _____ ratio results when a larger gear drives a smaller gear.

8._____

9. The two types of gears found in manual transmission are _____ gears and _____ gears.

9._____

_____

10. What is a *helical gear?* _____

_____

_____

11. Typically, _____ or _____ gear oil is recommended for manual transmissions.

11._____

12. Identify the types of gears and bearings shown in the illustration.

(A) _____

(B) _____

(C) _____

(D) _____

(E) _____

Manual Transmission Construction

Match the following terms and statements.

13. Supports transmission bearings and shafts.

14. Bolts to rear of case.

15. Covers front transmission bearing.

16. Transfers power from clutch disc to countershaft gears.

17. Also called cluster gear shaft.

18. Transfers power to drive shaft.

19. Prevents gear grinding or clashing.

(A) Bearing hub

(B) Pressure plate

(C) Idler shaft

(D) Output shaft

(E) Countershaft

(F) Input shaft

(G) Synchronizer

(H) Case

(I) Extension housing

13._____

14._____

15._____

16._____

17._____

18._____

19._____

Name _____

20. During gear engagement, the _____ rubs on the side of the gear cone,   20. _____
setting up friction between the two.
   (A) synchronizer sleeve
   (B) output shaft
   (C) shift fork
   (D) blocking ring

21. What is a *clutchless transmission?* _____

_____

_____

_____

_____

_____

22. Label the external parts of the manual transmission illustrated below.

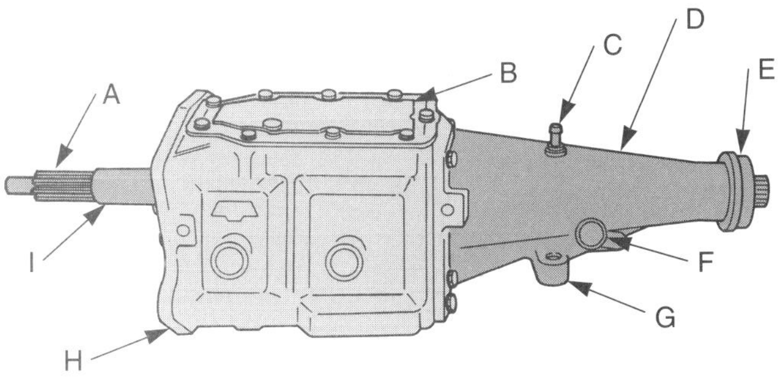

(A) _____

(B) _____

(C) _____

(D) _____

(E) _____

(F) _____

(G) _____

(H) _____

(I) _____

23. Label the parts and actions of the transmission synchronizer shown in the illustration.

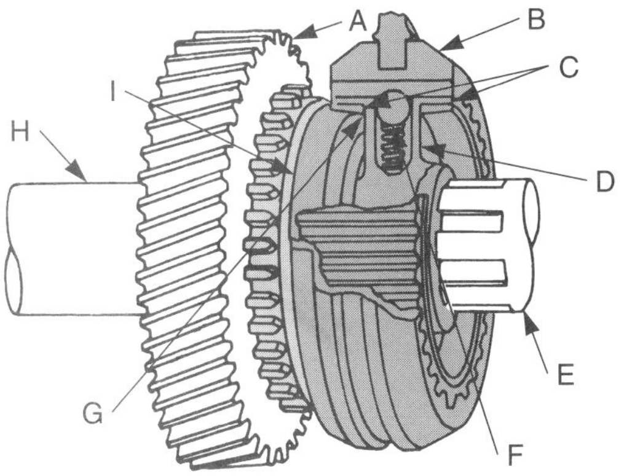

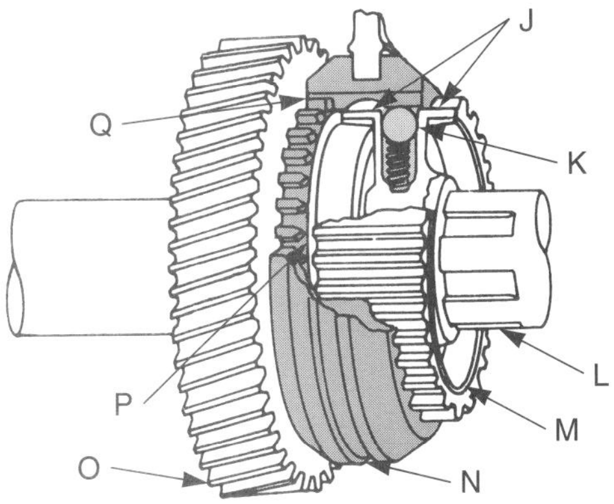

(A) _____

(B) _____

(C) _____

(D) _____

(E) _____

(F) _____

(G) _____

(H) _____

(I) _____

(J) _____

(K) _____

(L) _____

(M) _____

(N) _____

(O) _____

(P) _____

(Q) _____

24. Label the shafts inside the manual transmission shown in the illustration.

(A) _____

(B) _____

(C) _____

(D) _____

Manual Transmission Switches

25. An electric switch, known as a(n) _____ switch, is closed by the action of the reverse gear linkage.
    - (A) lamp
    - (B) back-up light
    - (C) ignition spark
    - (D) transmission

25. _____

26. Identify the parts of the all-wheel drive system shown in the illustration.

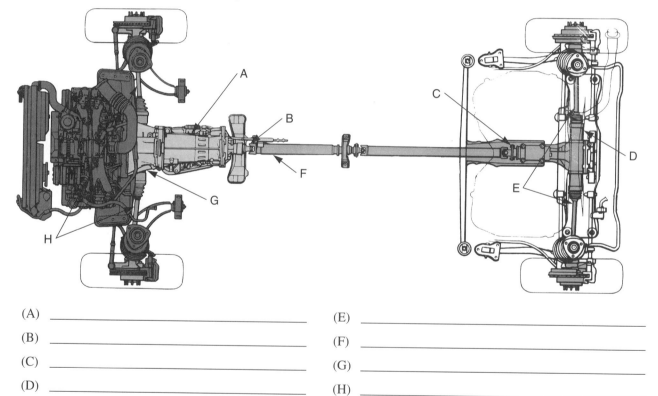

(A) _____   (E) _____

(B) _____   (F) _____

(C) _____   (G) _____

(D) _____   (H) _____

Chapter 56

Manual Transmission Diagnosis and Repair

Name: _____ Date: _____

Instructor: _____ Score: _____ Textbook pages 1037–1049

Objective: After studying this chapter, you will be able to troubleshoot and repair typical manual transmission problems.

Manual Transmission Diagnosis

1. Driver _____ and _____ after prolonged service can cause manual transmission failure.

   1._____

   _____

2. How should you begin diagnosis of a transmission problem?_____

   _____

   _____

3. On the illustration, label the types of problems that can develop in a manual transmission.

(A) _____   (E) _____

_____   (F) _____

(B) _____   (G) _____

(C) _____   (H) _____

(D) _____   (I) _____

_____   (J) _____

4. A grinding sound when shifting is commonly caused by incorrect transmission _____ or a _____ clutch.

4._____

_____

5. Which of the following is *not* a problem that can cause gear grinding during shifts?
   - (A) Worn or damaged synchronizers.
   - (B) Excess wear in shafts.
   - (C) Worn shift forks
   - (D) Low or contaminated lubricant.

5._____

6. If a transmission is noisy in all gears, what does that tell you? _____

_____

_____

_____

7. What may cause hard shifting? _____

_____

Manual Transmission Service

8. Many problems that seem to be caused by the transmission can be due to problems with the _____.
   - (A) clutch
   - (B) linkage
   - (C) driveline
   - (D) All of the above.

8._____

9. Explain how a heavy transmission can be a problem and may require help when removing or installing.

_____

_____

_____

_____

_____

10. In your own words, describe how to remove a manual transmission. _____

_____

_____

_____

_____

_____

_____

11. If gear tooth wear is uneven, check the shaft _____ and shafts.

11._____

12. Why replace all gaskets and seals in the transmission, even if they are not leaking, before teardown?

_____

13. *True or False?* With the transmission out of the vehicle, there is usually no reason to disassemble and inspect the condition of the clutch.

13._____

14. Before installation, place a small amount of grease in the _____ and the _____.

14._____

_____

15. *True or False?* Before installation, shift the transmission into high gear to help position the input shaft into the clutch disc.

15. _____

16. How do you adjust linkage-type shift levers on some manual transmissions? _____

_____

_____

_____

_____

_____

17. Identify the parts of the manual transmission shown in the illustration.

(A) _____

(B) _____

(C) _____

(D) _____

(E) _____

(F) _____

(G) _____

(H) _____

(I) _____

(J) _____

(K) _____

(L) _____

(M) _____

(N) _____

(O) _____

(P) _____

(Q) _____

(R) _____

(S) _____

(T) _____

(U) _____

(V) _____

(W) _____

(X) _____

Notes

Chapter 57

Automatic Transmission Fundamentals

Name: _____ Date: _____

Instructor: _____ Score: _____ Textbook pages 1050–1076

Objective: After studying this chapter, you will be able to explain the operation of an automatic transmission.

Basic Automatic Transmission

1. An automatic transmission performs the same functions as a manual transmission, but it _____ and _____ automatically.

    1._____

    _____

2. What are the three methods of power transfer in an automatic transmission?

    2._____

    _____

    _____

3. Explain the functions of the parts listed below.

    *Bell housing:*_____

    _____

    _____

    Transmission case: _____

    _____

    _____

    *Oil pan:*_____

    _____

    Extension housing: _____

    _____

    _____

4. *True or False?* In simple terms, a torque converter works like the force of moving air generated by one fan moving the blades of another fan.

    4._____

5. A(n) _____ is part of a modern torque converter.
    - (A) impeller
    - (B) turbine
    - (C) one-way clutch
    - (D) All of the above.

    5._____

6. A(n) _____ has an internal friction clutch for clamping the impeller to the turbine.

    6._____

7. What does a planetary gearset consist of? _____

_____

8. Automatic transmission _____ and _____ are friction devices that drive or lock planetary gearset members.

8. _____

_____

9. In your own words, describe how an *automatic transmission clutch* functions.

_____

_____

_____

_____

_____

10. How does a *servo* work? _____

_____

_____

_____

_____

_____

11. Label the basic parts of the automatic transmission.

(A)	_____	(G)	_____
(B)	_____	(H)	_____
(C)	_____	(I)	_____
(D)	_____	(J)	_____
(E)	_____	(K)	_____
(F)	_____		

12. Label the parts of the planetary gearset assembly.

(A)	_____
(B)	_____
(C)	_____
(D)	_____

Hydraulic System

13. List the two purposes of the automatic transmission hydraulic system. _____

_____

_____

14. The _____ produces the pressure to operate an automatic transmission.   14. _____

15. The _____ is operated by the driver's shift lever.   15. _____
    (A) manual valve
    (B) pressure regulator
    (C) modulator
    (D) governor

16. What are the two types of transmission oil pumps?   16. _____

_____

17. What is the function of the vacuum modulator valve? _____

_____

_____

18. The vacuum modulator valve is being phased out for _____ systems.   18. _____

19. The _____ sensor and _____ serve the same function as the vacuum   19. _____
    modulator.

_____

20. How do the shift or balanced valves operate? _____

_____

_____

_____

21. Define *valve body.* _____

_____

_____

_____

22. A(n) _____ is used to lock the transmission output shaft and keep the car   22. _____
    from rolling when not in use.

Electronic Transmission Control

23. Explain the basic operation of *electronic transmission control.* _____

_____

_____

_____

_____

_____

24. The _____, stored as data in ECM _____, determines when the electroni-   24. _____
    cally-controlled transmission changes gears.

_____

25. Transmission control sensors have replaced the _____.   25._____
    (A) governor
    (B) vacuum modulator
    (C) kickdown rod or linkage
    (D) All of the above.

26. What functions can electric solenoids perform in an electronically-controlled transmission?

    _____

    _____

    _____

    _____

27. What functions does the computer typically monitor in an electronically-controlled transmission?

    _____

    _____

    _____

    _____

28. Identify the parts of the computer control system.

(A) _____   (G) _____

(B) _____   (H) _____

(C) _____   (I) _____

(D) _____   (J) _____

(E) _____   (K) _____

(F) _____

Chapter 58

Automatic Transmission Service

Name: _____ Date: _____

Instructor: _____ Score: _____ Textbook pages 1077–1096

Objective: After studying this chapter, you will be able to describe common testing and service methods for automatic transmissions.

Automatic Transmission Diagnosis

1. What are some causes of incorrect shift points in an automatic transmission?

   (1) _____

   (2) _____

   (3) _____

   (4) _____

   (5) _____

   (6) _____

2. Automatic transmission mushy shifts are frequently caused by _____.   2._____
   - (A) worn bands or clutches
   - (B) valve body problems or low oil level
   - (C) misadjusted linkage
   - (D) All of the above.

3. What are some precautions to take when transmission service requires raising the vehicle on a lift?_____

   _____

   _____

   _____

   _____

   _____

   _____

4. Before road testing the vehicle, what checks should you make? _____

   _____

   _____

5. When inspecting the transmission oil, check for signs of _____ or _____.   5._____

   _____

6. What does a light brown coating on the transmission dipstick indicate? _____
_____

7. In your own words, explain how to perform a *stall test.* _____
_____
_____
_____
_____
_____
_____

8. Label the problems that can develop in the automatic transmission shown in the illustration.

(A) _____	(G) _____
(B) _____	(H) _____
(C) _____	(I) _____
(D) _____	(J) _____
(E) _____	(K) _____
(F) _____	(L) _____

9. List the steps for performing a pressure test.

(A)_____
_____

(B)_____
_____

(C)_____
_____

(D)_____
_____

10. Air tests will let you detect _____ or blocked passages.   10._____
    (A) leaks
    (B) stuck components
    (C) bad check valves
    (D) All of the above.

Automatic Transmission Maintenance

11. List the steps for changing automatic transmission oil.

    (A)_____
_____

    (B)_____
_____

    (C)_____
_____

    (D)_____
_____

    (E)_____
_____

    (F)_____
_____

    (G)_____
_____

    (H)_____
_____

    (I)_____
_____

    (J)_____
_____

12. List the steps for adjusting a neutral safety switch.

    (A)_____
_____

    (B)_____
_____

    (C)_____
_____

    (D)_____
_____

    (E)_____
_____

13. *True or False?* Check the automatic transmission oil with the engine off and the shift selector in park.

13._____

14. *True or False?* Transmission fluids vary; you must use the type specified in the service manual.

14._____

15. _____ adjustment is needed to set the correct clearance between the friction material and the drum.
   - (A) Clutch
   - (B) Servo
   - (C) Converter
   - (D) Band

15._____

Electronic Control System Service

16. What type of malfunction should you look for when troubleshooting electronically controlled transmissions?
   - (A) Mechanical
   - (B) Hydraulic
   - (C) Electrical
   - (D) All of the above.

16._____

17. How do you begin diagnosis of an electronically controlled transmission?

_____

_____

_____

_____

_____

_____

18. What is an automatic transmission *limp-in mode?* _____

_____

_____

_____

_____

_____

19. If the malfunction indicator light is glowing, connect the _____ to the computer diagnostic connector. Check for stored _____ or abnormal electrical values.

19._____

_____

20. Where can automatic transmission solenoids and sensors be located?

_____

21. Why do some automatic transmissions use an oil temperature sensor? _____

_____

_____

_____

_____

_____

Chapter 59

Drive Shafts and Transfer Cases

Name: _____ Date: _____

Instructor: _____ Score: _____ Textbook pages 1097–1109

Objective: After studying this chapter, you will be able to explain the construction and operation of drive shafts and transfer cases.

Drive Shaft Assembly

1. *True or False?* Drive shafts are required only on vehicles with rearwheel drive and engines in front.

   1._____

2. Explain the answer you gave in Question 1. _____

   _____

   _____

   _____

3. What causes a change in distance between a transmission and a differential?

   _____

   _____

4. What is another name for the drive shaft?

   4._____

5. How are some drive shafts designed for increased performance?_____

   _____

   _____

   _____

6. Why must a drive shaft be straight and perfectly balanced? _____

   _____

   _____

   _____

7. What are *balancing weights?*_____

   _____

   _____

8. Sometimes a drive shaft _____ is used to absorb torsional vibrations in a drive shaft.

   8._____

9. What is a *universal joint?* _____

_____

_____

_____

_____

10. The _____ is the most common type of drive shaft U-joint.   10. _____

11. Why is a constant velocity U-joint sometimes used? _____

_____

_____

_____

12. A(n) _____ is needed to hold the middle of a two-piece drive shaft.   12. _____

13. _____ is a type of driveline with an open drive shaft that operates a rear   13. _____
axle assembly mounted on springs.
    (A) Constant velocity
    (B) Torque tube
    (C) Variable velocity
    (D) Hotchkiss

14. Identify the major parts of the drive shaft assembly.

(A) _____

(B) _____

(C) _____

(D) _____

(E) _____

(F) _____

(G) _____

Transfer Cases

15. A transfer case sends power to both the _____ in a four-wheel-drive   15. _____
vehicle.

16. The transfer case usually mounts behind and is driven by the _____.   16. _____

17. What is an *all-wheel drive system?* _____

_____

_____

_____

_____

18. Label the parts of the four-wheel drive and all-wheel drive systems.

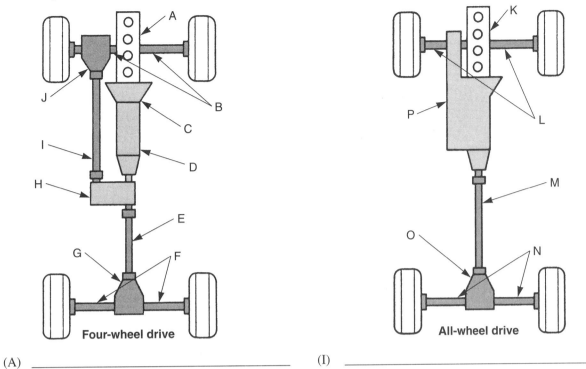

Four-wheel drive

All-wheel drive

(A) _____   (I) _____

(B) _____   (J) _____

(C) _____   (K) _____

(D) _____   (L) _____

(E) _____   (M) _____

(F) _____   (N) _____

(G) _____   (O) _____

(H) _____   (P) _____

19. Label the parts of the all-wheel drive system.

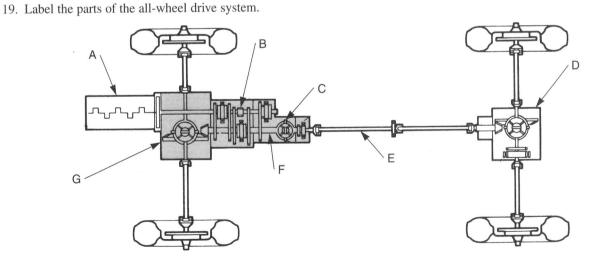

(A) _____   (E) _____

(B) _____   (F) _____

(C) _____   (G) _____

(D) _____

Notes

Drive Shaft and Transfer Case Diagnosis, Service, and Repair

Name: _____Date: _____

Instructor: _____Score: _____Textbook pages 1110–1122

Objective: After studying this chapter, you will be able to repair common drive shaft troubles.

Drive Shaft Problems

1. Squeaking from the drive shaft may be caused by worn _____. 1._____

2. Suggest causes for a *clunking* sound in a drive shaft. _____

_____

_____

_____

3. What is a symptom of a worn, dry center support bearing? _____

_____

_____

4. Vibration is caused by problems that affect drive shaft _____. 4._____
   - (A) angle
   - (B) runout
   - (C) straightness and balance
   - (D) All of the above.

Drive Shaft Inspection

5. How do you inspect a drive shaft for problems? _____

_____

_____

_____

_____

6. How do you check for worn universal joints in a drive shaft? _____

_____

_____

_____

_____

Drive Shaft Service

7. When removing a drive shaft, wrap _____ around the two _____ to keep the needle bearings from being dropped.

7. _____
   _____

8. A(n) _____ and two _____ can be used to disassemble and reassemble a universal joint.

8. _____
   _____

Transfer Case Service

9. Label the parts of the transfer case.

(A) _____   (G) _____

(B) _____   (H) _____

(C) _____   (I) _____

(D) _____   (J) _____

(E) _____   (K) _____

(F) _____

Chapter 61

Differential and Rear Drive Axle Fundamentals

Name: _____ Date: _____

Instructor: _____ Score: _____ Textbook pages 1123–1138

Objective: After studying this chapter, you will be able to summarize the operation and construction of differentials and rear axle assemblies.

Basic Rear Drive Axle Assembly

1. Explain the basic parts of a simple rear drive axle assembly.

Pinion drive gear: _____

_____

Ring gear: _____

_____

Differential case assembly: _____

_____

Rear drive axles: _____

_____

_____

Rear axle bearings: _____

_____

_____

Axle housing: _____

_____

_____

2. Power enters the rear axle assembly from the _____.   2. _____

3. List the functions of a *rear drive axle.* _____

_____

_____

_____

_____

_____

4. Label the parts of the rear axle assembly illustrated below.

(A) _____

(B) _____

(C) _____

(D) _____

(E) _____

(F) _____

(G) _____

(H) _____

Differential Construction

5. The differential must be able to transfer power to both axles, even when they are _____

_____.

6. The pinion gear turns the _____ when the shaft is turning.

6. _____

7. The pinion gear is normally mounted on tapered _____.

7. _____

8. _____ is a small amount of pressure applied to the bearings to remove play and excess clearance.

8. _____

9. The pinion _____ helps the two tapered roller bearings support the pinion gear during periods of heavy load.

9. _____

10. The ring gear transfers rotating power through an angle change of _____.

10. _____

11. The ring gear and pinion gear are often _____ at the factory to produce quieter operation and longer gear life.

11. _____

12. Most ring and pinion gears are _____.
    (A) hunting gearset
    (B) nonhunting gearset
    (C) spiral bevel gears
    (D) Both A and B.

12. _____

13. Hypoid gears have replaced _____ gears because they allow for a lower hump in the vehicle floor and improve gear meshing action.

13. _____

14. Explain how to calculate *rear axle ratio.* _____

_____

_____

_____

15. A rear axle ratio is usually determined by automakers as a compromise between what two factors?

_____

16. What is the average rear axle ratio?

16. _____

17. What would occur if a *higher* than average rear axle ratio was maintained? _____

_____

_____

18. What would occur if a *lower* than average rear axle ratio was maintained? _____

_____

_____

19. Explain the difference between the terms *rear axle ratio* and *final drive ratio.* _____

_____

_____

_____

20. What is the function of a *differential carrier?* _____

_____

_____

21. What are the two basic types of differential carriers? _____

_____

22. What does the *differential case* hold? _____

_____

_____

23. What do the *spider gears* include?

_____

24. What is the function of *differential lubricant*?

_____

_____

25. Differential lubricant, usually _____, is used to reduce friction inside the   25. _____
    rear axle assembly.

Differential Action

26. What problem is a differential designed to prevent? _____

_____

_____

_____

_____

27. When driving straight, both rear wheels turn at the _____ speed.   27. _____

Limited-Slip Differentials

28. There might not be adequate _____ on slippery pavement, in mud, or   28. _____
    during rapid acceleration with a conventional differential.

29. Summarize the construction of the most popular type of *limited-slip differential.*

_____

_____

_____

_____

_____

30. Identify the parts of the limited-slip differential illustrated below.

(A) _____

(B) _____

(C) _____

(D) _____

(E) _____

(F) _____

(G) _____

31. How does a *clutch pack type limited-slip differential* work? _____

_____

_____

_____

_____

32. What is a *cone clutch differential?* _____

_____

_____

33. What is a *Detroit Locker?* _____

_____

_____

_____

_____

_____

_____

34. What is a *Torsen differential?* _____

_____

_____

_____

_____

Rear Drive Axles

35. The rear axles connect the differential side gears to the _____.

35._____

36. A(n) _____ type axle turns the drive wheel and supports the weight of the vehicle.

36._____

37. The rear _____ reduce friction between the axles and axle housing.

37._____

38. The rear _____ keep lubricant from leaking out the ends of the axle housing.

38._____

Name _____

39. _____ are frequently used between the axle retainer plate and the housing to limit axle end play.
    (A) Axle retainer plates
    (B) Axle shims
    (C) Swing axles
    (D) Semifloating axles

39. _____

40. _____ axles are used when the differential is rigidly mounted on the car's frame.

40. _____

41. Drive axles are _____ (solid/flexible).

41. _____

42. A differential _____ vents pressure or vacuum in or out of the rear axle housing as temperature changes occur.

42. _____

43. Identify the parts of the rear drive axle.

(A) _____   (G) _____

(B) _____   (H) _____

(C) _____   (I) _____

(D) _____   (J) _____

(E) _____   (K) _____

(F) _____

Front, Four-Wheel Drive Axle

44. How is *front, four-wheel drive axle* assembly different from a *rear drive axle*?

_____

_____

_____

_____

45. Identify and describe the three basic types of locking hubs.

(1) _____

_____

(2) _____

_____

(3) _____

_____

46. What is an advantage of the front wheels being able to turn without turning the front axles?

_____

_____

_____

_____

47. Identify the parts of the semifloating, ball bearing type axle illustrated below.

(A) _____

(B) _____

(C) _____

(D) _____

(E) _____

(F) _____

(G) _____

(H) _____

(I) _____

(J) _____

48. Identify the parts of the full-floating axle illustrated below.

(A) _____

(B) _____

(C) _____

(D) _____

_____

(E) _____

(F) _____

_____

Chapter 62

Differential and Rear Drive Axle Diagnosis and Repair

Name: _____ Date: _____

Instructor: _____ Score: _____ Textbook pages 1139–1158

Objective: After studying this chapter, you will be able to summarize the diagnosis and repair of rear drive axle assemblies.

Differential and Rear Axle Diagnosis

1. Rear end problems usually show up as _____.

   1. _____

2. Identify some other problems that can produce symptoms similar to those caused by faulty rear drive axle components.

   _____

   _____

3. Using the exploded view below, identify the problems that can occur in a rear axle assembly.

(A) _____	(I) _____
(B) _____	(J) _____
(C) _____	(K) _____
(D) _____	(L) _____
(E) _____	(M) _____
(F) _____	(N) _____
(G) _____	(O) _____
(H) _____	

4. What should you listen for when road testing the vehicle? _____

_____

_____

5. A(n) _____ can be used to isolate the source of a differential or rear axle   5. _____
   bearing problem.

6. What are the symptoms of bad ring and pinion gears? _____

_____

_____

_____

7. If the backlash between the ring and pinion is too great, a(n) _____ sound   7. _____
   can be produced by the gears.

8. Rear axle lubricant leaks can occur at the _____.   8. _____
   (A) two axle seals
   (B) pinion gear seal
   (C) inspection cover gaskets
   (D) All of the above.

9. What can a technician do to tell the difference between a possible axle seal leak or a brake fluid leak?

_____

_____

10. When axle or carrier bearings are bad, a constant whirring or humming   10. _____
    sound can be heard while _____.
    (A) accelerating
    (B) coasting
    (C) decelerating
    (D) All of the above.

11. When do differential case problems frequently show up? _____

_____

12. Label the illustrations showing axle and bearing problems.

(A) _____

(B) _____

(C) _____

(D) _____

(E) _____

(F) _____

(G) _____

13. What is the cause of a chattering sound heard when a limited-slip differential turns a corner?

_____

_____

Differential Maintenance

14. Differential fluid should be checked or replaced at _____.

14. _____

15. A special type of fluid intended for the friction clutches should be installed in a(n) _____ differential.

15. _____

Rear Axle Service

16. Name three times when rear axle service is needed.

_____

_____

_____

_____

_____

17. A(n) _____ type axle is commonly used with a removable carrier.

17. _____

18. A(n) _____ type axle is frequently used with an integral carrier.

18. _____

19. Explain how to remove an axle that is secured with a retainer plate. _____

_____

_____

_____

_____

_____

_____

20. Identify the parts relating to rear axle removal.

(A) _____

(B) _____

(C) _____

(D) _____

(E) _____

(F) _____

(G) _____

(H) _____

(I) _____

(J) _____

21. What is a possible consequence if the backing plate is pulled off with the axle?

_____

_____

22. Explain how to remove an axle that is held in place with a C-clip.

_____

_____

_____

_____

_____

23. Once the axle is removed, what should be inspected?_____

_____

24. An axle with tapered ends may require a(n) _____ for removal of the hub.   24._____

25. Why are technicians cautioned *not* to use a cutting torch during removal of an old collar and axle bearing?

_____

26. Always press an axle bearing off using the _____ race.   26._____

27. What can cause bearing damage? _____

_____

28. Explain how to install a new bearing. _____

_____

_____

_____

_____

_____

29. What could result if the bearing and collar were pressed on at the same time?

_____

30. When should a new axle seal be installed?   30._____
    (A) Anytime the axle is removed for service.
    (B) Once a year.
    (C) Twice a year.
    (D) It is never required.

31. To remove a housing mounted rear axle seal, use a slide hammer puller   31._____
    equipped with a(n) _____.

32. Explain the steps in removal of a housing mounted seal. _____

_____

_____

_____

33. What is a *seal part number?* _____

_____

_____

34. What needs to be done before installing the new seal?_____

_____

_____

35. Why is it important *not* to bend the metal seal housing when installing an axle seal?

_____

36. What would indicate the need for installation of new lugs? _____

_____

_____

37. How do you replace axle studs?_____

_____

_____

38. During rear axle installation, what could result if the axle rubs on the new seal?

_____

39. When installing a rear axle, wiggle and move the axle up and down until
    its splines fit into the splines in the differential _____.

39. _____

40. Excess axle end play can cause a(n) _____ as the car rounds corners.

40. _____

41. Explain how to measure axle end play. _____

_____

_____

_____

_____

_____

42. What may be needed if there is too much end play?_____

_____

_____

43. What may be needed if the end play is too small? _____

_____

_____

_____

Differential Service

44. What should be inspected when differential troubles are suspected? _____

_____

_____

45. A differential _____ is provided to show the exact type of differential for
    ordering parts and looking up specifications.

45. _____

46. When using a service manual to repair a differential, what 12 basic procedures must you remember?

    (1) _____

    _____

    (2) _____

    _____

(3) _____

_____

(4) _____

_____

(5) _____

_____

(6) _____

_____

(7) _____

_____

(8) _____

_____

(9) _____

_____

(10) _____

_____

(11) _____

_____

(12) _____

_____

47. _____ torque is the amount of torque needed to make one axle or differential side gear rotate the limited-slip differential clutches.

47. _____

48. Identify the parts of the limited-slip differential.

(A) _____

(B) _____

(C) _____

(D) _____

(E) _____

(F) _____

(G) _____

(H) _____

(I) _____

(J) _____

(K) _____

(L) _____

(M) _____

(N) _____

(O) _____

49. How do you check the action of a limited-slip differential? _____
_____
_____
_____
_____

50. List six differential measurements and adjustments.
_____
_____
_____
_____

51. Pinion _____ refers to the distance the pinion gear extends into the carrier.   51. _____

52. How is *pinion bearing preload* frequently adjusted?_____
_____
_____
_____

53. Pinion bearing preload is commonly controlled by pinion _____ when a   53. _____
solid spacer is used.

54. All of the following are used to set pinion gear or bearing preload, *except:*   54. _____
    (A) a breaker bar.
    (B) a torque wrench.
    (C) a stethoscope.
    (D) a holding tool.

55. The amount of force pushing the differential case bearings together is the   55. _____
case bearing _____.

56. Ring gear runout is the amount of _____ produced when the ring gear is   56. _____
rotated.

57. Explain how to measure ring gear runout. _____
_____
_____
_____

58. What can happen if gear backlash is too small and the gears overheat?_____
_____
_____
_____
_____

59. Explain how to increase and decrease backlash. _____
_____
_____
_____
_____

60. A good ring and pinion gear contact pattern is located in the _____ of the   60. _____
    gear teeth.

61. Explain the names of the areas on ring gear teeth.

    Toe: _____

    _____

    Heel: _____

    _____

    Pitch line: _____

    _____

    Face: _____

    _____

    Flank: _____

    _____

    Drive side: _____

    _____

    Coast side: _____

    _____

62. Label the illustration showing ring and pinion adjustment on an integral carrier.

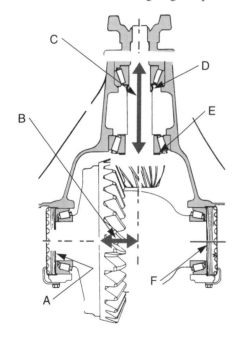

(A) _____

(B) _____

(C) _____

(D) _____

(E) _____

(F) _____

Chapter 63

Transaxle and Front Drive Axle Fundamentals

Name: _____Date: _____

Instructor: _____Score: _____Textbook pages 1159–1182

Objective: After studying this chapter, you will be able to describe the construction and operation of transaxles and front-drive axles.

Transaxles

1. What is a *transaxle?*_____

_____

_____

2. In what type of automobile is a transaxle most commonly found?_____

_____

_____

3. What are three possible advantages of a vehicle having a transaxle and front-wheel drive over a front engine vehicle with rear-wheel drive?

(1) _____

_____

(2) _____

_____

(3) _____

_____

4. List four possible disadvantages of front-wheel drive.

(1) _____

_____

(2) _____

_____

(3) _____

_____

(4) _____

_____

Manual Transaxle

5. Explain a *manual transaxle.* _____
_____
_____
_____

6. Explain the seven major parts of a manual transaxle.

Input shaft: _____
_____

Input gears: _____
_____

Output gears: _____
_____

Output shaft: _____
_____

Synchronizers: _____
_____

Differential: _____
_____

Transaxle case: _____
_____

7. A manual transaxle clutch is _____ (different from/identical to) the clutch
used with a manual transmission for a rear wheel drive vehicle.

7. _____

8. Sometimes high gear in a manual transaxle transmission can provide a(n)
_____ for increased fuel economy.

8. _____

■ *Items 9 through 11.* The names of shafts, gears, and other transaxle parts will vary depending on the location
and function of the components. Match the following terms to their other names.

9. Mainshaft

10. Pinion shaft

11. Clustergear assembly

(A) Sometimes called the input or
output shaft gears.

(B) Sometimes called the input
shaft.

(C) Sometimes called the output
shaft.

9. _____

10. _____

11. _____

12. Where are transaxle shafts normally mounted? _____
_____
_____

13. Explain how the gear becomes locked to the shaft when a shift fork moves a transaxle synchronizer into one of the free-
wheeling gears.
_____
_____

14. Like a rear axle differential, a(n) _____ differential transfers power to the axles and wheels while allowing one wheel to turn at a different speed than the other.

14. _____

15. The _____ is sometimes used to transfer crankshaft power to the transaxle, gearbox, or transmission.
    (A) transaxle shafts
    (B) transaxle differential
    (C) drive chain
    (D) pinion gear teeth

15. _____

16. What should be done to be able to diagnose manual transaxle problems quickly?

_____

_____

17. Briefly describe what occurs when the transaxle is in the following positions.

Transaxle in neutral: _____

_____

_____

Transaxle in first gear: _____

_____

_____

Transaxle in second gear: _____

_____

_____

Transaxle in third gear: _____

_____

_____

Transaxle in fourth gear: _____

_____

_____

Transaxle in reverse: _____

_____

_____

Automatic Transaxle

18. Explain the seven major parts of an automatic transaxle.

Torque converter: _____

_____

_____

Oil pump: _____

_____

_____

Valve body: _____

_____

_____

Pistons and servos: _____

_____

Bands and clutches: _____

_____

_____

Planetary gearsets: _____

_____

Differential: _____

_____

19. Modern transaxles often use _____ control to increase efficiency.   19. _____

20. What are the three basic sections of a transaxle electronic control system? _____

_____

_____

_____

21. Identify the basic parts of the manual transaxle illustrated below.

(A) _____   (H) _____

(B) _____   (I) _____

(C) _____   (J) _____

(D) _____   (K) _____

(E) _____   (L) _____

(F) _____   (M) _____

(G) _____

22. Some vehicles use a separate transaxle control module. Others use the _____ control module to analyze sensor inputs and determine the outputs needed to operate the automatic transaxle.

22._____

23. An electronically controlled transaxle uses _____ to alter hydraulic pressure to each circuit.

23._____

24. Sensors on the transaxle provide feedback concerning _____.
    (A) transaxle speed
    (B) fluid temperature
    (C) vehicle speed
    (D) All of the above.

24._____

25. With transaxles using manual type gearsets, the electric solenoids move the _____ to shift gears.

25._____

26. What is a *continuously variable transaxle (CVT)?* _____

_____

_____

_____

27. How does a CVT operate? _____

_____

_____

_____

_____

28. A computer controlled CVT can use _____ to operate the hydraulic control valve systems to move the variable pulley in or out, changing gear ratios.

28._____

Front Drive Axle Assembly

29. What do most modern front-drive axle assemblies include?_____

_____

_____

30. Front-drive axles turn about _____ the speed of a rear drive shaft.
    (A) one-half
    (B) one-third
    (C) one-eighth
    (D) one-fourth

30._____

31. Describe the three basic parts of an axle shaft.

Inner stub shaft: _____

_____

_____

Outer stub shaft: _____

_____

_____

Interconnecting shaft: _____

_____

_____

32. Front drive axle assembly transfers power from the _____ to the hubs and wheels of the vehicle.

32._____

33. Label the parts of the front-drive axle assembly.

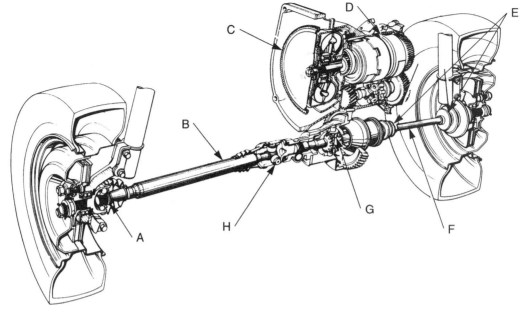

(A) _____   (E) _____

(B) _____   (F) _____

(C) _____   (G) _____

(D) _____   (H) _____

34. _____ in the front drive axle assemblies allow the shafts to operate through an angle without damage.

34._____

35. Explain the *outboard CV-joint.* _____

_____

_____

_____

36. What components does a tripod CV-joint include? _____

_____

_____

37. For what reasons are CV-joint boots used? _____

_____

_____

38. Why are CV-joint boots accordion shaped?_____

_____

_____

39. What function do retaining collars serve? _____

_____

_____

Chapter 64

Transaxle and Front Drive Axle Diagnosis and Repair

Name: _____ Date: _____

Instructor: _____ Score: _____ Textbook pages 1183–1205

Objective: After studying this chapter, you will be able to troubleshoot and repair common transaxle and drive-axle problems.

Transaxle Problem Diagnosis

1. Why is it difficult to correctly diagnose and isolate transaxle and front drive axle problems quickly?

_____

_____

_____

2. With electronic transaxle control, how can you use a scan tool to find problems? _____

_____

_____

3. Identify three problems found in manual transaxles.

_____

_____

_____

4. How is a manufacturer's diagnosis chart helpful in diagnosis of manual transaxles?

_____

_____

5. If a test drive does not pinpoint the trouble during diagnosis of an automatic transaxle problem, all of the following tests could be performed, *except:*
   (A) pressure tests.
   (B) air tests.
   (C) CV-joint test.
   (D) stall test.

5. _____

6. How do you use a hydraulic diagram to diagnose automatic transaxle problems?

_____

_____

_____

Front Drive Axle Problems

7. Front drive axle problems are usually noticed as _____ in the universals.
    (A) excessive play
    (B) abnormal noise
    (C) vibration
    (D) All of the above.

7. _____

8. Contamination and _____ will cause joint failure in a brief period of time.

8. _____

9. Describe a simple test to check for bad front drive axles. _____

_____

_____

_____

10. All of the following can be done when symptoms point to possible drive axle troubles, *except:*
    (A) check fluid pressures.
    (B) wiggle the joints to check for excessive play and wear.
    (C) inspect the axle shafts.
    (D) check the rubber boots for wear.

10. _____

11. What can happen if you operate the engine and transaxle with the suspension system hanging unsupported?

_____

_____

_____

Transaxle Maintenance

12. Identify some consequences if the transaxle lubricant is *not* changed at recommended intervals.

_____

_____

13. When should you check the lubricant level on both manual and automatic transaxles?

_____

14. Describe how to check the lubricant level for an *automatic transaxle.* _____

_____

_____

_____

15. Describe how to check the lubricant level for a *manual transaxle.* _____

_____

_____

_____

16. Using the incorrect type of lubricant could cause severe _____.

16. _____

17. When changing transaxle fluid, the fluid should be _____.
    (A) cooled
    (B) thinned
    (C) warmed to operating temperature
    (D) None of the above.

17. _____

18. What is a potential danger when draining transaxle fluid? _____

_____

_____

19. A few automatic transaxle bands have a(n) _____ inside the pan.   19. _____

Front Drive Axle Service

20. How do you remove a front drive axle? _____

_____

_____

_____

_____

21. With some transaxles, the inner ends of the axles are held with _____.   21. _____

22. What is included in a CV-joint *repair kit?* _____

_____

_____

23. The slightest dent in a hollow axle shaft could cause _____.   23. _____

24. A CV-joint requires the recommended type of _____ or else boot deterio-   24. _____
    ration and joint failure could occur.

25. Describe the steps to follow when servicing a tripod CV-joint. _____

    (1) _____

    _____

    (2) _____

    _____

    (3) _____

    _____

    (4) _____

    _____

    (5) _____

    _____

    (6) _____

    _____

    (7) _____

    _____

    (8) _____

    _____

    (9) _____

    _____

    (10) _____

    _____

26. How do you replace a *Rzeppa type CV-joint?*

_____

_____

_____

27. Installing a front drive axle is the _____ of the directions used in axle removal.

27._____

28. The _____ is the bushing between axle and seal.

28._____

29. _____ replacement is normally recommended during front drive axle service.

29._____

Transaxle Removal

30. A transaxle can be removed from a vehicle _____.
    (A) from the bottom of the engine compartment
    (B) through the top of the engine compartment
    (C) Both of the above.
    (D) Neither of the above.

30._____

31. If recommended, mount a(n) _____ on the vehicle to keep the engine from dropping during transaxle removal.

31._____

32. An engine supporting subframe is called a(n) _____.

32._____

Transaxle Service

33. Identify three of the general rules to follow when repairing or rebuilding a transaxle.

    (1) _____

    _____

    (2) _____

    _____

    (3) _____

    _____

Transaxle Installation

34. During transaxle installation, align the engine crankshaft centerline with the transaxle _____ centerline.

34._____

35. If you have a manual transaxle, the _____ must be in new or good condition.

35._____

36. If you have an automatic transaxle, you may have to align the _____ with the flywheel while fitting the transaxle.

36._____

37. Explain what could occur if the torque converter is not fully in position. _____

_____

_____

_____

_____

_____

Chapter 65

Tire, Wheel, and Wheel Bearing Fundamentals

Name: _____ Date: _____

Instructor: _____ Score: _____ Textbook pages 1207–1221

Objective: After studying this chapter, you will be able to explain tire, wheel bearing, and hub construction and operation.

Tires

1. What forces must a tire deliver to the surfaces on which it travels? _____
   _____
   _____
   _____
   _____

2. Today's tires are filled with air, meaning they are _____.   2. _____

3. Explain the six basic parts of a tire.

   Beads: _____
   _____

   Body plies: _____
   _____

   Tread: _____
   _____

   Sidewall: _____
   _____

   Belts: _____
   _____

   Liner: _____
   _____

4. What is a benefit of a *footprint* on a radial tire? _____
   _____
   _____
   _____

■ Match the terms on the right with the definitions on the left.

5. Has plies and belts running at different angles; the belts lie under the tread area only.

6. Has plies running at an angle from bead to bead; the angle is reversed from ply to ply.

7. Has plies running straight across the beads, with stabilizer belts directly beneath the tread.

(A) Bias ply tire

(B) Radial ply tire

(C) Belted bias tire

5. _____

6. _____

7. _____

8. Identify the two common size designations for tires. _____

_____

_____

9. What does GR 78-15 mean on a tire sidewall?

G: _____

R: _____

78: _____

15: _____

10. Identify and label the three types of tire construction.

A   B   C

(A) _____   (C) _____

(B) _____

11. The height to width ratio, known as the _____ ratio, is the most difficult value to understand in the tire size designation.

11. _____

12. Identify the point of measurement on a tire.

(A) _____

(B) _____

(C) _____

(D) _____

(E) _____

(F) _____

13. The amount of weight the tire can carry at the recommended inflation pressure is known as the _____ rating.

13. _____

14. A maximum recommended inflation pressure of _____ psi is common for many tires.

14. _____

15. What does a greater number of plies or higher ply rating generally indicate? _____

_____

16. What is the significance of *DOT* on the tire sidewall? _____

_____

17. The higher the tread wear number, the _____ (more/less) resistant the tire is to wear.

17. _____

18. Which tire rating provides the *least* traction?

18. _____

19. Explain *tire speed ratings.* _____

_____

_____

_____

20. Explain how *wear bars* indicate a critical amount of tread wear. _____

_____

_____

21. Which kind of spare tire is used on most new cars?

21. _____

22. Most modern spare tires are designed only for _____ use.

22. _____

23. How do *self-sealing tires* work? _____

_____

_____

24. What vehicles often receive retreads and why? _____

_____

_____

25. Tires with an extremely stiff sidewall construction so they are still usable with a loss of air pressure are _____ tires.

25. _____

26. How does a *tire inflation monitoring system* work? _____

_____

_____

_____

_____

_____

Wheels

27. Varieties of wheels may be made with all of the following materials, *except:*

27. _____

    (A) cast aluminum.
    (B) silver.
    (C) magnesium.
    (D) steel.

28. Why is a *drop center wheel* commonly used? _____

_____

_____

_____

29. A _____ rim has small ridges that hold the tire beads in place.   29._____
    (A) safety
    (B) ridge
    (C) two-piece
    (D) mag wheel

30. Explain the difference between a tire *blowout* and a *flat.* _____

_____

_____

_____

_____

Valve Stems and Cores

31. A valve stem snaps into a hole in the wheel of a(n) _____ tire.   31._____

32. The valve _____ is an air valve inside the valve stem.   32._____

33. Explain what happens when the air chuck is removed from the valve stem. _____

_____

_____

34. What is the function of a *valve stem cap?* _____

_____

_____

_____

Lug Nuts, Studs, and Bolts

35. Explain why the *inner face* of the lug nut is tapered. _____

_____

36. Lug _____ are special studs that accept the lug nuts.   36._____

37. What is the function of *wheel weights*? _____

_____

_____

Hub and Wheel Bearing Assemblies

38. Describe the three basic parts of a wheel bearing.

    Outer race: _____

_____

_____

Balls or rollers: _____

_____

_____

Inner race: _____

_____

_____

39. Describe the basic parts of a nondriving hub assembly.

Spindle: _____

_____

_____

Wheel bearings: _____

_____

_____

Hub: _____

_____

_____

Grease seal: _____

_____

_____

Safety washer: _____

_____

_____

Spindle adjusting nut: _____

_____

_____

Nut lock: _____

_____

_____

Cotter pin: _____

_____

_____

Dust cap: _____

_____

_____

40. Describe the basic parts of a drive hub and wheel bearing assembly.

Outer drive axle: _____

_____

_____

Ball or roller bearings: _____

_____

_____

Steering knuckle (bearing support): _____

_____

_____

Drive hub: _____

_____

_____

Axle washer: _____

_____

_____

Hub or axle locknut: _____

_____

_____

Grease seal: _____

_____

_____

41. Name the components of the driving hub and wheel bearing assembly.   41. _____

(A) _____

(B) _____

(C) _____

(D) _____

(E) _____

(F) _____

(G) _____

Chapter 66

Tire, Wheel, and Wheel Bearing Service

Name: _____ Date: _____

Instructor: _____ Score: _____ Textbook pages 1222–1242

Objective: After studying this chapter, you will be able to service tires, wheels, and wheel bearings.

Tire, Wheel, and Bearing Diagnosis

1. When noting problems in a steering assembly such as vibration, abnormal tread wear, or steering wheel pull, make sure that symptoms are not caused by _____ problems.
    (A) steering
    (B) suspension
    (C) front wheel alignment
    (D) All of the above.

1. _____

2. When inspecting tires, what should you look for? _____
   _____
   _____

3. Which of the following is *not* included in impact damage?
    (A) Punctures
    (B) Cuts
    (C) Cracking
    (D) Tears

3. _____

4. A tire _____ can usually be studied to find wear causes.

4. _____

5. Underinflation wears the _____ of the tread while overinflation wears the _____ of the tread.

5. _____

6. What can happen with tire *underinflation?* _____
   _____
   _____
   _____
   _____

7. What can happen with tire *overinflation?* _____
   _____
   _____
   _____
   _____

8. How do you tell the difference between *tire noise* and *wheel bearing noise?*

_____

_____

9. How do you check for a loose wheel bearing? _____

_____

_____

_____

_____

10. Label the types of tire damage.

(A) _____

(B) _____

(C) _____

(D) _____

(E) _____

(F) _____

(G) _____

Tire Maintenance

11. Tire maintenance involves periodic _____.
    (A) rotation
    (B) inspection
    (C) checking of inflation pressure
    (D) All of the above.

11._____

12. How do you know how much pressure to put in tires? _____

_____

_____

_____

_____

13. Most tire manufacturers recommend cold inflation pressure of _____ to _____ psi below the maximum listed air pressure.

13._____

_____

14. Define *tire load index.* _____

_____

_____

_____

_____

_____

15. Why is *lug nut torque* critical on new vehicles? _____

_____

_____

16. Draw arrows to show proper rotation for bias ply and radial tires.

Bias tires   **Radial tires**

LF   Forward   RF   RF   Forward   LF   LF   RF   LF   RF

LR   RR   LR   RR   LR   RR   LR   RR

4 Tires   ← Spare   ← Spare

5 Tires

Wheel Runout and Balance

17. Define the following terms.

Tire runout: _____

_____

_____

Wheel runout: _____

_____

_____

Lateral runout: _____

_____

_____

Radial runout: _____

_____

_____

18. Give typical specifications for the following runouts.

Tire radial runout: _____

Tire lateral runout: _____

Wheel radial runout: _____

Wheel lateral runout: _____

19. What does *static imbalance* cause the tire to do? _____

_____

20. What does *dynamic imbalance* cause the tire to do? _____

_____

21. How do you balance a wheel assembly? _____
_____ _____
_____

Tire Puncture Repair

22. What are the two requirements for correct tire puncture repair?_____
_____
_____

23. *True or False?* You should always dismount a punctured tire and patch the   23. _____
inner liner.

Wheel Bearing Service

24. In your own words, explain how to disassemble a nondriving wheel bearing assembly.

_____
_____
_____
_____
_____

25. *True or False?* All-purpose grease can be used to lubricate wheel bearings.   25. _____

26. How do you pack wheel bearings? _____
_____
_____
_____

27. *True or False?* Front wheel bearings on front-wheel drive vehicles are not   27. _____
as easily serviced as those on rear-wheel drive vehicles.

28. Label the drawings showing wheel bearing problems.

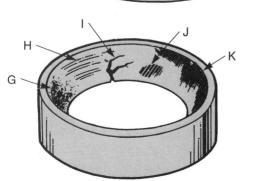

(A) _____

(B) _____

(C) _____

(D) _____

(E) _____

(F) _____

(G) _____

(H) _____

(I) _____

(J) _____

(K) _____

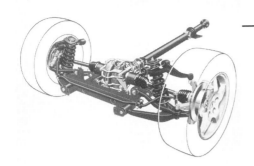

Chapter 67

Suspension System Fundamentals

Name: _____ Date: _____

Instructor: _____ Score: _____ Textbook pages 1243–1264

Objective: After studying this chapter, you will be able to explain the construction and operation of modern suspension systems.

Basic Suspension System

1. What is *chassis stiffness* and how is it measured? ___quiet $ smooth, Chassis hertz ↑___
   ___The stiffer_____

   _____

   _____

2. Define the six basic parts of a suspension system.

   Control arm: _____

   Steering knuckle: _____

   Ball joint: _____

   Spring: _____

   Shock absorber or damper: _____

   Control arm bushing: _____

3. Independent suspension systems allow one wheel to move up and down   3. ___min. effect___
   with _____ on the _____.   ___other wheels___

4. What is *understeer?* ___pushing, not turning_____

   _____

   _____

5. What is *oversteer?* ___loose, rear tries to pass front_____

   _____

   _____

6. Explain *lateral acceleration* and how it is measured. ___amount of side force before___
   ___tires lose traction — g-force_____

   _____

   _____

   _____

Suspension System Springs

7. Suspension system springs must _____ and _____ with bumps and holes in the road.

7. *Compress*
   extend

8. What are the four types of suspension system springs?

   (A) *coil*

   (B) *leaf*

   (C) *air*

   (D) *torsion*

Suspension System Construction

9. A control arm holds the _____ in position as the wheel moves up and down.
   - (A) steering knuckle
   - (B) bearing support
   - (C) axle housing
   - (D) All of the above.

9. *D.*

10. What is a *strut rod?* *fastens control arm to unibody or frame*

11. Without shock absorbers, the vehicle would continue to _____ after striking a dip or hump in the road.

11. *bounce up & down*

12. What is the advantage of *gas-charged shock absorbers?* *keeps shock from foaming*

13. How does a gas-filled shock absorber operate? *gas has pressure on oil and piston operates in oil*

14. What components does a *strut assembly* consist of? *shock, coil spring, damper*

15. How does a *sway bar* work? *connects to control arms & body*

16. A(n) _____ keeps the suspension system from hitting the frame structure.

16. *bound bumper*

17. If you hear a loud bang or thud when going over a large bump in the road, what might be happening and what might this be telling you?
    bottoming out

Name _____

18. Explain the construction, operation, and adjustment of a torsion bar suspension system. *turn adjust bolt to raise & lower*

19. Explain the construction/operation of a MacPherson strut suspension system.
spring, strut, dampener all one unit that ~~makes~~ connects to knuckle

20. Explain these three basic parts of an electronic height control system.

Height sensor: *senses height*

Sensor link: *connects from sensor to suspension*

Solenoid valve: *opens & closes to operate air suspension*

21. Explain these major parts of a typical electronic shock absorber system.

Steering sensor: *senses steering position*

Brake sensor: *input*

Acceleration sensor: *input*

Mode switch: *adjusts shocks - manually*

Electronic control unit: *Brain*

Shock actuators: *actuators*

22. How can a *sonar* sensor be used in an electronically controlled suspension system?
find dips & bumps and adjust before you get there

23. A(n) _____ suspension system uses computer controlled hydraulic rams instead of conventional suspension system springs and shock absorbers.

23. *active*

24. What purpose do *ball joints* serve? *to allow connections that allow limited rotation in all directions*

25. Spring _____ are limited by a vehicle's shock absorbers.

25. *oscillations*

26. Shock absorber _____ occurs when the vehicle's tire is forced upward upon hitting a bump.

26. *Compression*

27. Label the parts of the control arm.

(A) *control arm bushings*
(B) *steering knuckle*
(C) *wheel bearing bore*
(D) *seal*
(E) *Ball joint*
(F) *control arm*
(G) *" " bushing*

Suspension Leveling Systems

28. What is the main function of a suspension leveling system? *maintain same altitude*

29. A(n) _____ suspension leveling system uses air shocks and an electric compressor to maintain curb height.

29. *manual*

30. What is a *height sensor*? *lever-operated switch that reacts to changes in body height & suspension*

31. Identify the parts of the double-wishbone suspension system.

(A) *Top view trailing arm*
(B) *upper control arm Sway bar*
(C) *lower Control arm upper*
(D) *↑ lower*
(E) *trailing arm*
(F) *lower control arm*
(G) *strut*
(H) *upper Control arm*

Electronic and Active Suspension Systems

32. What is a *mode switch*? *Dash mounted switch that allows driver to choose shock action*

33. An active suspension system uses computer-controlled _____ instead of conventional springs and shock absorber actuators to control ride characteristics.

33. *hydraulic rams*

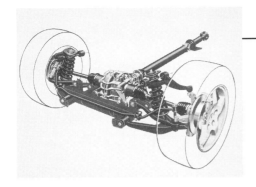

Chapter 68

Suspension System Diagnosis and Repair

Name: _____ Date: _____

Instructor: _____ Score: _____ Textbook pages 1265–1286

Objective: After studying this chapter, you will be able to troubleshoot and repair common suspension system problems.

Suspension System Diagnosis

1. List and explain common suspension system problems. _____

_____

_____

_____

_____

2. Label the types of problems that can develop in a suspension system.

(A) _____

(B) _____

(C) _____

_____

(D) _____

(E) _____

(F) _____

_____

(G) _____

(H) _____

_____

(I) _____

(J) _____

(K) _____

(L) _____

_____

3. What are the symptoms of bad shock absorbers? _____

_____

_____

_____

4. Describe how to perform a *shock bounce test*. _____

_____

_____

_____

_____

Suspension Spring Service

5. Describe the special tool sometimes used to service coil springs. _____

_____

_____

_____

_____

6. A(n) _____ tool or _____ is commonly used to force the ball joint away from the steering knuckle.

6. _____

_____

7. *True or False?* When replacing a rear coil spring, a spring compressor may *not* be needed.

7. _____

Ball Joint Service

8. What are some symptoms of worn ball joints? _____

_____

_____

9. Why must you be careful not to inject too much grease into a ball joint equipped with a balloon seal?

_____

_____

10. What are two ways of checking ball joint wear? _____

_____

_____

_____

11. *True or False?* Always use a new cotter pin when servicing a component.

11. _____

12. List the three steps in replacing a riveted ball joint.

(A) _____

(B) _____

(C) _____

Suspension Bushing Service

13. How do you check for control arm bushing wear? _____

_____

_____

_____

_____

_____

14. What is *sticktion?* When can it be heard? _____

_____

_____

_____

_____

_____

_____

MacPherson Strut Service

15. *True or False?* The most common trouble with a MacPherson strut suspension is spring fatigue.

15. _____

16. Label the parts of the strut assembly.

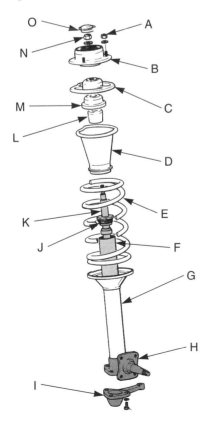

(A) _____

(B) _____

(C) _____

(D) _____

(E) _____

(F) _____

(G) _____

(H) _____

(I) _____

(J) _____

(K) _____

(L) _____

(M) _____

(N) _____

(O) _____

17. In your own words, explain how to replace a strut shock absorber. _____

_____

_____

_____

_____

18. How do you safely dispose of gas-filled shocks? _____

_____

_____

_____

_____

19. Always _____ all suspension systems bolts and nuts to factory specs.   19. _____

Computerized Suspension Diagnosis

20. How would you start troubleshooting an electronically controlled suspension system?

_____

_____

_____

21. What faulty parts might a scan tool locate on a suspension system?

_____

_____

_____

22. What can go wrong with a height sensor? _____

_____

_____

23. *True or False?* When replacing the shocks on electronic suspension   23. _____
    systems, you may be able to transfer some of the electronic parts from the
    old units onto the new ones.

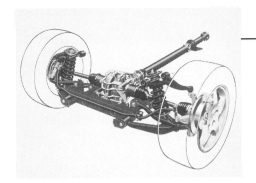

Steering System Fundamentals

Name: _____ Date: _____

Instructor: _____ Score: _____ Textbook pages 1287–1309

Objective: After studying this chapter, you will be able to summarize the construction and operation of steering systems.

Basic Steering Systems

1. Today's steering systems are very sophisticated. They may use _____ and _____ to improve steering precision.

   1._____

   _____

2. List five functions of a steering system.

   _____

   _____

   _____

   _____

   _____

   _____

3. What are the two basic types of steering systems? _____

   _____

Match the linkage steering system part to its corresponding description.

4. Connects steering gearbox to steering knuckles and wheels.

5. Supports steering wheel and steering shaft.

6. Transfers turning motion from steering wheel to steering gearbox.

7. Allow linkage arms to swivel up and down for suspension action and from left to right for turning.

8. Changes turning motion into straight-line motion to the left or right.

9. Used by driver to rotate steering shaft that passes through steering column.

(A) Steering wheel

(B) Steering shaft

(C) Steering column

(D) Steering gearbox

(E) Steering linkage

(F) Ball sockets

4._____

5._____

6._____

7._____

8._____

9._____

343

10. Describe a *rack-and-pinion* steering system. _____

_____

_____

_____

_____

11. Label the parts of the linkage steering system.

(A) _____

(B) _____

(C) _____

(D) _____

(E) _____

(F) _____

(G) _____

Steering Column Assembly

12. The steering column assembly consists of a _____.
    (A) column and ignition key mechanism
    (B) steering wheel and steering shaft
    (C) flexible coupling and universal joint
    (D) All of the above.

12. _____

13. What components typically make up the steering column assembly? _____

_____

_____

14. Label the steering column components.

(A) _____

(B) _____

(C) _____

(D) _____

(E) _____

(F) _____

(G) _____

(H) _____

(I) _____

(J) _____

(K) _____

Name _____

15. A(n) _____ steering wheel commonly uses a steel pin and a slotted disc to prevent the steering wheel from being turned.

15. _____

16. List the three types of collapsible steering columns in use today. _____

_____

_____

17. A(n) _____ steering wheel uses a flex joint that allows the top of the column and steering wheel to be positioned at different angles.

17. _____

Steering Gear Principles

18. The _____ gearbox is the most common type used with a linkage type system.

18. _____

19. *True or False?* The sector shaft is the input gear connected to the steering column shaft.

19. _____

20. A bearing _____ is usually provided to set worm shaft bearing preload.

20. _____

21. What is *gearbox ratio?* _____

_____

_____

_____

22. A manual gearbox will have a _____ (high/low) gearbox ratio to reduce the amount of effort needed to turn the steering wheel.

22. _____

23. A(n) _____ gearbox changes the internal gear ratio as the front wheels are turned from the center position.

23. _____

Steering Linkage

24. The _____ transfers gearbox motion to the steering linkage.

24. _____

25. The steel bar that connects the right and left sides of the steering linkage is called the _____.

25. _____

26. What purpose does the *idler arm* serve? _____

_____

27. What is used to fasten the center link to the steering knuckles?

27. _____

Rack-and-Pinion Steering

28. What function does the flexible coupling serve? _____

_____

29. Power steering systems normally use a(n) _____ to assist steering action.
    (A) hydraulic system
    (B) engine-driven pump
    (C) electric motor
    (D) All of the above.

29. _____

30. A(n) _____ is used in a power steering system to control maximum oil pressure.

30. _____

31. Explain the difference between *integral* and *external* cylinder power steering.

_____

_____

_____

_____

_____

32. Explain these four basic parts of a power rack-and-pinion system.

Power cylinder: _____

_____

Power piston: _____

_____

Hydraulic lines: _____

_____

Control valve: _____

_____

33. How can a steering system intentionally affect engine idle speed?_____

_____

_____

_____

_____

_____

34. What is *road feel?* _____

_____

_____

35. _____ steering systems alter steering wheel effort as road speed changes.   35._____

36. Label the parts of the four-wheel steering system.

(A) _____

(B) _____

(C) _____

(D) _____

(E) _____

(F) _____

(G) _____

(H) _____

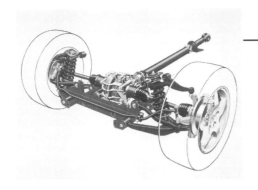

Chapter 70

Steering System Diagnosis and Repair

Name: _____ Date: _____

Instructor: _____ Score: _____ Textbook pages 1310–1330

Objective: After studying this chapter, you will be able to summarize how to diagnose and repair steering system troubles.

Steering System Service

1. After prolonged use, what parts of the steering system wear, and what are the results?

_____

_____

_____

_____

_____

_____

2. Label the problems that can occur in the steering system.

(A) _____

(B) _____

(C) _____

(D) _____

(E) _____

(F) _____

(G) _____

(H) _____

(I) _____

(J) _____

(K) _____

(L) _____

(M) _____

(N) _____

3. Explain two methods of checking the causes of steering wheel play. _____

_____

_____

_____

_____

_____

4. How do you remove a steering wheel? _____

_____

_____

5. How do you service an inner tie-rod end on a rack-and-pinion assembly?

_____

_____

_____

_____

_____

_____

_____

6. How do you remove a rack-and-pinion assembly from a vehicle? _____

_____

_____

_____

_____

7. *True or False?* An idler arm is a very common wear point on linkage type   7. _____
   steering.

8. Label the possible problems in the linkage system.

(A) _____

(B) _____

(C) _____

(D) _____

(E) _____

(F) _____

(G) _____

(H) _____

(I) _____

(J) _____

(K) _____

(L) _____

(M) _____

9. A power steering pressure test checks the operation of the _____.   9._____
    (A) power steering pump
    (B) pressure relief valve
    (C) control valve
    (D) All of the above.

10. *True or False?* Most automotive technicians rebuild a power steering pump   10._____
    in-shop.

11. With electronic assist, a scan tool might show codes for _____.   11._____
    (A) power steering pump pressure
    (B) lateral acceleration sensor
    (C) fluid pressure control solenoid
    (D) All of the above.

12. Label the parts that can cause power steering system leakage in a rack-and-pinion system.

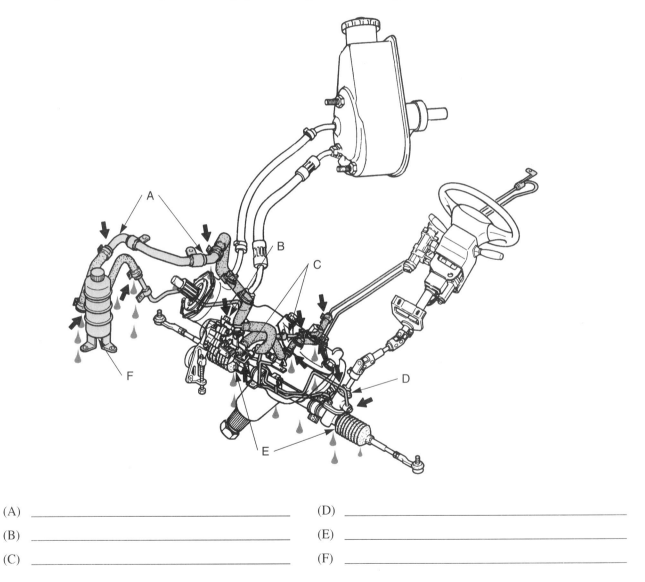

(A) _____   (D) _____

(B) _____   (E) _____

(C) _____   (F) _____

13. Label the parts that can cause power steering system leakage in a linkage system.

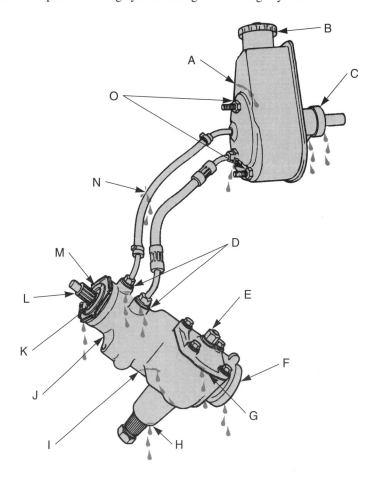

(A) _____

(B) _____

(C) _____

(D) _____

_____

(E) _____

_____

(F) _____

(G) _____

_____

(H) _____

_____

(I) _____

(J) _____

_____

(K) _____

(L) _____

(M) _____

_____

(N) _____

_____

(O) _____

Chapter 71

Brake System Fundamentals

Name: _____ Date: _____

Instructor: _____ Score: _____ Textbook pages 1331–1355

Objective: After studying this chapter, you will be able to describe the operating principles of an automotive brake system.

Basic Brake System

1. Automotive _____ provides a means of using friction to either slow, stop, or hold the wheels of a vehicle.

   1._____

2. What is a *master cylinder?*_____

   _____

   _____

   _____

3. A(n) _____ is a vacuum- or power steering-operated device that assists brake pedal application.

   3._____

4. Which of the following is used for brake lines?
   - (A) Metal tubing
   - (B) Rubber hose
   - (C) Plastic lines
   - (D) Both A and B.

   4._____

5. Technician A says when the driver pushes on the brake pedal, lever action pushes a rod into the brake booster. Technician B says it does this, but also continues pushing into the master cylinder. Who is right?
   - (A) A only.
   - (B) B only.
   - (C) Both A and B.
   - (D) Neither A nor B.

   5._____

6. _____ are frequently used on the two front wheels of a vehicle. _____ are sometimes used on the rear wheels.

   7._____

   _____

7. Describe the function and purpose of an *emergency brake system.* _____

   _____

   _____

   _____

   _____

8. All of the following are parts of a disc brake assembly, *except:*   8._____
    (A) wheel cylinder.
    (B) caliper.
    (C) brake pads.
    (D) rotor.

9. What are *brake pads?*_____

_____

_____

_____

10. Technician A says a wheel cylinder assembly is a hydraulic piston forced   10._____
    outward by fluid pressure. Technician B says a brake drum rubs against
    brake shoes to stop wheel rotation and vehicle movement. Who is right?
    (A) A only.
    (B) B only.
    (C) Both A and B.
    (D) Neither A nor B.

Braking Ratio

11. Define *braking ratio.* _____

_____

_____

_____

_____

_____

_____

12. How much braking power does the front wheel brakes handle?   12._____

13. Technician A says front-wheel drive cars can have a very low braking ratio   13._____
    at the front wheels. Technician B says front-wheel drive cars can have a
    very high braking ratio at the front wheels. Who is right?
    (A) A only.
    (B) B only.
    (C) Both A and B.
    (D) Neither A nor B.

Brake System Hydraulics

14. A hydraulic system uses a confined _____ to transmit motion and pressure.   14._____

15. List the three principles that apply to the operation of a hydraulic system.

_____

_____

_____

_____

16. When _____ of different sizes are used, motion and force can be increased   16._____
    or decreased.

Brake System Components

17. The _____ acts as a lever arm to increase the force applied to the master cylinder piston.
    - (A) push rod
    - (B) master cylinder
    - (C) firewall
    - (D) brake pedal assembly

17. _____

18. List the parts of a master cylinder. _____

   _____

   _____

   _____

19. The _____ master cylinder has two separate hydraulic pistons and two fluid reservoirs.

19. _____

20. Identify the parts of the master cylinder.

(A) _____

(B) _____

(C) _____

(D) _____

(E) _____

(F) _____

(G) _____

(H) _____

(I) _____

(J) _____

(K) _____

(L) _____

(M) _____

21. Technician A says in the dual master cylinder, the rear piston assembly is called the primary piston. Technician B says the front master cylinder piston is termed the secondary piston. Who is right?
    - (A) A only.
    - (B) B only.
    - (C) Both A and B.
    - (D) Neither A nor B.

21. _____

22. Describe what happens in a dual master cylinder if there was pressure loss in the primary section of the brake system.

   _____

   _____

   _____

23. What would be needed to slow and stop the vehicle if both primary and secondary hydraulic systems failed?

_____

24. Power brakes use a _____ to assist brake pedal application.   24. _____
    (A) booster
    (B) engine vacuum
    (C) atmospheric pressure
    (D) Both A and B.

25. Describe the operation of a power brake *vacuum booster.* _____

_____

_____

_____

_____

_____

_____

26. Name the two general types of brake boosters. _____

_____

27. A(n) _____ uses power steering pump pressure to help the driver apply the   27. _____
    brake pedal.

28. Technician A says Hydro-boost power brakes are commonly used with   28. _____
    vehicles equipped with diesel engines. Technician B says some gasoline
    powered vehicles also use Hydro-boost systems. Who is right?
    (A) A only.
    (B) B only.
    (C) Both A and B.
    (D) Neither A nor B.

29. Name the two organizations that write specifications for brake fluid.

_____

_____

30. What are six desirable properties of brake fluid?

_____

_____

_____

_____

_____

_____

31. Brake _____ and _____ transfer fluid pressure from the master cylinder to   31. _____
    the wheel brake assemblies.
                                                                            _____

32. What material is used to create brake hoses?   32. _____

33. A _____ is used when a single brake line must feed two wheel cylinders.   33. _____
    (A) junction block
    (B) fuse block
    (C) combination valve
    (D) diagonal valve

34. What is a *longitudinally split brake system?* _____

_____

_____

_____

_____

35. Disc brakes are like the brakes on a(n) _____.   35._____

36. The _____ is included in a brake caliper assembly.   36._____
    (A) piston seal
    (B) master cylinder
    (C) cylinder cups
    (D) return springs

37. Identify the components of the disc brake assembly.

(A) _____

(B) _____

(C) _____

(D) _____

(E) _____

(F) _____

(G) _____

(H) _____

38. Disc brake pads are _____ to which linings are riveted.   38._____

39. Technician A says newer vehicles use brake pad linings made of resistant   39._____
    semimetallic friction materials. Technician B says newer vehicles use pad
    linings made of asbestos. Who is right?
    (A) A only.
    (B) B only.
    (C) Both A and B.
    (D) Neither A nor B.

40. _____ are frequently used to keep the brake pads from vibrating and rattling.   40._____

41. Why is a *pad wear sensor* sometimes used? _____

_____

_____

42. What is a *brake disc?* _____

_____

_____

_____

_____

43. All of the following are true about brake discs, *except:*

    (A) it may be solid or vented.

    (B) the ventilated rib disc is hollow.

    (C) it may be an integral part of the wheel hub.

    (D) the brake disc is normally made of aluminum.

43._____

44. Define *floating caliper.* _____

_____

_____

45. Technician A says the sliding caliper uses more than one piston. Technician B says the fixed caliper disc brake is a one-piston caliper. Who is right?

    (A) A only.

    (B) B only.

    (C) Both A and B.

    (D) Neither A nor B.

45._____

46. Why are floating and sliding calipers used? _____

_____

_____

47. List the parts of a drum brake assembly. _____

_____

_____

_____

48. The backing plate holds all of the following drum brake components, *except:*

    (A) brake drum.

    (B) shoes.

    (C) wheel cylinder.

    (D) springs.

48._____

49. What is a *wheel cylinder?* _____

_____

_____

_____

50. What wheel cylinder component keeps road dirt and water out?

50._____

51. Explain the function of a wheel cylinder *bleeder screw.* _____

_____

_____

52. How are linings attached to brake shoes?

    (A) Rivets

    (B) Bonding agent

    (C) Spot welds

    (D) Both A and B.

52._____

53. Technician A says the secondary brake shoe has the shorter lining. Technician B says the primary shoe has the shorter lining. Who is right?

    (A) A only.

    (B) B only.

    (C) Both A and B.

    (D) Neither A nor B.

53._____

54. _____ pull the brake shoes away from the brake drums.

54. _____

55. Some manufacturers use _____ instead of hold-down springs and locking cups.

55. _____

56. What are brake springs made of? _____

_____

_____

57. Technician A says the brake shoe adjuster maintains the correct drum-to-lining clearance. Technician B says many vehicles use a star wheel-type brake shoe adjusting mechanism. Who is right?
    (A) A only.
    (B) B only.
    (C) Both A and B.
    (D) Neither A nor B.

57. _____

58. Explain how automatic *brake shoe adjusters* normally function. _____

_____

_____

_____

_____

_____

59. _____ provide a rubbing surface for the brake shoe lining.

59. _____

60. The brake shoes are drawn tighter against the drum by _____.
    (A) shoe action
    (B) self-energizing action
    (C) inertia action
    (D) servo action

60. _____

61. Define *servo action.* _____

_____

_____

_____

62. Because of servo action, _____ wheel cylinder hydraulic pressure is needed to apply the brakes.

62. _____

63. Name the three switches commonly used in brake systems. _____

_____

_____

64. Technician A says most modern cars use a mechanical stoplight switch. Technician B says most modern cars use a hydraulically operated stoplight switch. Who is right?
    (A) A only.
    (B) B only.
    (C) Both A and B.
    (D) Neither A nor B.

64. _____

65. What switch warns the driver of a pressure loss on one side of a dual master cylinder?

65. _____

66. The _____ is a small switch that often mounts in the master cylinder lid or cover.

66. _____

67. Many brake systems use *none* of the following to regulate the pressure to each wheel cylinder, *except:*
    (A) brake warning light switch.
    (B) check valves.
    (C) control valves.
    (D) metering valve.

67._____

68. The metering valve prevents the front brake from applying until the pressure reaches _____.

68._____

69. Technician A says a metering valve is designed to equalize braking action at each wheel during light braking. Technician B says a proportioning valve is used to equalize pressure in systems with front disc and rear drum brakes. Who is right?
    (A) A only.
    (B) B only.
    (C) Both A and B.
    (D) Neither A nor B.

69._____

70. Where is the proportioning valve normally located?_____

_____

_____

_____

71. Many late-model vehicles use a(n) _____ valve.

71._____

Parking Brakes

72. Parking brakes provide a(n) _____ means (cables and levers) of applying the brakes.

72._____

73. Describe the parking brake action on vehicles with disc brakes. _____

_____

_____

_____

_____

_____

_____

_____

_____

_____

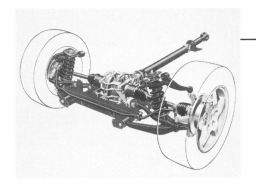

Chapter 72

Brake System Diagnosis and Repair

Name: _____ Date: _____

Instructor: _____ Score: _____ Textbook pages 1356–1382

Objective: After studying this chapter, you will be able to diagnose and repair typical brake system problems.

Brake System Problem Diagnosis

1. What symptoms should you use when diagnosing brake system troubles?

   _____

   _____

   _____

   _____

   _____

2. Technician A says many modern brake systems, especially those with ABS (anti-lock braking systems) provide on-board diagnostics. Technician B says no brake system has self-diagnostics. Who is right?
   - (A) A only.
   - (B) B only.
   - (C) Both A and B.
   - (D) Neither A nor B.

   2._____

3. All of the following can cause brake pedal vibration, *except:*
   - (A) hard spots on the brake disc.
   - (B) warped disc.
   - (C) out-of-round brake drum.
   - (D) air in the brake line.

   3._____

4. A vehicle's brakes grab. Which of the following is the *least likely* cause?
   - (A) Worn brake linings.
   - (B) Grease on the linings.
   - (C) Clogged brake hose or line.
   - (D) Malfunctioning brake booster.

   4._____

5. Technician A says excessive brake pedal effort may be caused by brake fluid on the linings. Technician B says excessive brake pedal effort may be caused by air in the brake system Who is right?
   - (A) A only.
   - (B) B only.
   - (C) Both A and B.
   - (D) Neither A nor B.

   5._____

6. What happens with *brake pull* and what is the most common cause? _____

_____

_____

_____

_____

7. What is the most common cause of a spongy brake pedal? _____

_____

8. What would be the cause of a dropping brake pedal with no fluid loss from the system?

_____

_____

_____

9. All of the following are causes of a low brake pedal, *except:*   9._____
    (A)   overadjusted parking brake.
    (B)   mechanical problem in the brake assemblies.
    (C)   inoperative brake adjusters.
    (D)   maladjusted master cylinder push rod.

10. What can cause *metal-on-metal grinding* when braking? _____

_____

11. What can cause *squeaking* when braking?_____

_____

_____

12. What can cause *rattling* when braking?_____

_____

_____

Brake System Inspection

13. Technician A says brake pedal height is the distance from the pedal to the   13._____
    floor with the pedal at rest. Technician B says brake pedal free play is the
    amount of pedal movement before the beginning of brake application. Who
    is right?
    (A)   A only.
    (B)   B only.
    (C)   Both A and B.
    (D)   Neither A nor B.

14. The brake pedal reserve distance on a vehicle is incorrect. Which of the   14._____
    following is the *most likely* cause?
    (A)   Weak return spring.
    (B)   Air in the system.
    (C)   Leaking power booster.
    (D)   Inoperative brake light switch.

15. What could happen if oil, grease, and other substances contaminated the brake fluid?_____

_____

_____

16. How will brake fluid leakage show up? _____

_____

_____

17. How do you check a parking brake? _____

_____

_____

_____

18. During a parking brake inspection, the cables were found to be frayed.   18. _____
Technician A says some fraying is okay. Technician B says the cables
should be replaced. Who is right?
- (A) A only.
- (B) B only.
- (C) Both A and B.
- (D) Neither A nor B.

19. How much wear would require brake pad or shoe replacement? _____

_____

_____

_____

20. Explain the danger of and precautions concerning asbestos dust on older brake shoes and pads.

_____

_____

_____

_____

_____

Vacuum Booster Service

21. Describe the inspection of a vacuum brake booster. _____

_____

_____

_____

22. Technician A says all vacuum boosters can be rebuilt. Technician B says   22. _____
most shops install new or rebuilt vacuum boosters. Who is right?
- (A) A only.
- (B) B only.
- (C) Both A and B.
- (D) Neither A nor B.

Hydraulic Booster Service

23. If a hydraulic booster is inoperative, what should be checked *first?* _____

_____

24. What should be done if a hydraulic booster is found to be faulty? _____

_____

Master Cylinder Service

25. When a master cylinder fails and leaks internally, what happens to the brake system?

_____

_____

26. Technician A says you can clean the hydraulic parts of a brake system with conventional parts cleaners. Technician B says you can clean brake parts in gasoline. Who is right?
    (A) A only.
    (B) B only.
    (C) Both A and B.
    (D) Neither A nor B.

26. _____

27. What tools should be used to measure master cylinder piston-to-cylinder clearance?

_____

_____

28. What is *brake system bleeding?* _____

_____

_____

29. How do you manually bleed a brake system? _____

_____

_____

_____

_____

_____

30. Technician A says you should start bleeding at the wheel brake assembly farthest from the master cylinder. Technician B says some brake systems require special procedures when bleeding. Who is right?
    (A) A only.
    (B) B only.
    (C) Both A and B.
    (D) Neither A nor B.

30. _____

31. All of the following are steps in pressure bleeding, *except:*
    (A) install a special adapter over the master cylinder reservoir.
    (B) pour enough brake fluid in the bleeder tank to reach the prescribed level.
    (C) fill the master cylinder with brake fluid.
    (D) charge the tank with 100–150 psi (690–1034 kPa) of air pressure.

31. _____

32. What is different about bleeding a brake system when the master cylinder has a plastic reservoir?

_____

_____

_____

_____

_____

_____

33. What type of tubing should you use when replacing brake lines? _____

_____

Disc Brake Service

34. All of the following are major operations needed for disc brake service,   34. _____
    except:
    (A) rebuilding caliper assembly.
    (B) replacing the wheel bearings.
    (C) turning (machining) brake discs.
    (D) replacing worn brake pads.

35. Technician A says you should hang the caliper by a piece of wire if it is not   35. _____
    being removed. Technician B says you can simply let the caliper hang by
    the brake hose. Who is right?
    (A) A only.
    (B) B only.
    (C) Both A and B.
    (D) Neither A nor B.

36. Why is it *not* advisable to service only the left or right brake assembly?

_____

_____

37. What should be done when a caliper piston is frozen? _____

_____

38. What is the technician doing in the above illustration?   38. _____
    (A) Pressure bleeding the caliper.
    (B) Checking the caliper for leaks.
    (C) Pushing the piston out of the caliper.
    (D) Cleaning the piston.

39. Technician A says light imperfections on a caliper cylinder wall can be   39. _____
    removed with a cylinder hone. Technician B says if excessive honing is
    required, the caliper should be replaced. Who is right?
    (A) A only.
    (B) B only.
    (C) Both A and B.
    (D) Neither A nor B.

Brake Disc (Rotor) Service

40. Minimum brake disc thickness will usually be printed on the side of the   40. _____
    _____.

41. How do you measure brake disc runout? _____

_____

_____

_____

42. What can happen if a brake disc is too thin? _____

_____

_____

_____

_____

43. What needs to be wrapped around the disc to prevent high-frequency vibration and squeal?

43. _____

44. How much metal should be machined from a brake disc?

44. _____

    (A) Enough to clean all imperfections.
    (B) Just enough to true the disc.
    (C) All the metal.
    (D) Enough to equal the number on the disc.

45. Label the parts of the brake lathe shown below.

(A) _____

(B) _____

(C) _____

(D) _____

(E) _____

(F) _____

(G) _____

46. When would an *on-car brake lathe* be a time-saver? _____

_____

_____

_____

_____

_____

47. All of the following are performed during disc brake reassembly, *except:*

47. _____

    (A) apply high temperature silicone on the friction linings.
    (B) fit the caliper assembly in place.
    (C) apply a small amount of grease to the caliper mounting bolt threads.
    (D) torque all fasteners to specs.

48. What can happen if you accidentally get oil or grease on a brake disc during installation?

_____

49. Technician A says brake rotors or discs can always be changed from right
   to left without problems. Technician B says rotors must be reinstalled on
   the side they came off. Who is right?
   (A) A only.
   (B) B only.
   (C) Both A and B.
   (D) Neither A nor B.

49. _____

Drum Brake Service

50. What should be done if a drum is rusted to the axle flange? _____
   _____
   _____
   _____

51. Describe drum brake disassembly. _____
   _____
   _____
   _____
   _____
   _____
   _____
   _____

52. A wheel cylinder shows signs of leakage when its boots were pulled back.
   Technician A says the wheel cylinder must be removed before disassembly.
   Technician B says the wheel cylinder can be serviced while bolted to the
   backing plate. Who is right?
   (A) A only.
   (B) B only.
   (C) Both A and B.
   (D) Neither A nor B.

52. _____

53. Describe how to hone a wheel cylinder. _____
   _____
   _____
   _____
   _____
   _____

54. Where is the wheel cylinder cup size printed? _____
   _____

55. What is *brake drum resurfacing?*_____
   _____
   _____

56. Why should you lubricate the small pads or bumps on the backing plate?_____
   _____

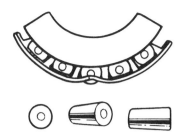

57. Technician A says the bearing shown above can be repaired. Technician B says this damage was caused by improper handling or tool use. Who is right?
    (A) A only.
    (B) B only.
    (C) Both A and B.
    (D) Neither A nor B.

57._____

58. Technician A says new brake shoes should rock slightly when moved in the drum. Technician B says they should conform perfectly when placed in the drum. Who is right?
    (A) A only.
    (B) B only.
    (C) Both A and B.
    (D) Neither A nor B.

58._____

59. A properly adjusted drum brake should _____ when turned by hand.

59._____

Parking Brake Adjustment

60. What must be tightened to adjust the parking brake? _____

_____

61. Technician A says the parking brakes should drag lightly when released. Technician B says the parking brakes should not drag when released. Who is right?
    (A) A only.
    (B) B only.
    (C) Both A and B.
    (D) Neither A nor B.

61._____

62. List the parking brake parts shown here.

(A) _____

(B) _____

(C) _____

(D) _____

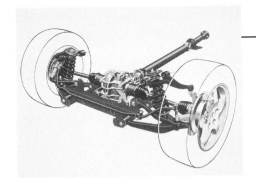

Anti-Lock Brakes, Traction Control, and Stability Control

Name: _____ Date: _____

Instructor: _____ Score: _____ Textbook pages 1383–1405

Objective: After studying this chapter, you will be able to explain the operation of anti-lock brakes, traction control, and handling systems.

Anti-Lock Brake Systems (ABS)

1. An anti-lock brake system uses wheel speed sensors, a computer (ECM), and a(n) _____ to prevent loss of tire adhesion during hard braking.

   1._____

2. For maximum stopping power, what do you want the tires to do during a panic stop? _____

   _____

   _____

3. Technician A says without ABS, a car would tend to skid to the right because of higher tire adhesion. Technician B says without ABS, the car would still travel straight ahead with hard braking. Who is right?

   3._____

   (A) A only.
   (B) B only.
   (C) Both A and B.
   (D) Neither A nor B.

4. How do wheel speed sensors produce a signal for the computer? _____

   _____

   _____

5. Technician A says the operation of a wheel speed sensor is similar to a coolant temperature sensor. Technician B says the operation of a wheel speed sensor is similar to a throttle position sensor. Who is right?

   5._____

   (A) A only.
   (B) B only.
   (C) Both A and B.
   (D) Neither A nor B.

6. What is the purpose of the *solenoid valve block* in an anti-lock brake system?_____

   _____

   _____

7. All of the following do not store fluid under pressure, *except:*

   7._____

   (A) fluid reservoir.
   (B) accumulator.
   (C) master cylinder-booster assembly.
   (D) solenoid valve block.

8. How does the ABS control module monitor system pressure? _____
_____

9. What is the *ABS dump mode?* _____
_____
_____
_____

10. Technician A says in the isolation mode, the modulator isolates the hydraulic circuit to any wheel that is locking up. Technician B says in the reapply mode, the modulator applies hydraulic pressure to one or more of the brake assemblies. Who is right?

    (A) A only.
    (B) B only.
    (C) Both A and B.
    (D) Neither A nor B.

10._____

11. Which channel ABS system has a separate hydraulic circuit for each wheel?

11._____

12. Technician A says that under normal braking conditions, ABS is not used. Technician B says ABS is used all the time for maximum braking control. Who is right?

    (A) A only.
    (B) B only.
    (C) Both A and B.
    (D) Neither A nor B.

12._____

13. When ABS takes over, what will the brake pedal do and why? _____
_____
_____

14. All of the following will occur if an ABS component malfunctions, *except:*

    (A) the brake system will not function.
    (B) the ABS warning light will light.
    (C) the ABS will be deactivated.
    (D) the brake system will still function normally.

14._____

Traction and Stability Control Systems

15. Most traction control systems work with the ABS to cycle _____ brake line pressure to the wheel spinning the fastest.

15._____

16. Technician A says the traction control system control module is capable of applying only one wheel brake at a time. Technician B says an indicator light will come on anytime the traction control system is activated. Who is right?

    (A) A only.
    (B) B only.
    (C) Both A and B.
    (D) Neither A nor B.

16._____

17. What is a *stability control system?*_____
_____
_____
_____
_____

18. Describe the additional sensors used in a stability control system.

Steering angle sensor: _____

_____

Lateral acceleration sensor: _____

_____

Yaw sensor: _____

_____

Throttle position sensor (TPS): _____

_____

Brake pressure sensor: _____

_____

ABS Service

19. Besides inspecting for conventional troubles, what should you check on an ABS system during troubleshooting?

_____

_____

_____

_____

_____

20. Technician A says the ABS light should glow for several minutes after the vehicle is started. Technician B says if the ABS light stays on, the ECM has detected an abnormal condition. Who is right?
    (A) A only.
    (B) B only.
    (C) Both A and B.
    (D) Neither A nor B.

20. _____

21. A scan tool will normally indicate problems with the following late-model ABS component(s).
    (A) Wheel speed sensor circuits.
    (B) System relays.
    (C) Modulator motors and brake switch circuit.
    (D) All of the above.

21. _____

22. You can use the scan tool to manually control all of the following ABS parts, *except:*
    (A) ABS motors.
    (B) relays.
    (C) brake pedal.
    (D) solenoids.

22. _____

23. If your scan tool indicates a problem with a wheel speed sensor, what should you do? _____

_____

_____

_____

_____

24. During the diagnosis for a defective wheel speed sensor, a pinpoint test shows the sensor to be okay, but the scan tool indicates a problem. What should be done next?

_____

_____

_____

25. What tool(s) should be used to check the wheel speed sensor air gap? _____

_____

26. Technician A says if the ABS modulator tests bad, most shops rebuild the unit. Technician B says if most shops rebuild ABS modulators, this would save customers money. Who is right?
    (A) A only.
    (B) B only.
    (C) Both A and B.
    (D) Neither A nor B.

26. _____

27. When the _____ forms an integral part of the modulator, you may need to use a very specific bleeding procedure.

27. _____

28. How can a technician determine if the ABS is working normally during a test drive? _____

_____

_____

_____

_____

_____

Traction and Stability Control Service

29. Technician A says when diagnosing a traction control problem, you can test drive the vehicle while scanning. Technician B says you should test the vehicle away from pedestrians and traffic. Who is right?
    (A) A only.
    (B) B only.
    (C) Both A and B.
    (D) Neither A nor B.

29. _____

30. When testing a traction or stability control system, what type of surface is best? _____

_____

31. When the traction control or stability control system energizes, what should you hear? _____

_____

32. All of the following should be checked after an ABS, traction control, or stability control repair, *except:*
    (A) clear trouble codes and rescan the system.
    (B) test drive the vehicle.
    (C) simulate a panic stop in traffic.
    (D) make sure the ABS indicator light stays off.

32. _____

Chapter 74

Wheel Alignment

Name: _____Date:_____

Instructor: _____Score: _____Textbook pages 1406–1427

Objective: After studying this chapter, you will be able to explain wheel alignment principles.

1. In reference to vehicles, what does the term *alignment* mean? _____
   _____
   _____

2. What does correct alignment provide for a vehicle? _____
   _____
   _____

Wheel Alignment Principles

3. What is the main purpose of wheel alignment?_____
   _____
   _____

4. Identify the six fundamental angles or specifications needed for proper wheel alignment.
   _____
   _____
   _____

Caster

5. Steering wheel pull caused by the hump in the center of the road is road   5._____
   _____.

6. Define *positive caster.* _____
   _____
   _____
   _____

7. It is typical for positive caster to be recommended for vehicles with _____   7._____
   steering.

8. Negative caster is recommended for vehicles with _____ steering.   8._____

9. Explain how the directional control angle of caster is used to offset the effect of road crown.

_____

_____

_____

Camber

10. Define *camber.* _____

_____

_____

11. What are the three reasons for camber?_____

_____

_____

_____

12. What is the difference between positive camber and negative camber? _____

_____

_____

_____

Toe

13. Toe is determined by the difference in _____ between the front and rear of   13._____
    the left and right-hand wheels.

14. Explain the difference between *toe-in* and *toe-out.* _____

_____

_____

_____

Steering Axis Inclination

15. Steering axis inclination is always a(n) _____ tilt, regardless of whether the   15._____
    wheel tilts inward or outward.

16. How does steering axis inclination aid directional stability?_____

_____

_____

Toe-Out on Turns (Turning Radius)

17. Explain how *toe-out on turns* works. _____

_____

_____

_____

18. _____ built into the steering system produce proper toe-out on turns.

18. _____

Tracking

19. With proper tracking, the rear tires follow in the tracks of the _____ tires, with the vehicle moving straight ahead.

19. _____

20. What can improper tracking cause in a vehicle? _____

_____

Prealignment Inspection

21. All of the following should be checked before attempting wheel alignment, *except:*
    - (A) worn tires.
    - (B) incorrect cradle alignment.
    - (C) dog tracking.
    - (D) loose wheel bearings.

21. _____

22. What are possible consequences of improper cradle location? _____

_____

_____

Adjusting Wheel Alignment

23. All of the following are common adjustable wheel alignment angles, *except:*
    - (A) tracking.
    - (B) toe.
    - (C) caster.
    - (D) camber.

23. _____

24. Explain how caster is adjusted. _____

_____

_____

25. Camber is usually adjusted after setting _____.

25. _____

26. How is toe usually adjusted? _____

_____

_____

27. Changing one tie-rod more than the other will _____ the steering wheel spokes.

27. _____

28. What could be the cause of rear wheels failing to track properly? _____

_____

_____

Turning Radius Gauges

29. What do turning radius gauges measure? _____

_____

_____

30. How do you check *toe-out on turns?* _____

_____

_____

_____

_____

Caster-Camber Gauge

31. To measure caster with a caster-camber gauge, turn one of the front wheels inward until the radius gauge reads _____ degrees.

31. _____

32. To measure camber with a caster-camber gauge, turn the front wheels _____.
    - (A) to the right
    - (B) to the left
    - (C) straight ahead
    - (D) None of the above.

32. _____

Tram Gauge

33. How does a *tram gauge* work? _____

_____

_____

_____

_____

34. When measuring toe with a tram gauge, the difference between the lines on the front and rear of the tires is _____ actual toe.
    - (A) two times
    - (B) three times
    - (C) four times
    - (D) five times

34. _____

Alignment Machines

35. What components does the alignment machine include? _____

_____

36. What does alignment equipment software include? _____

_____

_____

_____

_____

37. What should you check for as you test drive the vehicle after completing a wheel alignment?

_____

_____

_____

_____

Chapter 75

Heating and Air Conditioning Fundamentals

Name: _____ Date: _____

Instructor: _____ Score: _____ Textbook pages 1429–1452

Objective: After studying this chapter, you will be able to explain the operation of modern automotive air conditioning systems.

Air Conditioning Principles

1. Define *air conditioning.* _____

_____

_____

_____

2. What new refrigerant is being phased in because it is less damaging to the ozone layer?   2._____

3. What are the four phases through which a refrigerant passes? _____

_____

_____

Match the air conditioning component to its corresponding description.

4. Uses cooling action of vaporizing refrigerant to cool the air inside the vehicle.

5. Fan that forces air through the evaporator and into the passenger compartment.

6. Causes refrigerant to change from a gaseous state to a liquid state, causing it to give off its stored heat.

7. Removes moisture from and stores refrigerant.

8. Shuts the compressor off when the evaporator temperature nears freezing.

9. Substance that carries heat through the system to lower the air temperature in the vehicle.

10. Pump that pressurizes refrigerant and forces it through the system.

11. Expansion valve or tube that causes refrigerant pressure and temperature to drop, cooling the evaporator.

(A) Refrigerant

(B) Compressor

(C) Condenser

(D) Flow-control device

(E) Evaporator

(F) Receiver-drier or accumulator

(G) Blower

(H) Thermostatic switch

4. _____

5. _____

6. _____

7. _____

8. _____

9. _____

10. _____

11. _____

12. Identify the major parts of an air conditioning system.

(A) _____

(B) _____

(C) _____

(D) _____

(E) _____

(F) _____

(G) _____

(H) _____

(I) _____

(J) _____

(K) _____

(L) _____

Automotive A/C System

13. What are the four basic functions of an A/C system? _____

_____

_____

14. What is the *high side* of an A/C system? _____

_____

_____

15. A(n) _____ is a thin piece of metal that bends to open or close an opening.   15. _____
   (A) swash plate
   (B) vane
   (C) reed valve
   (D) desiccant

16. What is the purpose of a *receiver-drier?* _____

_____

17. What is an *expansion tube A/C system?* _____

_____

_____

18. What is an *expansion valve?* _____

_____

_____

19. What does *valves in receiver (VIR)* mean? _____

_____

_____

20. What is the purpose of *service valves?* _____

_____

_____

21. Label the parts of the A/C system.

(A) _____

(B) _____

(C) _____

(D) _____

(E) _____

(F) _____

(G) _____

(H) _____

(I) _____

(J) _____

(K) _____

(L) _____

Heating and Ventilation

22. Explain the three main parts of a heating system. _____

_____

_____

_____

_____

_____

23. Describe the operation of the four types of heating and air conditioning controls.

Electric switch: _____

_____

Mechanical levers and cables: _____

_____

Vacuum switch: _____

_____

Electronic control unit and sensors: _____

_____

24. List and explain the major parts of a solar ventilation system. _____

_____

_____

_____

_____

_____

_____

_____

25. How does a solar powered ventilation system operate? _____

_____

_____

_____

_____

_____

_____

26. Label the parts of the heating and ventilation system.

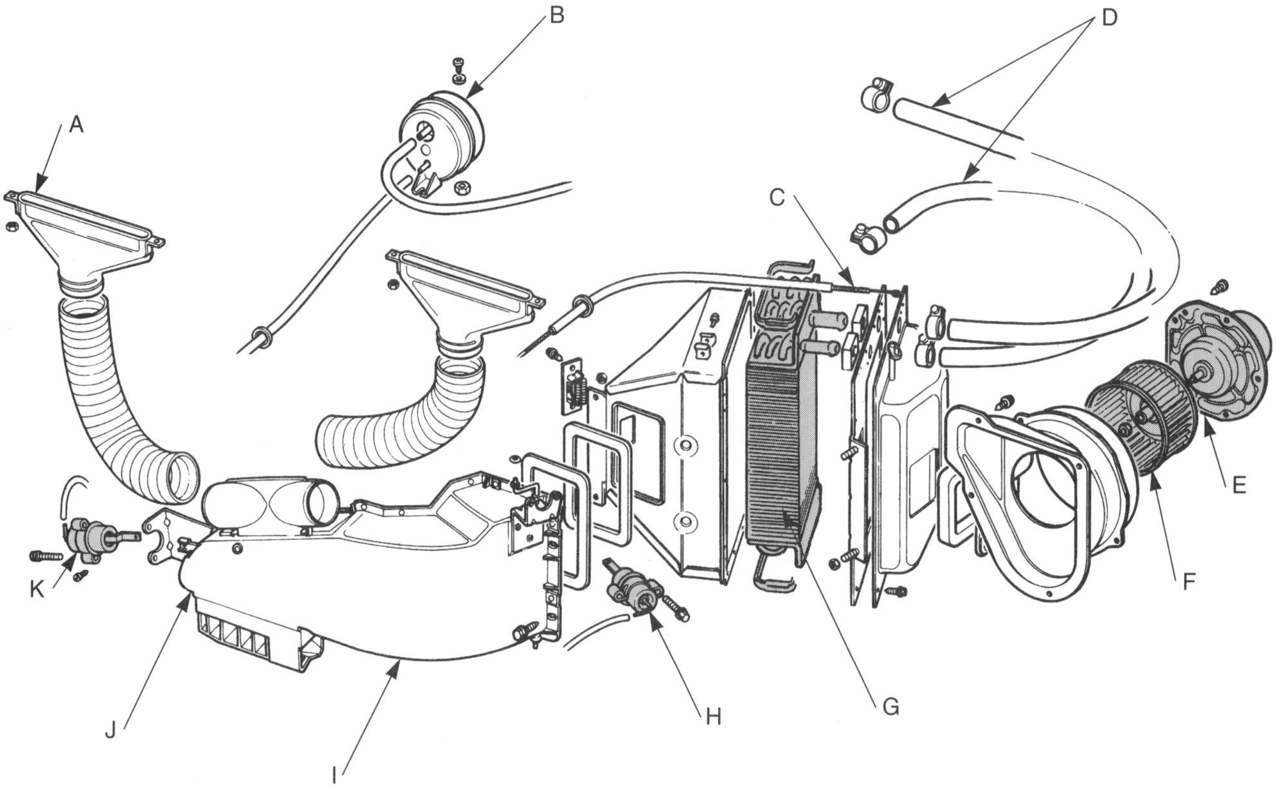

(A) _____   (G) _____

(B) _____   (H) _____

(C) _____   (I) _____

(D) _____   (J) _____

(E) _____   (K) _____

(F) _____

Chapter 76

Heating and Air Conditioning Service

Name: _____ Date: _____

Instructor: _____ Score: _____ Textbook pages 1453–1479

Objective: After studying this chapter, you will be able to do common service and repair operations on heating and air conditioning systems.

Inspecting an Air Conditioning System

1. List six obvious signs of air conditioning system trouble.

   (1) _____

   _____

   (2) _____

   _____

   (3) _____

   _____

   (4) _____

   _____

   (5) _____

   _____

   (6) _____

   _____

2. Many late-model climate control systems will produce _____ if the on-   2. _____
   board diagnostic system detects an abnormal circuit value or condition.

R-134a Service Differences

3. Why shouldn't flammable refrigerants like OZ-12 be used in a system designed for R-134a or R-12?

   _____

   _____

4. How can you tell the difference between tanks used for R-134a and R-12?

   _____

5. Tool fittings on R-12 systems use _____ threads.   5. _____

6. Are R-134a service fittings male or female?   6. _____

7. What type of fittings does an R-134a system use on charging valve joints?   7. _____

8. *True or False?* O-ring seals designed for R-12 and R-134a are interchangeable. 8. _____

9. Why shouldn't R-12 and R-134a be mixed? _____

_____

_____

_____

_____

Testing an Air Conditioning System

10. A pressure gauge or manifold assembly typically consists of a manifold,   10. _____
    two on-off valves, _____.
    - (A) three pressure gauges, and two service hoses
    - (B) two pressure gauges, and three service hoses
    - (C) one pressure gauge, and two service hoses
    - (D) All of the above.

11. Identify the parts of the pressure gauge assembly.

(A) _____

(B) _____

(C) _____

(D) _____

(E) _____

(F) _____

(G) _____

12. How can you tell by feeling line temperatures if refrigerant is moving through the system? _____

_____

_____

13. A _____ sight glass condition would indicate the system is low on refrigerant.   13. _____
    - (A) clear
    - (B) cloudy
    - (C) foamy or bubbling
    - (D) None of the above.

14. What does an *oil-streaked* sight glass indicate? _____

_____

_____

Service Valves and Pressure Gauges

15. Service valves provide a means of connecting the _____ to the A/C system.

15. _____

16. An R-134a service valve has a _____-_____ fitting that accepts a corresponding fitting on the service hose or gauge set.

16. _____

17. An R-12 service valve has _____ threads that accept a _____ fitting on the test hose.

17. _____

18. How do you connect the pressure gauge assembly to the system? _____

_____

_____

_____

_____

_____

Performance Testing A/C System

19. When performance testing an A/C system, the engine should be operated at approximately _____.
    (A) 800 rpm
    (B) 1500 rpm
    (C) 2500 rpm
    (D) The engine should not be running.

19. _____

20. What are typical system pressures for an orifice tube system at 70°F?
    (A) High-side pressure = __?__
    (B) Low-side pressure = __?__

20.(A) _____

(B) _____

21. Why might you need to measure wet- and dry-bulb temperature to analyze the operation of an air conditioning system?

_____

_____

_____

_____

_____

_____

_____

Locating A/C System Leaks

22. If more than _____ of refrigerant must be added per year, the air conditioning system is in need of repair.

22. _____

23. Name four methods used to find leaks in an A/C system.

    (1) _____

    (2) _____

    (3) _____

    (4) _____

Recovering Refrigerant

24. *True or False?* It is against the law to allow old refrigerant to leak out into the atmosphere.

24. _____

25. Refrigerant must be processed through a(n) _____ if it is contaminated or to be used in another A/C system.

25. _____

Common A/C Component Problems

■ Match the terms on the right with the descriptions on the left.

26. Will usually keep the compressor clutch from engaging.

(A) Shaft seal

26. _____

(B) Bad evaporator

27. Can leak refrigerant or become restricted internally.

(C) Bad condenser

27. _____

(D) Faulty expansion valve

28. Trouble normally shows up as inadequate cooling.

(E) Bad thermostat

28. _____

29. Usually shows up as low pressure readings on both suction and discharge sides of system.

29. _____

30. Common leakage point, can sometimes be replaced without compressor removal.

30. _____

Evacuating an Air Conditioning System

31. List six reasons why you should replace a receiver drier.

    (1) _____

    (2) _____

    (3) _____

    (4) _____

    (5) _____

    (6) _____

32. A/C system evacuation involves using a(n) _____ to remove air and moisture from inside the system.

32. _____

33. Describe the only environmentally safe way to evacuate refrigerant from an A/C system.

_____

_____

_____

_____

Charging an Air Conditioning System

34. How do you fill an A/C system with refrigerant? _____

_____

_____

_____

_____

Air Conditioning System Service Rules

35. *True or False?* R-12 and R-134a use the same type of compressor oil.   35. _____

36. List the 10 air conditioning service rules.

(1) _____

_____

(2) _____

_____

(3) _____

_____

(4) _____

_____

(5) _____

_____

(6) _____

_____

(7) _____

_____

(8) _____

_____

(9) _____

_____

(10) _____

_____

Heater Service

37. What is a typical indication of heater problems?_____

_____

_____

_____

_____

38. A vehicle's owner is complaining of insufficient heating. Technician A   38. _____
says to run the engine at fast idle and to check for system blockage by
checking the temperature of both the inlet and outlet hoses. Technician B
says that the flow valve should be checked because it could be stuck
closed. Who is right?
    (A) A only.
    (B) B only.
    (C) Both A and B.
    (D) Neither A nor B.

Electronic Climate Control Service

39. Using your textbook, label the parts indicated on the component location drawing.

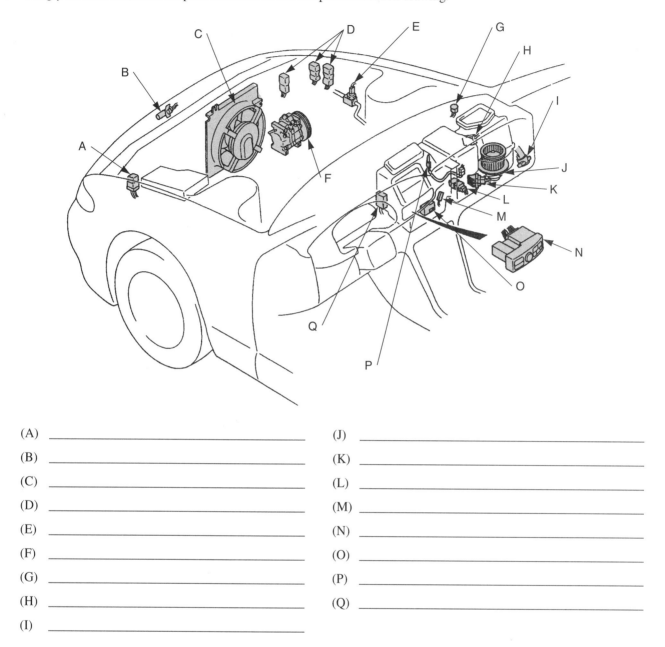

(A) _____   (J) _____

(B) _____   (K) _____

(C) _____   (L) _____

(D) _____   (M) _____

(E) _____   (N) _____

(F) _____   (O) _____

(G) _____   (P) _____

(H) _____   (Q) _____

(I) _____

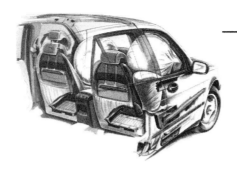

Chapter 77

Restraint Systems

Name: _____ Date: _____

Instructor: _____ Score: _____ Textbook pages 1481–1493

Objective: After studying this chapter, you will be able to explain the construction and operation of restraint systems.

Vehicle Collisions

1. What is the purpose of a *restraint system?* _____

   _____

   _____

2. What major parts are included in a restraint system? _____

   _____

   _____

   _____

3. Vehicle collisions normally result from _____ that causes the car or truck   3. _____
   to hit other objects (vehicles, trees, retaining walls, etc.).

4. What is a vehicle *crush zone?* _____

   _____

   _____

   _____

   _____

   _____

5. _____ are used by the auto manufacturer to measure how well the body-   5. _____
   frame structure protects the driver and passengers in a major collision.

Active and Passive Restraints

6. What is an *active restraint system?* _____

   _____

   _____

   _____

7. What is a *passive restraint system?* _____

_____

_____

_____

8. Seat belt _____ provide a means of bolting the seat belt to the body structure.

8. _____

9. A belt retractor takes slack out of the seat belt so it fits around your body snugly.

· 9. _____

10. Identify the parts of the seat belt assembly illustrated below.

(A) _____

(B) _____

(C) _____

(D) _____

(E) _____

(F) _____

(G) _____

(H) _____

(I) _____

Air Bag Systems

11. What is an *air bag system?* _____

_____

_____

_____

12. Explain the major parts of an air bag system.

Air bag system sensors: _____

_____

Air bag module: _____

_____

Electronic control module: _____

_____

Dash warning lamp: _____

_____

13. The air bag inflates in about _____, well before the driver's body flies forward from the collision.
    (A) 1/20 of a second
    (B) 1/10 of a second
    (B) 20 seconds
    (C) 45 seconds

13._____

14. The driver and passenger front air bags will only deploy during _____ impacts.

14._____

15. _____ air bags can be located in the door panels or on the seats.

15._____

16. What is an *air bag module?* _____

_____

_____

_____

_____

17. A deploying driver's side air bag forces the steering wheel cover to split open and the air bag shoots out at about _____.
    (A) 110 mph
    (B) 200 mph
    (C) 200 km/h
    (D) 425 mph

17._____

18. How does a *hybrid air bag* work? _____

_____

_____

_____

_____

_____

19. What is an advantage of a hybrid-type air bag?_____

_____

_____

_____

_____

20. Explain the operation of a *mechanical air bag system.* _____

_____

_____

_____

_____

21. Where are impact sensors often located?_____

_____

_____

22. What are *arming* or *safing sensors?*_____

_____

_____

_____

_____

_____

23. The trend is to replace several arming and impact sensors with one central _____ sensor that measures changes in motion or deceleration.

23._____

24. The air bag _____ uses inputs from the impact and safing sensors to determine if air bag deployment is needed.

24._____

25. Label the parts of the air bag module illustrated below.

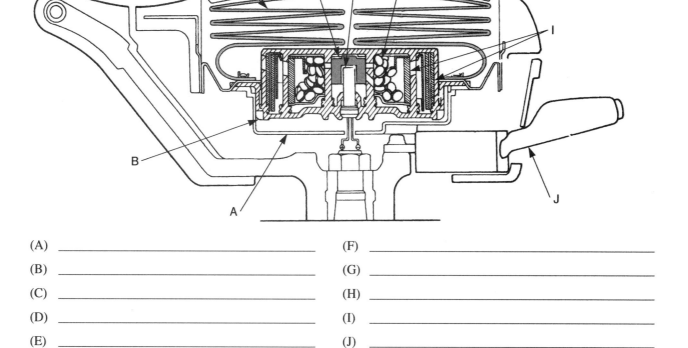

(A) _____	(F) _____
(B) _____	(G) _____
(C) _____	(H) _____
(D) _____	(I) _____
(E) _____	(J) _____

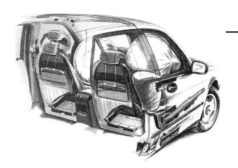

Chapter 78

Restraint System Service

Name: _____ Date: _____

Instructor: _____ Score: _____ Textbook pages 1494–1503

Objective: After studying this chapter, you will be able to service passive and active restraint systems.

Seat Belt Service

1. When is it especially important to inspect the seat belt mechanisms of a vehicle? _____
   _____
   _____

2. Summarize four steps for inspecting seat belts.

   (1) _____

   (2) _____

   (3) _____

   (4) _____

   (5) _____

3. Summarize four precautions that should be taken into account when performing seat belt service.

   (1) _____

   (2) _____

   (3) _____

   (4) _____

Air Bag Service

4. If the malfunction indicator light glows to show a problem and the bag is   4. _____
   not deployed, use a(n) _____ to analyze the system.

5. How and why do you disarm an air bag? _____
   _____
   _____
   _____
   _____
   _____

6. What danger does an air bag *reserve energy module* pose? _____

_____

_____

_____

7. When disposing of a deployed air bag, you should wear _____.   7._____
   - (A) rubber or plastic gloves
   - (B) safety glasses
   - (C) a respirator
   - (D) All of the above.

8. Why should you place pieces of tape over the vent holes of a deployed air bag? _____

_____

_____

_____

9. Of what use is a shop vacuum when working with deployed air bags? _____

_____

_____

_____

10. To remove the deployed air bag, remove the _____ from the rear of the   10._____
    steering wheel.

11. When replacing a deployed air bag, what related areas should be inspected?

_____

_____

_____

12. Why is it important to hold an air bag carrying a live (undeployed) air bag module with the trim cover away from your body?

_____

_____

13. *True or False?* After deployment from a collision or accident, some man-   13._____
    ufacturers recommend replacement of all air bag sensors.

14. *True or False?* Any air bag sensor arrow must face the rear of the vehicle.   14._____

15. To check your work on an air bag system, use your _____ to make a final   15._____
    sweep for trouble codes.

16. Label the drawing on air bag removal and installation.

(A) _____

(B) _____

(C) _____

(D) _____

(E) _____

(F) _____

(G) _____

(H) _____

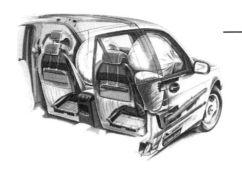

Security, Navigation, and Future Systems

Name: _____ Date: _____

Instructor: _____ Score: _____ Textbook pages 1504–1515

Objective: After studying this chapter, you will be able to summarize security systems, navigation systems, and future vehicle systems.

Security Systems

1. A security system basically uses motion _____ and _____ to feed signals to the electronic control unit.

    1._____

    _____

2. With a security system, the electronic control unit can _____ the vehicle and operate a warning _____ if someone tampers with the vehicle.

    2._____

    _____

3. Some security systems disable the _____ to keep the vehicle from being started and driven.
    - (A) transmission
    - (B) engine and starting system
    - (C) exhaust system
    - (D) All of the above.

    3._____

4. A remote hand-held _____ or dash _____ is used to activate and deactivate the system.

    4._____

    _____

5. How does a theft deterrent system *resistance key* work?_____

_____

_____

_____

_____

_____

_____

6. How does a security system *transponder key* work? _____

_____

_____

_____

_____

_____

_____

Navigation Systems

7. Navigation systems use a(n) _____ system to display the geographic location of the vehicle.

7._____

8. With most navigation systems, a(n) _____ of the area with a representation of the vehicle's _____ can then be shown to help the driver navigate.

8._____

_____

9. A vehicle tracking system can follow the location of a car or truck if stolen through the use of _____.
   (A) an on-board security control module
   (B) the vehicle's cellular telephone
   (C) a satellite system
   (D) All of the above.

9._____

Future Systems

10. *True or False?* We have the technology to allow motor cars to clean up or even modify out atmosphere as desired.

10._____

11. How does a *DUI box* function? _____

_____

_____

_____

_____

_____

_____

_____

_____

12. What is a *smog scrubbing radiator* and how does it operate?_____

_____

_____

_____

_____

_____

_____

_____

13. How would a *night vision system* help the driver see? _____

_____

_____

_____

_____

14. How do most *collision avoidance systems* operate? _____

_____

_____

_____

_____

_____

_____

_____

_____

_____

_____

Match the following terms with the statements that best identify them.

15. Uses a large, high efficiency motor and large storage batteries to power the automobile.

16. It combines hydrogen and water to produce electrical energy.

17. Its uses the power of the sun to generate electricity for propulsion.

18. Uses a special flywheel that spins on almost frictionless magnetic bearings.

19. Uses two different methods to generate power.

20. It produces little or no air pollution and is the same fuel that powers the sun.

21. Regenerative braking converts the inertia of the moving car into electrical energy to recharge the batteries.

(A) Hydrogen fuel

(B) Solar vehicle

(C) Regenerative braking

(D) Hybrid vehicle

(E) Inertia energy storage system

(F) Fuel cell

(G) Electric vehicle

15. _____

16. _____

17. _____

18. _____

19. _____

20. _____

21. _____

Notes

Shop Safety

Name: _____

Date: _____

Instructor: _____

Score: _____

Objective: With access to the auto shop, you will learn to locate and use fire extinguishers, the fire exit, safety glasses, and other shop safety equipment.

Tools and Equipment: Obtain a floor jack and jack stands.

Instructions: Study Chapter 5 in the text before starting this job. As you read the instructions, answer the questions and complete the tasks. Ask your instructor for any added details.

Eye Protection

Safety glasses or goggles should be worn in the shop *at all times*. Safety glasses are fine when used for most tasks with minimum danger. Goggles are preferred when there is a chance of a chemical being splashed in your face. A full face shield is best when debris could be thrown toward your face. Welding goggles have dark lenses that protect your eyes from the bright light of a welding flame or arc.

1. What types of eye protection are available in your shop? _____

_____

_____ Completed ☐

2. Where are the safety glasses and goggles kept in your shop? _____

_____

_____ Completed ☐

Clothing Safety

Always dress for safety. Loose clothing, jewelry, and long hair are very dangerous. They can be caught in drum lathes, wheel balancers, engine fans, a drill press, drive shaft universal joints, and other spinning objects.

Wear protective safety shoes. Tennis shoes and sandals are *not* safe in an auto shop. If a heavy part (engine flywheel, brake drum, etc.) were dropped on an unprotected foot, serious injury could result.

3. Are you properly dressed to work? _____

Explain. _____

_____

_____ Completed ☐

Battery Safety

Batteries can explode. Keep sparks and flames away from all batteries, especially during charging. Hydrogen gas is produced by batteries as part of their chemical reaction. If ignited, this gas can explode, possibly throwing the battery case and acid into your face.

4. What is a safe method of connecting jumper cables to a vehicle's battery? _____

_____

_____

_____ Completed ☐

5. When connecting a battery charger, what safety precautions should you take?_____

_____

_____

_____

_____

_____ Completed ☐

Fire Safety

Always take precautions to minimize the risk of fire. Store oily rags and gasoline in safety cans. Wipe up spilled gasoline and oil immediately. Hold a rag around the fitting when removing a vehicle's fuel line. Relieve fuel pressure before working on fuel injection systems. Remember, if you are badly burned, you can be scarred for life, blinded, or even killed. A few seconds can be a lifetime during a fire.

6. Walk around the shop and locate all fire extinguishers, fire exits, and fire alarms.   Completed ☐

7. Where are the fire extinguishers located? _____

_____

_____ Completed ☐

8. Where are the fire alarms located? _____

_____

_____ Completed ☐

9. Explain how to properly exit the shop in case of a fire. _____

_____

_____ Completed ☐

Grinder and Drill Press Safety

If misused, an electric grinder can cause serious injuries to your eyes, face, and hands. Always keep the tool rest adjusted close to the grinding wheel. Hold small objects with vise-grip pliers. Wear a face shield and thick leather gloves. Keep the machine face shield in position close to the wheel. Be careful not to strike the grinding wheel. It can shatter and explode when spinning.

10. Inspect the electric grinder closely. Locate the power switch. Observe the position of the tool rest and face shield. Also, check the condition of the grinding wheel.   Completed ☐

11. Is the electric grinder in your shop safe? _____

    Explain. _____

    _____ Completed ☐

12. Locate and inspect the operation of your shop's drill press. Find the on/off button, feed lever, chuck, and other components.   Completed ☐

⚠️ **Warning**
Never leave the chuck key in the drill chuck. If the drill press is accidentally turned on, the chuck key could fly out and hit someone.

13. How should a workpiece be secured on the drill press?_____

_____

_____

_____ Completed ☐

Name _____

Compressed Air Safety

Use compressed air with caution. Shop air hoses can have more than 100 psi (689 kPa) air pressure. If abused, this is enough pressure to blind, deafen, or even kill. *Never* point an air nozzle at yourself or anyone else.

14. What is the air pressure setting on your shop compressor? _____

_____ Completed ☐

Shop Cleanliness

The auto shop floor must be kept clean at all times. Oil or water on the floor could cause a serious fall or injury. Wipe up or place quick dry (oil absorbent) on spilled oil or antifreeze. Use a squeegee and rags to remove spilled water. When your hands become oily or greasy, wash them off or wipe them dry with a clean rag.

Never leave tools, creepers, or parts on the floor. Place them on, against, or under the workbenches. You can judge a technician by the condition of his or her tools and work area. If a technician looks sloppy, he or she probably does sloppy work.

15. Is the shop area clean and organized? _____

List any unsafe conditions found. _____

_____

_____ Completed ☐

Carbon Monoxide

When an engine is running, it produces carbon monoxide, a colorless, odorless, toxic gas. Always install an exhaust hose over the tailpipe of a vehicle running in an enclosed shop, **Figure 1.**

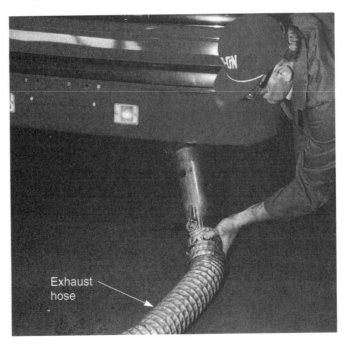

Exhaust hose

Figure 1. Place an exhaust hose over tailpipe of any vehicle running in enclosed shop. This will prevent shop from filling with poisonous fumes.

16. Where are the exhaust hoses in your shop? _____

_____ Completed ☐

17. Where do you turn on the fan for the exhaust hoses?_____

_____

_____ Completed ☐

Tool Safety

Tool safety involves keeping your tools clean and well maintained. Greasy or oily tools are very dangerous. Your hand could slip, causing serious injury. Always wipe off your tools with a clean shop rag after use and organize them neatly in your toolbox. Tool safety also involves selecting the right tool for the job. If you are using the wrong tool, an accident is more likely to occur.

18. Where are your tools stored?_____

_____

_____ Completed ☐

Floor Jack and Jack Stand Safety

⚠️ **Warning**
Never work under a vehicle only supported by a floor jack. If someone were to hit the jack handle or a jack seal were to fail, the vehicle would fall and crush you. Use jack stands to secure the vehicle before working under it. See **Figure 2.**

Figure 2. Never work under a vehicle supported only by a floor jack. A—A jack is only used for initial lifting. B—Jack stands must be used to secure the vehicle before working. Place them under recommended lift points. (Subaru)

19. *Without* lifting a vehicle, practice operating a floor jack. Close the valve on the jack handle. Pump the handle up and down slowly. It is important that you know how to control the lowering action of the jack. This will help you lower a vehicle safely off the jack stands. Completed ☐

20. After getting your instructor's approval, place the jack under a proper lift point on the frame, rear axle housing, suspension arm, or reinforced unibody section. Completed ☐

📋 **Note**
If in doubt about where to position the jack, refer to a service manual for the vehicle at hand. Lifting instructions are usually given in one of the front sections of the manual.

21. Make sure the vehicle is on a level shop floor and will not roll. Place the transmission in neutral and release the emergency brake. This will let the vehicle roll slightly as the jack goes up. If the vehicle cannot roll and the small wheels on the jack catch in the shop floor, the vehicle could slide off the jack saddle. Completed ☐

22. Pump the jack handle slowly to raise the vehicle. Completed ☐

Name _____

23. When the vehicle is high enough, place jack stands under the suggested lift points. Lower the vehicle slowly onto the stands. Check that they are safe. Then, block the wheels, place the transmission in park, and apply the emergency brake. Finally remove the floor jack. It should now be safe to work under the vehicle.   Completed ☐

24. Raise the vehicle and remove the jack stands. Lower the vehicle to the floor and return the equipment to its storage areas.   Completed ☐

25. Where did you position the floor jack saddle when raising this particular vehicle?

_____

_____   Completed ☐

Lift Safety

Most shops have a lift for raising vehicles during repairs. If used improperly, a lift can be very dangerous. The vehicle could fall off the lift.

26. *After* obtaining permission from your instructor, raise your shop lift (no vehicle on it). Practice raising it slowly and steadily.   Completed ☐

27. Where is the control for raising and lowering the lift? _____

_____

_____   Completed ☐

28. Position a vehicle on the lift so that its center of gravity is over the center of the lift. Position the lift arms on service manual recommended lift points under the vehicle. Raise the vehicle until the tires are about an inch off the shop floor.   Completed ☐

29. Go to the front and jounce the vehicle a few times. There should be no substantial movement or noise from the vehicle leaving the lift pads. If the vehicle does not seem secure, lower it back down and recheck the lift arm placement.   Completed ☐

30. If the lift arms are positioned properly, continue to raise the vehicle slowly. When the vehicle is in the air, double-check that the safety leg or catch has kicked out, **Figure 3.** This will ensure the lift does not drop with a loss of air pressure or other failure.   Completed ☐

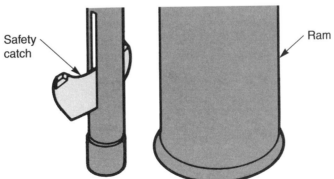

Figure 3. Most lifts have a safety catch. It must be engaged before working under vehicle.

Air Bag Safety

An air bag can be dangerous if mishandled. By following some simple rules, air bags can be safely serviced. When servicing a vehicle that has an undeployed air bag, follow the manufacturer's instructions for disarming the system. You should disarm the system when installing a new air bag.

31. List the precautions that should be taken when working with air bags.

_____

_____

_____

_____ Completed ☐

32. Summarize the procedure for disarming an air bag on a particular late-model vehicle.

_____

_____

_____

_____

_____ Completed ☐

33. Clean your work area and return all tools to their proper storage locations.   Completed ☐

34. Ask your instructor to sign this job.

Instructor's Signature _____

Shop Measurement

Name: _____

Date: _____

Instructor: _____

Score: _____

Objective: Using your textbook, conversion charts, proper gauges, and instruments, you will learn to perform both U.S. Conventional and SI Metric measurements.

Tools and Equipment: You will need a ruler, pencil, micrometer, feeler gauge, dial indicator, instructor prepared parts, and your textbook.

Instructions: Study Chapter 6 in the text before starting this job. Refer to the examples as required. If you need help getting started, ask your instructor for assistance. Good measurement skills are very important to your success as an automotive technician.

Using a Ruler

1. Use a ruler to measure the following lengths. Measure from point zero to the small marks on the lines.
   Give answers in both inches and millimeters. Write your answers in the chart below.   Completed ☐

0   A   B   C   D   E   F   G   H   I   J   K   L   M   N   O   P   Q R

──────▶ Measure along this line.

0   S   T   U   V   W   X   Y   Z AA   AB AC AD AE   AF AG AH AI

──────▶ Measure along this line.

	A	B	C	B	E	F	G	H	I	J	K	L	M	N	O	P	Q	R
INCH	1/4"																	
MILLIMETER	6 mm																	

	S	T	U	V	W	X	Y	Z	AA	AB	AC	AD	AE	AF	AG	AH	AI
INCH																	
MILLIMETER																	

Using Conversion Charts

2. Using the information found in textbook Figure 6-3, calculate the equivalents for the following.   Completed ☐

   (A) 2″ = _____ mm

   (B) 10 mm = _____ inches

   (C) 3′ = _____ meter

   (D) 12 miles = _____ kilometers

   (E) 10 kilometers = _____ miles

   (F) 6 psi = _____ kPa

   (G) 10 kPa = _____ psi

   (H) 50 hp = _____ kW

   (I) 3 quarts = _____ liters

   (J) 179 cubic inches = _____ liters

   (K) 45 pounds = _____ kg

   (L) 55 mph = _____ km/h

3. Using textbook Figure 6-1, fill in the proper U.S. Customary and SI Metric abbreviations.   Completed ☐

Quantity	U.S. Customary (abbreviation)	Metric (abbreviation)
(A) Road speed		
(B) Length		
(C) Temperature		
(D) Torque		
(E) Pressure		
(F) Weight		
(G) Power		

4. Use the chart in Figure 6-4 of the text to determine the equivalents for the following.   Completed ☐

(A) 1/16″ = _____ mm   (F) 9/16″ = _____ decimal inch

(B) 1/32″ = _____ decimal inch   (G) 45/64″ = _____ mm

(C) 7/8″ = _____ decimal inch   (H) 22.6 mm = _____ decimal inch

(D) .43750″ = _____ ″ (fraction)   (I) 5.1 mm = _____ ″ (fraction)

(E) 25/32″ = _____ mm   (J) 1.1 mm = _____ decimal inch

Using a Micrometer and Caliper

5. What are the four steps for reading a micrometer?_____

_____

_____

_____   Completed ☐

6. Inspect the feeler gauge set. Ten of the blades should have the blade sizes removed (ground off, taped over, etc.). These blades should be renumbered (engraved, labeled using tape, or notched) from one to ten.   Completed ☐

7. Before measuring the unsized blades, practice measuring a few of the sized blades. Then, you can get feedback about measuring accuracy by comparing your micrometer readings to the actual size written on the blades.   Completed ☐

8. Using the micrometer, measure the thickness of the ten unsized feeler gauge blades and record your measurements in the following chart. If needed, ask your instructor for help getting started.   Completed ☐

Feeler gauge blade number	1	2	3	4	5	6	7	8	9	10
Your "Mike" measurement										

9. Locate the six engine valves. Check that they are numbered from one to six.   Completed ☐

10. Measure the valve stems using both the micrometer and sliding caliper. Try to measure the largest (least worn) and the smallest (most worn) part of each stem. Only measure on the operational, machined, or shiny portion of the stem.   Completed ☐

11. Record your results in the chart below.   Completed ☐

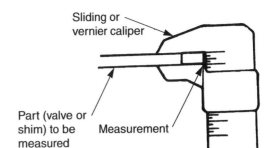

Sliding or
vernier caliper

Part (valve or
shim) to be
measured   Measurement

Valve Number	1	2	3	4	5	6	Reading
Caliper reading							Largest
							Smallest
"Mike" reading							Largest
							Smallest

12. Repeat this procedure of measurement on the six valve spring shims and write your answers in the chart below.   Completed ☐

Shim Number	1	2	3	4	5	6	Reading
Caliper reading							Largest
							Smallest
"Mike" reading							Largest
							Smallest

Using a Dial Indicator

13. Check out a dial indicator setup. It should have a clamp, base, or magnet for mounting the indicator on various assemblies.   Completed ☐

14. Ask your instructor which differential will be used in this section of the job. Preferably, you will have a bench mounted unit.   Completed ☐

15. Go to the differential assembly. Mount the dial indicator as shown in **Figure 1.** The indicator stem should contact the smooth, backside of the ring gear. The base of the indicator should be clamped to or placed on the outer edge of the carrier.   Completed ☐

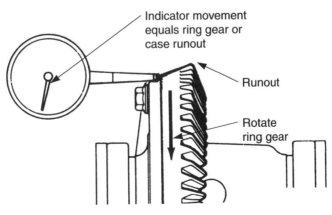

Indicator movement
equals ring gear or
case runout

Runout

Rotate
ring gear

Figure 1. Mount dial indicator as shown. This will measure any wobble or runout at ring gear.

16. Adjust indicator dial to read zero. The face of the indicator should turn and adjust to zero.   Completed ☐

17. Slowly rotate the ring gear while watching the movement of the indicator needle. The amount of needle movement indicates the runout (wobble) of the ring gear in thousandths of an inch.   Completed ☐

18. How much runout is present on the ring gear?

_____ Completed ☐

19. Without changing the indicator mounting, use screwdrivers or small pry bars to move the ring gear sideways. Pry one way and then the other while watching the indicator needle. This will measure gear end play.   Completed ☐

20. How much side or end play is there in the case bearings?

_____ Completed ☐

21. To measure the gear backlash, mount the indicator as shown in **Figure 2.** The indicator stem should contact one of the ring gear teeth. Hold the pinion gear solid to prevent any movement while moving (wiggling) the ring gear back and forth gently. Do not turn the ring gear, however. The amount of dial indicator needle movement indicates gear backlash.

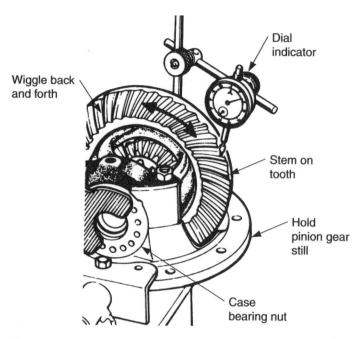

Figure 2. Play or gear backlash can be measured as shown. Hold the pinion while wiggling the ring gear.

22. What is the amount of backlash between the differential gears?

_____ Completed ☐

Temperature Measurement

Special thermometers or temperature gauges are frequently used to measure the temperature of numerous components such as the air conditioning output temperature and radiator temperature. A temperature gauge can read in either conventional Fahrenheit (°F) or metric Celsius (°C). The temperature obtained with the gauge can be compared to specs. Then, if the temperature is too low or too high, you would know that a repair or adjustment is needed.

23. Use a thermometer or digital pyrometer to measure and record the following temperatures: Completed ☐

    Shop room temperature: _____

    Engine operating temperature (fully warmed): _____

    Air conditioning vent temperature (on cool high): _____

24. Clean your work area and return all tools to their proper storage location.   Completed ☐

25. Have your instructor initial this job for credit.

Instructor's Signature: _____

Using Digital Multimeters

Name: _____

Date: _____

Instructor: _____

Score: _____

Objective: After completing this job, you will be able to properly use a digital multimeter to complete electrical tests.

Tools and Equipment: You will need a digital multimeter, access to a vehicle or battery and battery charger, piece of wire and vacuum hose, ballast resistor or thermistor, eight spark plug wires, jumper wires, light socket and bulb, an on/off switch, three alternator diodes, three ignition system pickup coils, and your textbook.

Instructions: Study textbook Chapters 8 and 19 before doing this job. It will give you information essential to the full understanding of this learning exercise. Ask your instructor for the location of the equipment to be used for added details. Only connect the circuits and tests described. This job may require more than one class period.

Digital Multimeters

1. Check out the multimeter and study its controls. It will have settings for different measurements and scales. It is important that you have the meter set properly *before* connecting it to a source of voltage or current. Completed ❑

2. You will be using the ohmmeter part of your multimeter first. Set the meter controls to measure resistance. Completed ❑

3. Measure the resistance of the following components.

   Piece of wire = _____ ohms

   Piece of rubber hose = _____ ohms Completed ❑

4. Using what you learned in the text about conductors and insulators, explain your ohmmeter readings for Step 3.

   _____

   _____

   _____

   _____

   _____

   _____

   _____

   _____ Completed ❑

Resistance Measurement

5. A ballast resistor or thermistor can be used to control the amount of current flowing into a circuit, depending upon temperature. Both a thermistor and ballast resistor's internal resistance is altered by temperature. Measure and record the resistance of your ballast resistor or thermistor at room temperature.

   Ballast resistor or thermistor = _____ ohms Completed ❑

6. Touch your ohmmeter leads on each resistor or thermistor terminal. If you were to heat either device, its ohm value would change. When testing the ballast resistor or thermistor, you would compare your ohm value to specifications. Completed ❑

7. For this job, assume that specifications call for your ballast resistor or thermistor to have between 10–12 ohms at room temperature. Would the resistor or thermistor you tested be good or bad? _____

   Explain: _____

   _____

   _____

   _____

   _____

   _____

   _____ Completed ☐

Testing Spark Plug Wires

A good spark plug wire should *not* have excessive resistance (depending on manufacturer, below 25,000–100,000 ohms). When the carbon filled center of a plug wire fails, the resistance of the spark plug wire will increase tremendously.

A defective plug wire will often have an almost infinite amount of resistance and current will not flow through the wire. The engine cylinder with the bad plug wire would develop a "dead miss" and the engine would idle roughly.

8. Locate the numbered spark plug wires. Measure the resistance of the wires to determine if they are defective. Record your results in the following chart.   Completed ☐

Spark plug wire	1	2	3	4	5	6	7	8
Resistance								

9. How many spark plug wires were good?   Completed ☐

10. How many spark plug wires were defective?   Completed ☐

Diode Testing

A diode is an electrical check valve. It will allow current to flow in one direction only. The condition of a diode can be tested with an ohmmeter.

A good diode will show high resistance with the meter leads connected in one direction and low resistance with the meter leads reversed. A bad diode may be either open or shortened. An open diode will exhibit an extremely high resistance when tested in both directions. A shorted diode will have low resistance in both directions.

11. Measure the resistance of three diodes. Connect the ohmmeter leads in both directions and record your readings in the chart below. Unless instructed otherwise, set your ohmmeter range switch to resistance. Some meters have test settings specifically designed for testing diodes.   Completed ☐

Diode	1	2	3
Forward reading			
Reverse reading			

12. Explain the condition of the diodes. _____

    _____

    _____

    _____ Completed ☐

Pickup Coil Testing

A pickup coil is one of the more problem prone components in an electronic ignition or computer system. Due to heat, cold, vibration, and movement, coil windings and output wires can break. When this happens, the ignition or computer system can malfunction.

13. Connect an ohmmeter to the pickup coil as shown in **Figure 1.** Depending upon the manufacturer, the resistance specification for your pickup coils may vary from 150–1500 ohms. Wiggle the pickup coil wires and tap the coil with a screwdriver. If the ohmmeter reading does not remain steady and within specifications, replace the pickup coil.

Completed ☐

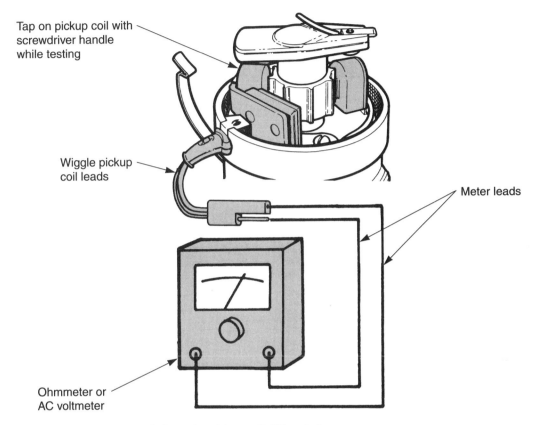

Tap on pickup coil with screwdriver handle while testing

Wiggle pickup coil leads

Meter leads

Ohmmeter or AC voltmeter

Figure 1. Connect an ohmmeter to leads from the pickup coil. (Chrysler)

14. Measure and record the resistance of three pickup coils. It is a good idea to *wiggle* the pickup coil's output wires while testing. An internal wire break may only show up when the wires are moved.

Completed ☐

Pickup coil	1	2	3
Ohmmeter reading			

15. Explain the condition of the pickup coils._____

_____

_____

_____   Completed ☐

16. Have your instructor sign this sheet for credit on this section of the job.   Completed ☐

Instructor's Signature _____

Measuring Voltage

17. Set your meter to measure dc volts. If the meter is capable of measuring volts on a scale, make sure the meter is set to read at least 15 volts dc. A voltmeter, as with any meter, must always be set to measure slightly above the expected maximum value. This will prevent the meter from being damaged.   Completed ☐

18. With the engine off, connect your test leads across the battery posts. *Do not* reverse your leads or meter damage could occur. The red meter lead should go to positive, black to negative.   Completed ☐

19. What is the voltage of your battery?

    _____   Completed ☐

20. Connect a battery charger (trickle charger) to the battery. Measure the voltage across the battery posts with the charger on. For a battery to be charged, it must have an input voltage higher than its standing potential of 12.6 volts. By forcing voltage into the battery, the battery can be returned to a full state of charge.   Completed ☐

21. What was your charging voltage reading?

    _____   Completed ☐

22. How much higher was the charging voltage reading than the standing battery voltage (step 19)?

    _____   Completed ☐

 Tech Tip
Whenever you think of voltage, relate it to water pressure. Voltage is the force that pushes electrons (electricity) through a circuit. It is much like the pressure that pushes water through a garden hose. As water pressure is increased, the amount of flow (current) and the distance that the water will spray is increased.

23. Connect the light circuit as shown in **Figure 2.** Take your time and try to keep everything organized. Avoid winding all the wires into a confusing bundle. Make sure that none of your "hot wires" are touching ground and shorting out.   Completed ☐

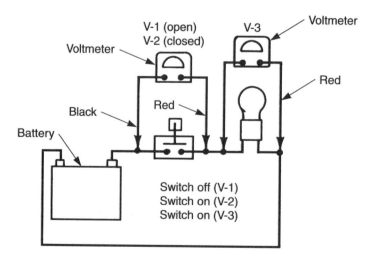

Figure 2. Study required voltage measurements.

24. Before trying out your circuit or connecting your meter, ask your instructor to check your work. Also, ask whether the remainder of the job is to be performed with or without the battery charger in operation.   Completed ☐

25. After obtaining instructor approval, turn on the switch. The lightbulb should light every time the circuit path is connected with the switch. If not, recheck your connections and bulb.   Completed ☐

26. Connect your voltmeter as shown in V-1 of **Figure 2.** Leave the switch open.   Completed ☐

27. Record your meter readings in the chart. Then with the switch closed (on), repeat this process on the other two voltage drop measurements (V-2 and V-3).   Completed

Voltmeter Connection	V-1 Switch Off	V-2 Switch On	V-3 Switch On
Reading			

A voltage drop is an indicator of circuit resistance. For example, the voltage drop across an open switch represents full battery voltage. The voltage drop across the closed switch will be zero.

A voltage drop is proportional to the internal resistance of the tested circuit or component (open switch = infinite resistance = maximum voltage drop and a closed switch = zero resistance = zero voltage drop.) In many instances, a voltmeter (voltage drop) is much easier, faster, and more desirable than an ohmmeter. You do not need to disconnect the circuit and voltage source to check for high resistance.

Current Measurement

28. Change your meter controls (range and function) to measure maximum dc current (mA or A). On some meters, you may need to change the location of the meter test leads in their jacks (plug-in sockets). If your meter does not measure 10 A or more, check with your instructor to prevent meter damage.   Completed

29. Unlike the ohmmeter and voltmeter, which must be connected in parallel, a conventional ammeter *must* be connected in series with the circuit. Connect your ammeter in series with the circuit, as shown in **Figure 3.** You must break (disconnect) the circuit at the positive of the battery and insert your meter between the two connections.   Completed

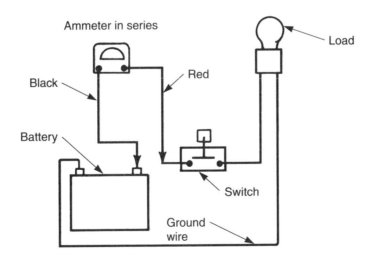

Figure 3. Check that your ammeter is in series and that negative and positive connections are not reversed.

 Caution
Never connect an ammeter in parallel with a circuit as it could damage the meter. Also, a short circuit may be produced, causing an electrical fire.

30. Before turning on the power, double-check your meter connections and settings. If they check OK, turn on the switch and measure the current in your circuit.   Completed

31. Record the meter readings for the open and closed switch positions.   Completed ☐

Switch Settings	Switch Open	Switch Closed
Meter amps reading		

From these extremes (infinite resistance with switch open and normal resistance with only resistance of the lightbulb in the circuit), you can easily see the relationship between current and resistance. A high resistance will lower current. A lowered resistance will increase current.

You will use this principle when using an ammeter. You will measure the actual current flowing in a circuit and compare it to specifications. If the tested circuit current is high, then the circuit resistance is low (short faulty resistor, electric motor, etc.) and vice versa. As a technician, you can then diagnose which component or connection is defective.

32. Clean your work area and return all tools to their proper storage location.   Completed ☐

33. Ask your instructor to sign this job.

Instructor's Signature _____

Vehicle Safety Inspection

Name: _____

Date: _____

Instructor: _____

Score: _____

Objective: Using this job, and an assigned vehicle, you will learn to perform a basic vehicle safety inspection.

Tools and Equipment: Ask your instructor for details of the job. You may have to inspect your own vehicle, your parent's vehicle, a shop-owned vehicle, or a customer's vehicle.

Instructions: After inspecting the condition of each checkpoint, place an X in the appropriate column. Identify whether the vehicle passes or fails each checkpoint. In the space for comments, tell why the vehicle passed or failed the checkpoint. Make sure you explain the results for all inspection points.

Note
Before inspecting a vehicle, obtain approval from your instructor. Ask your parents for written permission before inspecting their vehicle.

Vehicle Safety Inspection

1. List the following information for the vehicle to be inspected.   Completed ☐

   Make: _____

   Model: _____

   Year: _____

   VIN: _____

   Color: _____

   Owner: _____

   License Number: _____

2. Where is the vehicle located? _____

   _____   Completed ☐

3. How old is the vehicle? _____   Completed ☐

4. If applicable, ask the owner for his or her signature before completing the inspection. If you are inspecting a shop-owned vehicle, ask for your instructor's initials before beginning this job. Remember to explain each passed or failed condition.   Completed ☐

Inspection Item	Passed	Failed	Reason for Failure
5. **Horn** Horn should be audible at a distance of 200′ (61 m) and work from steering wheel.			
6. **Glass** All windows should not be broken, cracked, or obstructed in any way.			
7. **Mirrors** Mirrors should not be broken or cracked. They should be clear and stay in position when angled properly.			
8. **Windshield wipers** Check that blades are not hardened or cracked. Make sure the wipers operate properly.			
9. **Headlights** Check that the high and the low beams operate and are aimed properly. Lenses should not be broken.			
10. **Parking lights** Make sure all lights operate and lenses are not broken. Make sure that side and license plate lights work.			
11. **Turn signal** All turn signals should blink at a reasonable rate of speed. All lights must flash and be clearly visible.			
12. **Stop lights** All brake lights must be visible at a distance of 500′ (152 m).			
13. **Seat belts** They should be properly anchored and in working condition.			
14. **Engine** Engine should start quickly and idle normally. There should be no unusual noises or leaks.			

Inspection Item	Passed	Failed	Reason for Failure
15. **Transmission or transaxle** Check that it shifts into each gear. Make sure the reverse indicator lights come on when in reverse.			
16. **Steering** There should not be excessive play in the steering wheel (1/4″ or 64 mm maximum). The engine should be running when checking a power steering system.			
17. **Brakes** The brake pedal should be solid and at correct applied height. The emergency brake must keep vehicle from rolling.			
18. **Struts and shock absorbers** Bounce each corner of the vehicle. It should stop in one or two motions if struts or shocks are good.			
19. **Suspension system** There should be no noise heard during the last test. Check for worn bushings or structural damage; there should be none.			
20. **Tires** There must be a minimum of 1/16″ (16 mm) of tread depth on all four tires. Wear pattern on tread should be even.			
21. **Drive axles** Check all drive shafts. There should be no excessive play. Boots should be clean with no grease leaks.			
22. **Exhaust system** The exhaust system must not leak. The tail pipe must not terminate beneath the vehicle. The catalytic converter(s) must be present.			

23. Clean your work area and return all tools to their proper storage location.   Completed ☐

24. Ask your instructor to sign this job.

Instructor's Signature _____

Notes

Checking Fluids

Name: _____

Date: _____

Instructor: _____

Score: _____

Objective: Using the tools and equipment listed here, you will learn to check the various fluids of a vehicle.

Tools and Equipment: Check out a pair of safety glasses, protective gloves, standard screwdriver, set of hand wrenches, 3/8″ drive ratchet set, ruler, shop rag, antifreeze tester, and an automobile.

Instructions: Ask your instructor for any added details for the job. You may have to work on a shop-owned vehicle or a vehicle assigned to you by your instructor. Follow all safety rules. Study textbook Chapter 10 before doing this job.

Checking Engine Oil

1. When checking the engine oil, the engine must be off. Find the oil dipstick; it should be on the side or front of the engine. Remove the dipstick and wipe it off. Then, reinstall the dipstick until fully seated. Completed ❑

2. Pull the dipstick back out. Hold it over your shop rag. Inspect the level of the oil on the stick. The oil should be between the full and add marks, **Figure 1.** Memorize the smell of engine oil. This will help you when diagnosing leaks. Completed ❑

Figure 1. Check oil with engine off. Oil should be between full and add marks on stick. Only add enough to bring to full mark.

3. When the oil is even with the add mark on the dipstick, add one quart of oil. If the oil is midway between the add and full marks, approximately one-half quart is needed. Never add too much oil or foaming and other problems may result. Completed ❑

4. Is the oil level in the engine OK? _____

    If not, how much oil is needed? _____ Completed ❑

5. If oil is needed, remove the oil filler cap. The oil fill is usually on or near the valve cover. Pour in the correct type and amount of motor oil. Reinstall the filler cap. Completed ❑

6. Where is the oil fill on this engine? _____

    _____ Completed ❑

Checking the Battery

7. Inspect the battery for problems. The top of the battery should be clean and dry. Moisture on the battery case top can cause battery leakage. Also check the condition of the battery terminals. They should be clean, and tight. Corroded terminals may keep the engine from cranking properly. Explain the condition of the battery case and terminals.

    _____

    _____

    _____ Completed ❑

To check the battery's state of charge, you can use a voltmeter. A fully charged battery will have 12.4–12.6 volts between its battery terminals. A lower voltage means the battery has been discharged or may have bad plates.

8. Use a voltmeter to check the state of charge of your battery. What is the state of charge? _____

_____   Completed ☐

9. Check the battery tray for corrosion and damage.   Completed ☐

Checking Engine Coolant

Modern cooling systems are closed. A closed system will have a plastic reservoir tank on one side of the radiator. The radiator cap may also be labeled: ***Do Not Open.*** Remember that many newer vehicles use the reservoir tank as part of the pressurized cooling system.

10. To check the coolant level, inspect the amount of coolant in the plastic reservoir tank. Compare the level with the marks on the side of the tank.   Completed ☐

11. To check the coolant level in an open system, make sure the radiator is cool. If warm, do *not* remove the cap. Hot coolant could blow into your face, causing serious injury. The coolant in an open system should be about one inch down in the radiator.   Completed ☐

12. Was the level of coolant in your cooling system OK? _____

_____   Completed ☐

13. If the system needs coolant, add the correct mixture of antifreeze and water. Modern cooling systems have a reservoir tank. Compare the coolant level to the marks on the side of the reservoir.   Completed ☐

14. Check out an antifreeze tester. Draw coolant into the tester. Use the directions with the particular tester to determine the freeze-up protection of the coolant.   Completed ☐

15. How much freeze-up (low temperature) protection does your coolant provide for the system?

_____   Completed ☐

16. Inspect the coolant for rust or discoloration. After prolonged use, antifreeze can break down and become very corrosive. It can cause rapid rust formation and damage to the cooling system. For this reason, antifreeze must be drained and replaced at recommended intervals. Is your coolant rusty?

_____   Completed ☐

17. Install a pressure tester on the filler neck and pressurize the system to check for leaks. Pump the tester until the gauge reads about 12 psi (83 kPa). Do not exceed cap pressure.   Completed ☐

Tech Tip
To increase your troubleshooting skills, try to memorize the smell of antifreeze. Then, when a leak is found, the smell will tell you whether it is antifreeze or another liquid.

18. Did you find leaks? _____ If so, explain. _____

_____

_____   Completed ☐

Power Steering Fluid

If your vehicle has manual steering, skip steps 19–22.

19. With the engine off, inspect the power steering fluid reservoir. The fluid should be between the full and add marks. If the reservoir is on the pump itself, remove the power steering fluid cap and wipe off the dipstick. Reinsert dipstick and pull it back out. Holding the dipstick over your shop rag, inspect the fluid level.   Completed ☐

20. If needed, add enough recommended power steering fluid to reach the full mark. Do *not* add too much, or fluid will blow out the pump after engine starting.   Completed ☐

21. If the power steering fluid is excessively low, check the power steering system for leaks. Look near the pump, line fittings, and other components containing fluid.   Completed ☐

22. Did your power steering fluid level check OK? _____ Explain: _____

_____

_____   Completed ☐

Automatic Transmission/Transaxle Fluid Service

If your vehicle has a manual transmission or transaxle, skip steps 23–26 or locate a vehicle with an automatic transmission or transaxle.

23. To check the automatic transmission or transaxle fluid, start and warm the engine. Move the transmission selector through the gears. Apply the parking brake, shift the transmission into park, and block the wheels. You may have to leave some vehicles in neutral to check the fluid. Leave the engine running.   Completed ☐

24. Remove and wipe off the transmission/transaxle dipstick. It will usually be at the rear of the engine on one side. Reinsert the dipstick and pull it back out. Hold it over your rag while you check the fluid level on the stick. Note the smell of the fluid. If the fluid smells burned, the bands or clutches may be worn and damaged.   Completed ☐

25. Describe the condition and level of fluid in your automatic transmission or transaxle.

_____

_____   Completed ☐

26. If necessary, add transmission fluid. When adding fluid to an automatic transmission, make sure you use the correct type of fluid. Different transmissions sometimes require different fluids. *Do not* overfill the transmission or transaxle. Overfilling can cause fluid foaming, poor operation, and seal leakage.   Completed ☐

Manual Transmission/Transaxle Lubricant Service

If your vehicle has an automatic transmission or transaxle, skip steps 27–29 or locate a vehicle with a manual transmission or transaxle.

27. Check the lubricant in a manual transmission or transaxle. Remove the filler plug on the side of the transmission. The lubricant should be slightly below or almost even with the filler hole, **Figure 2.** Some units may have a dipstick.   Completed ☐

28. If needed, add the recommended type of gear oil, or fluid, for the particular transmission/transaxle. Also, learn to identify the smell of gear oil. Note that some transaxles do not have a provision for checking fluid level. Refer to the service manual if in doubt.   Completed ☐

Figure 2. Manual transmissions will have a fill plug for checking fluid level. Fluid should be almost even with hole when the fluid is warm. Check the service manual for details.

29. Was the lubricant level in the manual transmission or transaxle OK? _____

Explain: _____   Completed ☐

Checking Differential Lubricant

Ask your instructor for approval before checking the differential lubricant. If your vehicle has a transaxle, skip steps 30 through 32.

30. Raise the vehicle on a lift or secure it on jack stands. Remove the differential filler plug, *not* the drain plug, **Figure 3.** The filler plug will be on the front or rear of the housing, about halfway up on the differential. The differential fluid should be approximately 1/2″ (12.7 mm) below the fill hole. This can vary with some vehicles so always refer to exact specification. Stick your finger in the filler hole to check the lubricant level.   Completed ☐

31. If needed, add just enough of the recommended differential lubricant to meet factory recommendations. Memorize the smell of differential fluid so you can quickly diagnose leaks.   Completed ☐

Figure 3. The differential fill hole allows checking of lubricant level. Do not accidentally remove the drain plug.

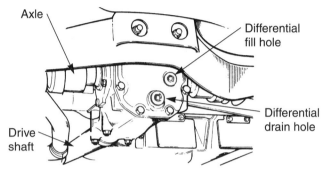

32. Was the lubricant in your differential low? _____ If so, what type of gear oil was added?

_____   Completed ☐

Checking Brake Fluid

33. Locate the brake master cylinder. It is normally bolted to the firewall on the driver's side of the vehicle. Clean and remove the master cylinder cover. If spring clips are used to secure the cover, pry them off with a screwdriver. A wrench is needed if the cover is bolted in place.   Completed ☐

34. Inspect the level and condition of the brake fluid. If the master cylinder reservoir is clear plastic, simply compare the fluid level to the marks on the side of the reservoir. On older master cylinder reservoirs and those without markings, the brake fluid should *not* be more than 1/4″ (6.4 mm) below the top of the reservoir. Keep oil, water, dirt, and grease out of the brake fluid. Oil, water, dirt, and grease can ruin the cups and seals in a brake system. To improve your troubleshooting ability, memorize the smell of brake fluid. Then, if fluid leakage is found, you can quickly identify the type of leak.   Completed ☐

35. Is the master cylinder full or low? _____   Completed ☐

36. Inspect your brake system for leaks. Look behind the wheel backing plates, at the brake line fittings, and anywhere else a leak might occur. Did you find any brake system leaks? _____

Explain: _____   Completed ☐

 Caution
If you spill brake fluid, wipe it up immediately. Brake fluid can ruin the paint on a vehicle. It dissolves paint in a matter of minutes.

Checking Windshield Washer Fluid

37. Check the windshield washer fluid. It will be in a plastic reservoir on one side of the engine compartment. The fluid should be almost even with the full mark on the side of the container.   Completed ☐

38. Clean your work area and return all tools to their proper storage location.   Completed ☐

39. Ask your instructor to sign this job for credit.

Instructor's Signature _____

Engine Oil and Filter Service, Chassis Lubrication

Name: _____

Date: _____

Instructor: _____

Score: _____

Objective: Given a vehicle and the listed tools, you will learn to change an engine's oil and filter and perform a chassis "lube job."

Tools and Equipment: Check out an oil filter wrench, box end wrench, funnel, grease gun, oil squirt can, spray lithium grease, oil drain, some door latch lubricant, a few shop rags, and eye protection. If you are servicing a customer's vehicle, you should obtain the manufacturer's designated type and amount of oil and an oil filter.

Instructions: Ask your instructor for details of the job. Your instructor may want you to perform this job for a customer vehicle or use a shop-owned auto or stand-mounted engine.

Draining Engine Oil

During an oil change, the engine should be warmed to operating temperature. Then, any dirt or contaminants will be picked up, suspended, and drained out of the engine.

1. Raise the vehicle on a lift or with a jack and then secure it on jack stands. The vehicle should be level to allow all the oil to drain from the pan. To prevent accidentally starting the engine without oil, remove the key from the ignition.   Completed ☐

2. Place an oil drain under the engine oil pan. Make sure you are *not* looking at the transmission pan. Put the drain slightly to one side of the oil pan.   Completed ☐

3. With the correct size box end wrench, turn the oil drain plug counterclockwise and remove it. Allow oil to pour into the catch pan. Keep your arm out of the way of the hot oil as it flows from the engine.   Completed ☐

4. While the oil is draining, inspect the drain plug. The plastic washer or seal should not be cracked or split or it will leak. Check the bolt threads for damage and wear. During an actual oil change, you would have to replace a damaged washer seal or drain plug.   Completed ☐

5. What is the condition of your drain plug threads? _____

   _____

   _____   Completed ☐

6. Is the drain plug seal smashed or split?

   _____ Explain:_____

   _____

   _____   Completed ☐

7. Being extremely careful not to overtighten and strip the threads, install and snug the oil drain plug. The drain plug only needs to be tight enough to slightly compress the plug seal. Overtightening will cause thread damage and leakage.   Completed ☐

8. Move the oil drain under the engine oil filter. Using your filter wrench, loosen the oil filter (counterclockwise). Being careful not to let hot oil run down your arm, spin the filter the rest of the way off.   Completed ☐

Replacing the Engine Oil Filter

9. Wipe off the mounting base for the oil filter to remove any dirt and contaminated oil. Also, check that the oil filter seal is not stuck on the engine. Completed ❑

10. Make certain the new filter is the proper replacement. Always check that the rubber O-ring seals are identical. The diameters of each should measure the same. Completed ❑

11. What is the measured diameter of your oil filter seal? _____
_____ Completed ❑

12. What is the measured diameter of the threaded hole in the filter? _____
_____ Completed ❑

Caution
If the filter fits on the engine upright, fill the new filter with oil. This prevents a temporary lack of oil pressure while the empty filter is filling. If the filter mounts sideways or upside down, do *not* fill it with oil.

13. At what angle is your oil filter mounted on the engine?_____
_____ Completed ❑

14. Where is the oil filter located on your engine?_____
_____ Completed ❑

15. Wipe some clean engine oil on to the new oil filter rubber seal. This will ensure proper filter tightening and help prevent leaks. Completed ❑

16. Without crossthreading, screw on and hand tighten the new oil filter (reuse the old filter if this is just an exercise). Your hands and the filter should be clean and dry. After the seal makes contact with the engine base, use a rag or towel to help turn the filter an additional 1/2–3/4 turn. Completed ❑

Caution
Do *not* tighten the filter with an oil filter wrench or the rubber seal may be smashed, causing a serious oil leak.

17. Using a funnel to minimize spillage, fill the engine with the proper weight and amount of oil. Your instructor may want you to install the same oil if this is simply a learning exercise. Completed ❑

18. Referring to a service manual, how much oil does your engine hold?_____
_____ Completed ❑

19. What weight oil is recommended? _____
_____ Completed ❑

20. Replace the filler cap and wipe off any oil that might have dripped on the engine, workbench, or floor. Completed ❑

21. Start the engine and watch the oil pressure indicator light or gauge. The oil warning light should go out within 5–10 seconds. A gauge should begin to register almost immediately. If not, *shut off the engine* and find the problem. Completed ❑

22. How long did it take for the engine to develop oil pressure? _____
_____ Completed ❑

23. Shut off the engine. Wipe off the hood and fenders. Completed ❑

24. Wipe up any spilled oil and empty your oil drain. Allow the oil filter to drain or dispose of it properly after crushing the filter in a self-contained filter crusher. Completed ❑

25. If this is an actual oil change, fill out a service sticker including the date, mileage, type, weight, and brand of oil. Depending on the type of sticker, place it in the upper left-hand corner of the windshield or on the edge of the driver's door above the latch. Completed ❑

Chassis Lubrication

26. Using either a front end training unit or a vehicle, prepare to perform chassis lubrication, often called a "grease job." Locate components that need lubrication. These include ball joints, tie-rod ends, idler arms, and universal joints. If the vehicle has never been lubricated, one or more small hex head screws may have to be removed so that fittings can be installed.   Completed ❑

⚠ Caution
Do not overfill or the boots can rupture. As soon as you see them swell a little, stop.

27. How many grease fittings did you find? _____   Completed ❑

28. Where were they located? _____

_____

_____

_____   Completed ❑

29. Using a grease gun, slowly force grease into all chassis fittings.   Completed ❑

30. Wipe up any spilled oil or grease.   Completed ❑

Lubricate Body Hinges and Locks

31. Place a small amount of grease between the parts that rub on the hood hinges and hood latch. Spray a small amount of lithium grease or oil on the door hinges and rub a little nonstain lubricant on the door latches and posts.   Completed ❑

Checking Belts and Hoses

💡 Tech Tip
During an oil change service, it is usual to check the condition of all belts and hoses. Being made of rubber, these parts frequently cause on-the-road breakdowns.

32. Inspect belts for glazing, cracking, and fraying. Twist the belt over and check its operating surface.   Completed ❑

33. Did you find any wear problems on your belts? _____

Explain: _____

_____

_____

_____   Completed ❑

34. Belts should not be too loose or too tight. Belts tend to loosen after prolonged use. Loose belts can slip, flop, and squeal. To adjust, loosen correct mounting bolts and adjustment bolt. Using the directions in the service manual, pry component outward and tighten adjusting bolt. Then, tighten mounting bolts. Recheck belt tightness.   Completed ❑

35. Were all of the belts adjusted properly? _____

Explain: _____

_____   Completed ❑

36. Check the condition of the cooling system and fuel system hoses. Squeeze them to check for hardness or excessive softness. Hoses in either condition require replacement.   Completed ❑

37. Are your hoses in satisfactory condition? _____

    Explain: _____

    _____

    _____ Completed ❑

Environmental Protection

Tech Tip

The Environmental Protection Agency (EPA) guidelines and state regulations affect how you must handle and dispose of used fluids, solvents, and other shop chemicals. Used oil and other potentially hazardous used fluids must be stored and sent to a recycling or treatment facility to prevent pollution to the environment.

38. Where do you store used chemicals for recycling?_____

    _____

    _____

    _____ Completed ❑

39. Clean your work area and return all tools to their proper storage location.　Completed ❑

40. Ask your instructor to sign this job.

    Instructor's Signature _____

Using Scan Tools

Name: _____

Date: _____

Instructor: _____

Score: _____

Objective: After completing this job, you will be able use a scan tool to retrieve trouble codes and read datastream information from a computer-controlled vehicle system.

Tools and Equipment: You will need a scan tool and related harness adapters, a car or light truck, and the appropriate service manual.

Instructions: After getting your instructor's approval, use the shop's scan tool to analyze the operation of the vehicle's computerized engine control system. You should have studied Chapter 18 of your textbook before performing this job.

Scan Tools

1. Examine your test vehicle and fill in the following service information. If necessary, use a service manual.

    Make: _____

    Model: _____

    Year: _____

    VIN: _____

    Engine size: _____

    Transmission type: _____   Completed ☐

2. Check out a scan tool and take it to the vehicle. It will come with a variety of harness adapters.   Completed ☐

3. What is the name of the scan tool you will be using for this job? _____   Completed ☐

    Late-model vehicles use one of two on-board diagnostic systems—OBD I or OBD II. OBD I was used on all production vehicles until 1994. In 1994, manufacturers began phasing in OBD II systems. Since 1996, all vehicles have been equipped with OBD II systems.

4. What type of on-board diagnostic system does your test vehicle have? (Check the service manual.)

    _____   Completed ☐

5. Locate the vehicle's data link connector (DLC). If the vehicle was manufactured before 1996, the DLC may be located in either the passenger compartment or the engine compartment. If the vehicle was manufactured in 1996 or later, the DLC is located under the dash in the passenger compartment. You may need to consult the service manual to locate the data link connector.   Completed ☐

6. Where is the vehicle's data link connector located? _____   Completed ☐

7. Look at the data link connector and find a harness adapter that will connect to the DLC. OBD II vehicles use a standardized 16-pin adapter. OBD I vehicles use one of a variety of connectors, depending on the manufacturer. Consult the scan tool user's manual or the service manual for assistance.   Completed ☐

8. Connect the adapter to the scan tool harness as shown in **Figure 1.** You may need to connect a power adapter cord to the scan tool harness. The cord will have a single plug on one end with a cigarette lighter adapter on the other. Most OBD II vehicles will power the scan tool directly through the DLC. How does your scan tool receive power?

    _____

    _____   Completed ☐

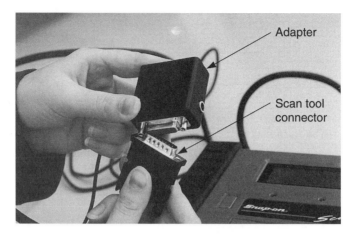

Figure 1. An adapter is sometimes needed between the scan tool cable and the vehicle's data link connector. As OBD II vehicles become more commonplace, these adapters will be needed less.

Scan Tool Program Cartridges

Many scan tools come equipped with several removable program cartridges that contain specific information about the vehicle to be scanned. Most scan tools use one program cartridge at a time. Some scan tools can access two cartridges at the same time. This permits the use of a troubleshooting cartridge.

9. Look in the scan tool manual. How many cartridges can the scan tool access? _____ Completed ☐

10. Carefully install the cartridges for the vehicle to be scanned. Slide the cartridge straight into the tool to prevent damage. Completed ☐

11. What is the title of the scan tool cartridge(s)? _____ Completed ☐

Most scan tools have an LCD screen that can display two or more items. Scan tools also have a keypad or buttons that allow the user to enter vehicle information and commands. See **Figure 2.** Some scan tools have a rotary knob, which is used to move the screen information up and down.

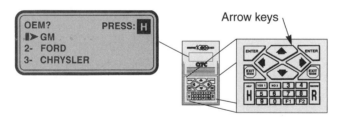

Figure 2. Controls on a scan tool will vary by manufacturer. This scan tool uses a keypad and arrow keys for inputting requested information about the vehicle and desired tests. (OTC)

12. What type of controls does the scan tool have? _____

_____

_____

_____ Completed ☐

Connecting the Scan Tool to the Vehicle

13. After setting up the scan tool, you are ready to connect it to the vehicle. The ignition switch should be *off.* As shown in **Figure 3,** connect the DLC harness first; then connect the power adapter, if used. Do *not* force the connector on the DLC. If the DLC harness does not attach easily, check the pins and the adapter. Make sure you are using the correct adapter. Completed ☐

Name _____

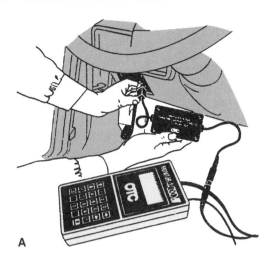

A

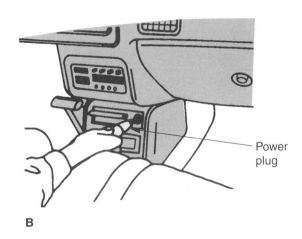

Power plug

B

Figure 3. A—Connect the scan tool cable to the data link connector. Make sure the pins match up; do not force them together. B—Scan tools can be powered by a cigarette lighter plug or they can be directly powered by the DLC.

14. After the necessary connections are made, the scan tool display should light. The scan tool will perform a short power on self-test; then the display will show some information. What information does the scan tool display show?

_____

_____

_____ Completed ☐

   Before the scan tool can communicate with the vehicle's computer(s), you must enter some information about the vehicle. Most scan tools will ask you to enter certain numbers and letters from the vehicle identification number (VIN). Others will ask you for the vehicle make, model, year, and engine type.

15. What information did you enter into the scan tool. If VIN information was entered into the scan tool, which numbers and letters did you enter?

_____

_____

_____ Completed ☐

16. What does your scan tool prompt you to do next? _____

_____

_____ Completed ☐

17. If you entered the vehicle information correctly, you will see a menu screen. List the information choices displayed on the menu screen. You may need to scroll down to see all the choices.

_____

_____

_____

_____ Completed ☐

Engine-Off/Key-On Scan

   Accessing trouble codes with the engine off and the key on is often the first step a technician takes when diagnosing a computer system problem. The technician usually looks for codes because the vehicle's malfunction indicator light was on. In some cases, however, the MIL does not light all the time.

18. To perform an engine-off/key-on scan, turn the ignition key to the run position, but do not crank the engine. Command the scan tool to retrieve stored trouble codes, **Figure 4.** If needed, disconnect a sensor wire and operate the engine to produce a fault in the system.

Completed ☐

```
┌─────────────────────────────────┐        ┌─────────────────────────────────┐
│  FAULT CODE REVIEW        [H]    │        │  P0400                    [H]    │
│     P0400 1/3                    │        │  EGR FLOW MALFUNCTION            │
│     P0401 2/3             ↕      │        │      21                          │
│  press ENTER for info            │        │  Code 01 of 01                   │
│                                  │        │                                  │
│  A                               │        │  B                               │
└─────────────────────────────────┘        └─────────────────────────────────┘
```

Figure 4. This is an example of what you might see on the display of a scan tool. A—The scan tool will give you the trouble code numbers. B—If you request information on the stored trouble codes, the tool will explain what each code means. (OTC)

19. What trouble code number(s) are given? _____

_____ Completed ☐

20. Using the scan tool or a service manual, explain what the trouble code number(s) indicate.

_____

_____

_____ Completed ☐

Engine-On/Key-On Scan

21. To perform an engine-on/key-on scan, start and warm the engine to full operating temperature to bring the computer system into the closed loop operating mode.

Completed ☐

22. Trigger the scan tool to read trouble codes. You may disconnect another sensor or an actuator to produce another trouble code.

Completed ☐

23. What trouble codes were given? _____

_____ Completed ☐

24. Scanning the computer system while the engine runs allows you to examine the datastream entering and leaving the computer. When a code is not stored, this is the next place to look for a problem. Select the datastream setting on the scan tool and look over the datastream values for each device.

Completed ☐

25. In the spaces provided below, list the datastream values displayed by your scan tool. Your scan tool may not display all the values listed.

Oxygen sensor (O₂S): _____   Mass airflow (MAF) sensor: _____

Throttle position sensor (TPS): _____   Open/Closed loop: _____

Intake air temperature (IAT) sensor: _____   Injector pulse: _____

Coolant temperature sensor (CTS): _____   Idle air control (IAC) solenoid: _____

Vehicle speed sensor (VSS): _____   Torque converter clutch (TCC): _____

Engine RPM: _____   PROM or Program ID number: _____

Manifold absolute pressure (MAP) sensor: _____   Completed ☐

26. Clean your work area and return all equipment to their proper storage locations.   Completed ☐

27. Ask your instructor to sign this job.

Instructor's Signature _____

Computer System Service

Name: _____

Date: _____

Instructor: _____

Score: _____

Objective: Given the needed tools and equipment, you will be able to test and perform diagnostic operations on a computer-controlled vehicle system.

Tools and Equipment: You will need a basic set of hand tools, a thermometer, multimeter, heat gun, scan tool, and a car or light truck.

Introduction: Computers are now used to monitor and control all major systems of a modern vehicle, including the engine, transmission, suspension, anti-lock brakes, air conditioning, air bags, even the seat and steering column presets. This makes it critical for today's technician to be well versed in using scan tools and repairing computer troubles. You should have studied Chapters 17 through 19 of your textbook before starting this job.

Service Manual Information

1. Record the vehicle information below. Using a service manual, look up and read the service information on the computer system for your test vehicle. Completed ❏

   Make: _____ VIN: _____

   Model: _____ Engine size: _____

   Year: _____ Transmission type: _____

2. Look in the service manual. How many computers does this vehicle use? _____ Completed ❏

3. What are the names in the service manual of the computers that control the following systems? If the vehicle's system is not computer-controlled or the vehicle is not equipped with a particular system, write the word *none* in the blank.

   Engine: _____ Air conditioning/heating: _____

   Transmission: _____ Air bags: _____

   Anti-lock brakes: _____ Cruise control: _____

   Traction control: _____ Anti-theft system: _____

   Suspension: _____ Other: _____

   Steering: _____ Completed ❏

   As discussed in Job 8, there are two types of on-board diagnostic systems, OBD I and OBD II. OBD I was used on almost all production vehicles until 1996. Beginning in 1996, vehicles were required to be equipped with the OBD II diagnostic system.

4. Which on-board diagnostic system does the test vehicle have? _____ Completed ❏

Computer System Diagnostics

After connecting the scan tool and entering the necessary vehicle information, retrieve any trouble codes that are stored. If there are any trouble codes stored in memory, write them down. Then, if available, go to the code history to determine which codes have occurred the most often. This may give you an indication of where the problem lies. You or your instructor may want to unplug a sensor to set a code.

5. List all stored codes and the number of times each was set. _____

_____

_____

_____

_____

_____ Completed ☐

Along with the scan tool, you can also access many computer systems without a scan tool. Depending on the manufacturer, you can do this by grounding two or more pins on the DLC, turning the key on and off in a certain sequence, or pressing certain buttons on the electronic dash control. However, an OBD II computer can only be accessed using a scan tool.

6. If you were *not* going to use a scan tool, how could you pull up trouble codes on the test vehicle? If the vehicle is OBD II compliant, write *OBD II compliant; access codes using scan tool only.*

_____

_____

_____ Completed ☐

7. Clear the codes and test drive the vehicle. See if any codes reset. If one or more codes reset, they are considered "hard failures." Codes that do not reset are considered "soft failures." Completed ☐

8. List all codes that reset in memory.

_____

_____

_____

_____ Completed ☐

If no codes were present or reset, the problem is most likely intermittent or is not caused by the computer system. You may want to try performing a snapshot to locate the problem. When diagnosing any stored codes, start with the lowest number code and work up. Often, you can eliminate one or more of the higher number codes by starting with the low number codes first.

Visual Inspection and Wiggle Test

9. Look over the engine compartment. Check for disconnected sensors, damaged actuators, and other obvious problems. Completed ☐

10. Did you find any problems? _____

Explain: _____

_____

_____ Completed ☐

11. Do a wiggle test. This is done by wiggling wires to sensors and actuators while scanning for trouble codes. The wiggle test might help you find an intermittent problem. Completed ☐

⚠ **Warning:**
If you perform this test while the engine is running, stay clear of belts and pulleys. If you cannot reach a sensor or other device safely, do not try. Be careful when wiggle testing oxygen sensors as the exhaust manifold will be extremely hot

12. Did you find any other problems during the wiggle test? _____

Explain: _____

_____

_____ Completed ☐

Switch Tests

13. If possible, do a switch self test. Follow scan tool instructions to turn each switch on and off. The scan tool will then tell you if each switch is working properly.

Can you do a switch test on this vehicle? _____

If so, summarize the results of the test. _____

_____

_____

_____

_____ Completed ☐

14. Test at least three switch devices. Candidates for switch tests include the brake pedal, air conditioning system, cruise control, and transmission shift lever. Make sure you put the parking brake on and step on the brake pedal when doing the transmission shift test. List the device(s) tested and your test results.

_____

_____

_____ Completed ☐

Sensor Pinpoint Tests

After you have retrieved trouble codes, you must do pinpoint tests to find the exact source of the trouble. A trouble code simply indicates which circuit might be at fault.

15. To simulate a test of the sensor, use your heat gun to change the sensor's temperature while measuring its internal resistance with your ohmmeter, **Figure 1.** Take resistance readings at the following temperatures and record them in the chart. Concentrate the heat on the sensor tip, *not* the plastic plug.   Completed ☐

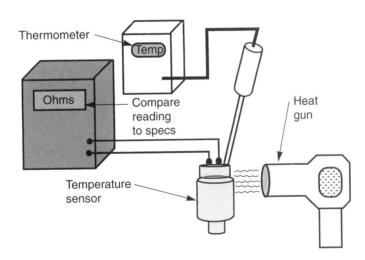

Figure 1. An ohmmeter can be used to measure resistance while heating the sensor with a heat gun.

Temperature	80°F	100°F	120°F	140°F	160°F
Sensor Resistance					

16. Using the service manual, find and remove the engine coolant temperature sensor.   Completed ☐

17. Does your service manual give resistance specifications for the coolant temperature sensor? If so, how do your readings compare to them? _____

_____

_____

_____   Completed ☐

Actuator Tests

18. Perform an actuator self-test. Use the scan tool instructions to "fire" vehicle actuators. The scan tool will then signal the vehicle's computer to fire the injectors, idle solenoid, and other actuators. You can then listen to determine if they are working properly.   Completed ☐

19. Explain the results of your actuator test. _____

_____

_____

_____

_____   Completed ☐

20. Disconnect the wires to a fuel injector. Using your ohmmeter, measure and record the injector's internal resistance. Compare your readings to service manual specifications.   Completed ☐

21. Does the injector resistance indicate a good or bad injector? _____

Explain: _____

_____

_____   Completed ☐

Erasing Computer Trouble Codes

22. Read the service manual instructors for erasing stored trouble codes. Then, use this information to erase any codes in your test vehicle. Trouble codes in most OBD I vehicles can be cleared by disconnecting battery power from the ECM or by using the scan tool. You must use the scan tool to clear codes in an OBD II computer system.   Completed ☐

23. How do you erase stored trouble codes on your vehicle? _____

_____

_____

_____

_____

_____   Completed ☐

24. If you disconnected battery power or the ECM at any time, you may need to reset the idle air control solenoid and other devices. In most cases, this can be done by simply driving the vehicle. In a few cases, a special procedure is needed to reset these devices. Check the service manual for any special reset procedures.   Completed ☐

25. Clean your work area and return all equipment to the proper storage locations.   Completed ☐

26. Ask your instructor to sign this job.

Instructor's Signature _____

Name: _____

Date: _____

Instructor: _____

Score: _____

Fuel Injection Service

Objective: Given the needed tools and equipment, you will be able to troubleshoot and repair typical fuel injection system problems.

Tools and Equipment: You will need a basic set of hand tools, fuel pressure gauge, hand vacuum pump, stethoscope, injector noid light, injector balance tester, scan tool, and test vehicle, preferably shop-owned. Read Chapters 22 and 23 before completing this Job.

Instructions: Fuel injection systems have replaced carburetors on modern cars. This makes it critical that you know how to troubleshoot and repair these systems. Keep in mind that many parts in carburetor systems can be compared to the parts and operating modes of a fuel injection system. Knowledge about one can be transferred to the other when troubleshooting. After getting your instructor's approval, use the following instructions and a service manual to analyze the operation of the vehicle's fuel injection system. Be sure you wear eye protection at all times while performing this job.

Fuel System Inspection

1. Record the vehicle information below. Using a service manual, read the service information on the fuel injection system for your test vehicle.

   Make: _____

   Model: _____

   Year: _____

   VIN: _____

   Engine size: _____

   Transmission type: _____   Completed ☐

2. Begin your fuel injection system service by inspecting for obvious problems. If possible, start the engine. Look for fuel leaks, disconnected wires, leaking vacuum hoses, and similar troubles.   Completed ☐

3. Could you find any visible problems with the fuel injection system? _____

   Explain: _____

   _____

   _____

   _____

   _____   Completed ☐

⚠️ **Warning**
Do not smoke in the shop or create sparks or flame.

4. If the fuel pump is operating, you may be able to hear the fuel pump running. Most fuel pumps used with injection systems are located in or near the fuel tank. Have someone turn the ignition key to the run position (do not crank the engine) while you listen for the electric fuel pump. If the pump is in the fuel tank, you may want to remove the fuel fill cap to better hear the pump.   Completed ☐

5. Could you hear the fuel pump running? _____   Completed ☐

6. If the engine runs, use a stethoscope to listen to each of the injectors. Start the engine and place the stethoscope lead near each injector. Each injector should be clicking to indicate that it is open and closing. The noise from each injector should also be similar. Record your observations in the following chart.

Completed ☐

Cylinder Number	1	2	3	4	5	6	7	8
Sound								

7. Did the stethoscope test reveal problems with any of the injectors? _____

Explain: _____

_____

_____

_____   Completed ☐

Fuel Injector Harness Testing

The fuel injectors receive their power through a feed circuit. This circuit commands the injector to spray fuel into the engine. Occasionally, these circuits become shorted or open. These circuits can be checked by using a noid light, which is a special test light used to check EFI feed circuits. They are also used to check that the injectors are receiving a "pulse" when diagnosing no-start problems.

8. Disconnect the wiring harness from one injector. Be sure to release the locking mechanism. *Do not force the harness off.* Fit the correct style noid light into the injector harness connector, **Figure 1.** Start the engine and check the light.

Completed ☐

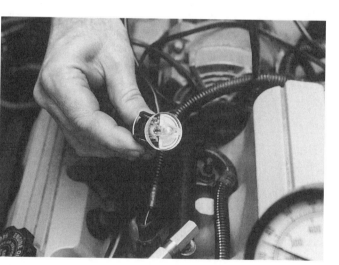

Figure 1. Install the noid light into the injector connector.

9. Did the light flash after the engine was started? _____   Completed ☐

10. Reconnect the injector wiring harness.   Completed ☐

Checking Fuel Pressure

11. Locate the fuel pressure test fitting on the engine. On multiport fuel injection systems, it is usually on the fuel rail. If the engine is throttle body injected, there may not be a test fitting. You will have to install a fuel pressure gauge in the line itself.

Completed ☐

Name _____

12. Does the fuel injection system have a test fitting? _____

 Where is it located? _____

 _____

 _____

 _____ Completed ☐

13. Using service manual instructions, relieve fuel pressure from the fuel system.   Completed ☐

 ⚠ **Warning:**
 Modern fuel systems operate under high pressure. Keep this in mind at all times. Always relieve pressure before opening the fuel system

14. Connect your fuel pressure gauge to the injection system, **Figure 2.** Make sure all fittings are tight.   Completed ☐

Figure 2. Connect the pressure gauge before the injectors. (Ford)

 Many fuel pumps receive a 2–5 second operating voltage "pulse" from the ECM. This is to charge the fuel system and provide extra fuel for cold start-up. This pulse can be checked by turning the ignition key to run without starting the engine. Performing this test first ensures your fuel pressure gauge is connected properly.   Completed ☐

15. Turn the ignition key to run (do not start the engine).   Completed ☐

16. What does the fuel pressure gauge read? _____   Completed ☐

17. Shut off the key, but do not relieve fuel pressure. One common cause of extended cold crank problems is fuel bleeding back into the fuel tank. This is caused by a small check valve in the fuel pump becoming weak over time. This condition can also occur if the pressure regulator is defective. Normally, the fuel system should maintain pressure for 5–7 minutes with minimal decrease.   Completed ☐

18. Did the fuel pressure reading decrease significantly after 5 minutes? _____   Completed ☐

19. To check running pressure, start the engine and read fuel pressure at idle. Write down fuel system pressure.   Completed ☐

20. How does your fuel pressure reading compare to specifications? _____

 _____

 _____ Completed ☐

21. If the fuel pressure regulator is vacuum assisted, you can remove the vacuum line to test the regulator's performance. The regulator is usually located on the fuel rail. Remove the vacuum line from the regulator and cap the line. If your vehicle has a throttle body injection system, skip to step 24, as most of these systems do not use a vacuum-assisted pressure regulator.   Completed ❑

22. What happened to the fuel pressure when you removed the regulator's vacuum supply?_____

    _____

    _____   Completed ❑

23. Install a hand vacuum pump on the fuel pressure regulator's vacuum fitting. Measure pressure as you apply vacuum to the regulator. Explain what happened as you applied vacuum. When you are finished, leave the fuel pressure gauge connected, as you will use it later in this job.

    _____

    _____

    _____   Completed ❑

Checking Fuel Filters

24. The fuel filter is an overlooked source of fuel system problems, even though it is frequently replaced as part of routine maintenance. If clogged, it can reduce fuel pressure. Shut off the engine and remove the main fuel filter, *not* the in-tank filter. Be sure to relieve fuel pressure before disconnecting the fuel filter's fittings.   Completed ❑

25. Where is the main fuel filter located?_____

    What is its condition? _____

    _____

    _____   Completed ❑

26. Reinstall or replace the fuel filter and check for fuel leaks.   Completed ❑

Testing Fuel Injectors

An injector balance tester can measure the amount of fuel flowing through each injector. It can tell you if any of the injectors are clogged or not operating.

27. What kind of injector balance tester are you going to use? _____

    _____

    _____   Completed ❑

28. Read the owner's manual for the injector tester.   Completed ❑

29. Install the injector balance tester on the engine. How did you do this? _____

    _____

    _____

    _____

    _____   Completed ❑

30. With the fuel pressure gauge you used earlier still installed, start the engine and use the injector balance tester to check the volume of fuel leaving each injector, **Figure 3.** Record your test results in the following chart.   Completed ❑

Figure 3. Connect the test harness to each injector. Press the tester button and notice the reading on the fuel pressure gauge.

	Balance Tester Results	Scan Tool Results
Injector 1		
Injector 2		
Injector 3		
Injector 4		
Injector 5		
Injector 6		
Injector 7		
Injector 8		

31. In some cases, you can perform an injector balance test using a scan tool. Read the scan tool user's manual to make sure it can perform this task. Repeat step 30, but this time, use the scan tool to disable each injector. Make sure the scan tool is disabling the injectors and not the ignition system to each cylinder.   Completed ☐

32. Did the scan tool test results match those you obtained using the injector balance tester? _____   Completed ☐

Removing Fuel Injectors

33. Remove and reinstall one of the fuel injectors. Describe how this was done. Be aware that injector removal on some vehicles is quite complicated and may take more than one class period to complete. Your instructor may tell you to skip this part of the job.

_____

_____

_____

_____

_____

_____   Completed ☐

34. Remove all test equipment from the engine. Make sure you clean up any spilled fuel and reconnect all vacuum hoses and wiring harnesses.   Completed ☐

35. Clean your work area and return all equipment to the proper storage locations.   Completed ☐

36. Ask your instructor to sign this job.

Instructor's Signature _____

Notes

Job 10

Charging and Starting System Testing

Name: _____

Date: _____

Instructor: _____

Score: _____

Objective: After completing this exercise, you will be able to test the operating condition of a battery, starting system, and charging system using a modern inductive-type load tester.

Tools and Equipment: You will need access to an operating shop vehicle, a VAT (volt-amp tester), a digital multimeter capable of 10 A reading, safety glasses, and the shop area.

Instructions: During this job you will actually test the battery, charging system, and starting system of a running vehicle. You will do this using a modern inductive tester. You should perform this job on a shop vehicle as you will be placing high amperage loads on the battery.

Battery Load Test

1. Check out the load tester and move it to the test vehicle. Ask your instructor for added details if needed. Completed ☐

2. Is your load tester an inductive type? _____

   If the load tester is *not* an inductive type, you will have to read the operating instructions for the unit and modify the instructions in this job for your particular tester. Completed ☐

3. Connect the load tester to the battery. If an inductive type is used, connect the two battery leads to the battery posts or side terminals. Clip the amps pickup over the negative battery cable, **Figure 1.** Completed ☐

4. Does your battery have top posts or side terminals? _____ Completed ☐

Figure 1. Modern load testers are connected as shown. (Marquette)

5. Determine the rating of the battery you are going to load test. The rating should be printed somewhere on the battery. If you cannot find its rating, ask your instructor for help or refer to the textbook. Completed ☐

6. What is the rating of your battery? _____ Completed ☐

437

7. Using the chart in **Figure 2,** how many amps should be drawn through the battery when load testing?

_____ Completed ☐

Battery ratings			Load test amps
Cold cranking current	Amp-hour (approx.)	Watts	
200	35–40	1800	100 amps
250	41–48	2100	125 amps
300	49–62	2500	150 amps
350	63–70	2900	175 amps
400	71–76	3250	200 amps
450	77–86	3600	225 amps
500	87–92	3900	250 amps
550	93–110	4200	275 amps

Figure 2. This chart lists different battery ratings and calculated current values for load testing. (Marquette)

8. What rating is given for your battery (cold cranking, amp-hour, and watts)? _____

_____

_____ Completed ☐

9. Before load testing, make sure the battery is fully charged. A charged battery should have an open circuit voltage (OCV) of at least 12.4 volts. Completed ☐

10. What is the OCV of your battery? _____ Completed ☐

11. Is your battery fully charged? _____ Completed ☐

12. Turn the load tester control knob until the ammeter reads the correct load test amps determined from the chart in **Figure 2.** Hold the load for 15 seconds. Then, read the voltmeter and turn off the load. Completed ☐

Tech Tip

A good battery should keep voltage at about 9.5 volts or higher during the load test. A bad or discharged battery will let the voltage drop below 9.5 volts.

13. What did your voltmeter read during the load test? _____

14. Did your battery test good or bad? _____

Explain: _____

_____

_____ Completed ☐

Parasitic Draw Test

A parasitic draw test is often performed when diagnosing an unexplained battery discharge and when replacing a discharged battery. All modern vehicles have some parasitic draw in the milliamps range.

15. To perform the test, plug your meter leads into the fused 10 A terminal and common ground on your meter and set the meter to measure dc amperage. Disconnect the negative battery cable from the battery and connect the meter in series. Completed ☐

16. What is the amperage reading on the meter? _____ Completed ☐

17. If the meter does not read an abnormally high draw, create a draw by opening one of the vehicle's doors. Completed ☐

> **Caution**
> If the meter reads over 10 amps, disconnect the meter immediately and make sure no high amperage circuits are on. Do *not* turn on the vehicle's headlights or other high amperage device to create a draw as it could damage the meter.

18. What is the amperage reading on the meter with one of the vehicle's doors open? _____   Completed ☐

19. Disconnect the meter and reconnect the negative cable to the battery.   Completed ☐

Starting Current Draw Test

A load tester can also be used to measure the current draw from the starting motor. For example, if an engine cranks slow, the tester can be used to find out if the starter motor itself is defective.

A good starting motor should draw a specific amount of amps. **Figure 3** lists typical current draw values for starting motors. If during the test, current draw is high or low, it indicates problems with the motor or circuit.

20. How much current should your starting motor draw? Use the chart in **Figure 3.** _____   Completed ☐

ENGINE DISPLACEMENT	12-VOLT SYSTEM MAX. CURRENT
Most 4–6 Cylinders	125–175 Amps Max.
Under 300 C.I.D.	150–200 Amps Max.
Over 300 C.I.D.	175–250 Amps Max.

Figure 3. Chart shows typical current draw values for different engine sizes. (Marquette)

21. To prevent engine starting, disable the ignition system. This can be done by disconnecting the primary wires feeding current to the coil.   Completed ☐

22. With the load tester connected properly (as in the first test of the battery with an inductive-type tester), measure starting current draw. Crank the motor for about 10 seconds and note the ammeter reading. The initial readings should be ignored until the current draw stabilizes.   Completed ☐

23. What was the ammeter reading while you were cranking the engine?_____   Completed ☐

24. Was your starting current draw within acceptable limits? _____

Explain: _____

_____

_____   Completed ☐

Charging System Output Test

A load tester is also commonly used to test charging system condition. It can be used to load the system while measuring alternator output.

25. If you are using an inductive-type tester, your test connections do not have to be changed. Set the tester controls properly.   Completed ☐

26. Turn the ignition key switch to *run*. Note this ammeter reading.

What did the ammeter read? _____   Completed ☐

27. Start the engine. Adjust the idle speed to the test specifications (about 2000 rpm).   Completed ☐

28. Adjust the load control on the tester until the ammeter reads specified current output but *do not* let voltage drop below specifications (about 12 volts). Note (write down) this ammeter reading.

_____ Completed ☐

29. Rotate load control to off. Evaluate readings. Completed ☐

30. Add your two ammeter readings (steps 26 and 28) to get system output. _____ Completed ☐

31. Look up the specifications for your alternator current output.
    Did your system check good or bad? _____

    Explain: _____

    _____

    _____ Completed ☐

    If the system tested bad, other tests would be needed to pinpoint the problem. Refer to the text for more information.

32. Clean your work area and return all tools to their proper storage location. Completed ☐

33. Ask for your instructor's signature.

Instructor's Signature _____

Ignition System Service

Name: _____

Date: _____

Instructor: _____

Score: _____

Objective: Using the tools and equipment listed below, you will learn to explain the principles and basic service procedures for ignition systems.

Tools and Equipment: For the first part of the job, check out a shop-owned distributor, flat feeler gauge, and standard screwdriver. For the second part of the job, you will also need a 3/8″ drive speed handle, safety glasses, ignition coil, two jumper wires, remote starter switch, spark plug, spark plug wire, a battery or 12 V power supply, ballast resistor, ignition coil, electronic ignition distributor, piece of vacuum hose, fender cover, and a dwell meter.

Instructions: This is a very informative learning exercise; so take your time. Follow the job procedures carefully and answer all the job questions. During this job, you will actually build and observe the operation of an ignition system. You will connect the parts of an ignition system with jumper wires at a workbench. Then, by spinning the distributor with a speed handle, you can inspect the firing of a spark plug. You will also learn to use a dwell meter, adjust pickup coil air gap, and set spark plug gaps.

Review of Distributor

This job requires several hours for completion. Unless the length of your class permits, only attempt to finish the first section of the job.

Even though you may never have to work on one, a contact point ignition system is an excellent way for you to better understand modern electronic and computer-controlled ignition systems. Many of the parts (spark plugs, secondary wires, ignition coil, etc.) and operating principles are the same.

1. Check out a distributor and other components listed for part one of the job.   Completed ☐

2. Lightly clamp the distributor housing in a vise. See **Figure 1.** The distributor shaft must be free to turn.
   On some vises, the distributor should be placed to one side of the jaws so the distributor gear will clear.   Completed ☐

Figure 1. The vise jaws must clamp on the distributor housing, preferably on an unmachined portion of the housing. Vise caps, rags, or small pieces of wood should be used to protect the distributor from damage.

3. Check the distributor for wear. Wiggle the distributor shaft sideways. If the shaft is loose in the housing, the shaft or shaft bushings are worn. Also, check the base plate for looseness.   Completed ☐

4. Can you detect any wear in the distributor bushings? _____

   Explain: _____

   _____ Completed ☐

5. Check the condition of the vacuum advance diaphragm. Apply a vacuum to the diaphragm to make sure it does not leak. Also check that it moves the breaker plate properly.   Completed ☐

6. Does the vacuum advance diaphragm leak? _____   Completed ☐

7. Does the distributor plate advance? _____   Completed ☐

8. You are ready to gap your pickup coil or points. Turn the distributor shaft until a trigger wheel tooth is aiming at the pickup coil point or the running block is touching one of the cam lobes. See **Figure 2.**   Completed ☐

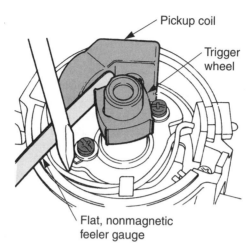

Figure 2. To set the pickup coil or point air gap, turn the distributor shaft until the points are fully open or the trigger wheel tooth is pointing at the pickup coil. Slide the correct thickness feeler gauge between the gap. Open or close the gap until the gauge just touches. (Mopar)

9. After wiping it clean, insert the proper size feeler gauge (around 0.017″ or 0.43 mm) between the pickup coil and trigger wheel tooth or contact points. Shift the pickup coil on its mount, or open or close the points until the feeler gauge just fits between the two. The blade should have a very light drag when pulled out.   Completed ☐

10. When set correctly, tighten the hold-down screws. Double-check the gap because it could change as the screws are tightened.   Completed ☐

11. Ask your instructor to check your pickup or point gap and sign this job for credit.

Instructor's Signature _____

Gapping Spark Plugs

12. Check out the rest of the tools and equipment listed at the beginning of the job.   Completed ☐

13. Set the spark plug gap. Insert a 0.035″ (0.89 mm) spark plug or wire feeler gauge between the electrodes. The gauge should touch both electrodes in the spark plug.   Completed ☐

14. To change the spark plug gap, bend the side electrode up or down. Many feeler gauges have a tool for grasping and bending the plug electrode. There should be a slight drag as the gauge is pulled through the spark plug gap.   Completed ☐

Ignition Circuit Wiring

15. Connect the parts of your ignition system using the jumper wires and remote starter switch. **Figure 13-5** illustrates how the wires and components must be connected. Depending on your distributor, you may or may not need a ballast resistor.   Completed ☐

Caution
When connecting the ignition system components, keep all the parts and wires organized on your workbench to prevent any connections from shorting. Also, do *not* connect the battery or power source until you are ready to test your circuit.

16. Start connecting your wires at the positive battery terminal and work your way through the ignition circuit. This will prevent you from forgetting to connect any component. Do *not* connect to the negative cable. As in **Figure 3,** the spark plug shell, distributor housing, and battery negative must be all *grounded together*. If you fail to ground any of these parts, the ignition system will not work.   Completed ☐

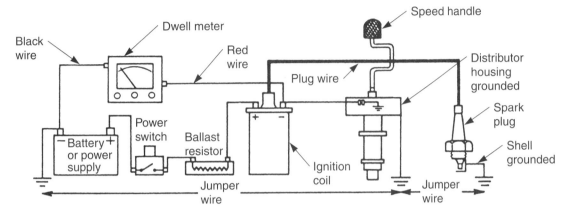

Figure 3. This drawing shows how parts of your ignition system should be connected. Note the jumper wires grounding major parts to the battery's negative terminal.

17. Read steps 15 and 16 again. Double-check all your connections. Make sure none of your "hot wires" are shorted to ground.   Completed ☐

Using a Dwell Meter

18. Make sure the dwell meter is connected to the negative side of the coil and to ground. Check that the meter settings (number of cylinders, dwell, etc.) are correct and, if required, calibrate the meter.   Completed ☐

19. Ask your instructor to check your circuit before connecting the power source.   Completed ☐

20. Connect your ignition system grounds to the negative battery terminal. Use the finger rule to determine the direction of distributor rotation. See **Figure 4.**   Completed ☐

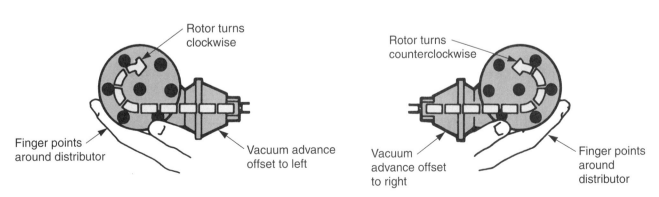

Figure 4. Use the finger rule to determine the direction of rotor rotation. Point around the distributor as shown. This will tell you how the rotor turns without removing the cap and watching the rotor. (Florida Dept. of Voc. Ed.)

21. What is the direction of rotation of your distributor shaft? _____

_____

_____   Completed ☐

22. Gap the distributor pickup coil or points to the setting given in the service manual for the vehicle it came from or approximately 0.020″ (0.51 mm).   Completed ☐

23. Force the end of your speed handle into the prepared distributor shaft. Turn the speed handle the correct direction while your partner presses the start switch. This should make the spark plug "fire" and the dwell meter register cam angle.   Completed ☐

24. While spinning the distributor, read the dwell meter. It will register dwell for your present point gap setting. What is the dwell meter reading? _____   Completed ☐

25. Ask your instructor to sign this job.

Instructor's Signature _____

Electronic Ignition System Service

26. Check out an electronic ignition system distributor, ignition module (if not attached to the distributor), and ignition coil. Read a service manual that covers the service of the distributor.   Completed ☐

27. Remove the distributor cap from the distributor body.

How is this done? _____

_____

_____

_____   Completed ☐

28. Inspect the inside of the cap for signs of cracks, carbon traces, and burning. Can you find any signs of failure? _____   Completed ☐

29. If necessary, remove the ignition coil from the distributor cap.   Completed ☐

30. Using an ohmmeter, check the internal resistance of the ignition coil windings. Record your readings below.

Coil Primary Winding Resistance _____

Coil Secondary Winding Resistance _____   Completed ☐

31. Is the coil resistance within specifications? _____   Completed ☐

32. Check the distributor shaft bushings for wear. Try wiggling the top of the shaft sideways while you watch for movement in the distributor body. If the shaft wiggles sideways, the shaft bushings are worn.   Completed ☐

33. Explain the condition of the distributor shaft bushings. _____

_____

_____

_____   Completed ☐

34. Remove the distributor shaft. Refer to your service manual if needed.   Completed ☐

35. What do you have to do before removing the distributor shaft?_____

_____

_____   Completed ☐

36. Inspect the shaft for signs of wear at the bushing bearing surfaces. Use a micrometer to measure shaft diameter at its most worn point and on an unworn point. Record your readings below.

    Shaft diameter (most worn): _____

    Shaft diameter (unworn): _____   Completed ❑

37. Is the distributor shaft worn beyond specifications? _____

    Explain: _____

    _____   Completed ❑

38. Use a telescoping gauge and micrometer to measure distributor bushing inside diameter. Record your measurements below.

    Lower bushing inside diameter: _____

    Upper bushing inside diameter: _____   Completed ❑

39. Use your ohmmeter to check the condition of the pickup coil. See **Figure 5.** Wiggle the pickup coil wires while measuring resistance. Sometimes the pickup coil wires can break internally and cause a resistance fluctuation. Record your readings below.

    Pickup coil resistance: _____   Completed ❑

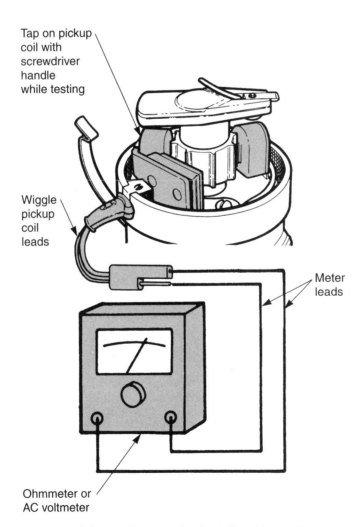

Figure 5. Using an ohmmeter to check the pickup coil.

40. Remove the ignition module, if attached.   Completed ☐

41. How many wires are connected to the module? _____   Completed ☐

42. Use a high-impedance ohmmeter to measure the resistance across the terminals of the ignition module.
    Record your readings. _____

    _____

    _____

    _____   Completed ☐

43. How does the service manual say to test an ignition module? _____

    _____

    _____

    _____

    _____   Completed ☐

44. Reinstall the module. In some cases, you may need to wipe a thin layer of dielectric grease across the
    bottom of the unit. This helps keep it from overheating. Install the module and tighten each fastener
    equally.   Completed ☐

45. Reassemble the distributor following service manual instructions.   Completed ☐

46. Clean your work area and return all tools to the proper storage locations.   Completed ☐

47. Ask your instructor to sign this job.

Instructor's Signature _____

Using Vehicle Analyzers

Name: _____

Date: _____

Instructor: _____

Score: _____

Objective: After completing this job, you will be able to utilize a vehicle analyzer when trying to find electrical-electronic related performance problems.

Tools and Equipment: You will need access to an analyzer, an ignition system training unit or running vehicle, exhaust vent system, set of basic hand tools, fender covers, wire feeler gauge, and access to the auto shop.

Instructions: During the job, you will connect an analyzer to an engine or ignition trainer. Then, by following the instructions, you will regap spark plugs, disconnect plug wires, and simulate other common causes of engine performance problems. This will let you see how the analyzer can detect and show engine performance problems. Study textbook Chapter 46 before doing this job.

Analyzer Type

1. Check out an analyzer. Ask your instructor whether an ignition system training unit or an engine will be used during the job. Completed ☐

2. What is the brand name of the analyzer? _____ Completed ☐

3. Give the following information for the vehicle or ignition system training unit to be tested. Ask your instructor for this data if you are using an ignition training unit. Completed ☐

   Make: _____   VIN: _____

   Model: _____   Engine size: _____

   Year: _____   Transmission type: _____

Note
Operating instructions for analyzers vary. The instructions in this job are general so you will have to modify them to meet your specific type of analyzer. Have the operating instructions for the analyzer handy and study them before beginning the job.

Figure 1 shows one make and model of analyzer. Although the controls may look different than the one you are using, both are similar. The lead connections, types of tests performed, etc., are almost the same.

Figure 1. Analyzers contain several test instruments in one housing.

4. What external differences can you see in *your* analyzer and the one in **Figure 1.**

_____

_____

_____

_____

_____

_____ Completed ☐

5. List the testing devices mounted on your analyzer.

_____   _____

_____   _____

_____   _____

_____   _____

_____   Completed ☐

As detailed in the text, the oscilloscope is the "heart" of an analyzer. It will measure voltages very accurately. Study your scope screen. Note the values given on the screen.

6. What values are given on the left vertical scale? _____ Completed ☐

7. What values are given on the right vertical scale? _____ Completed ☐

8. What values are given along the bottom horizontal scale? _____ Completed ☐

Connecting the Analyzer

9. Connect the analyzer to the vehicle or ignition training unit. Follow the operating instructions for your particular analyzer. Completed ☐

10. Does your ignition system have the coil mounted inside the distributor? _____ Completed ☐

11. Where did you connect the timing light pickup? _____

_____

_____ Completed ☐

12. How did you connect the ignition coil pickup? _____

_____

_____ Completed ☐

13. Where did you connect the analyzer ground? _____

_____

_____ Completed ☐

14. Does the analyzer have an exhaust gas probe? _____ Completed ☐

⚠ **Caution**
Make sure none of the analyzer leads are near the engine fan or hot engine exhaust manifolds. The leads are very expensive and can be easily damaged.

15. Are your analyzer test leads routed properly? _____ Completed ☐

Secondary Scope Patterns

As a review, study the parts of the waveform, in **Figure 2.**

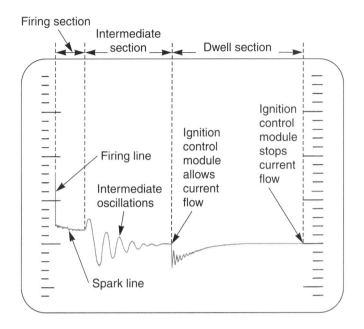

Figure 2. A secondary waveform for one cylinder. The firing line is voltage needed to fire the spark plug. The spark line is voltage needed to maintain the spark across the plug gap. Intermediate oscillations show the coil and condenser action. Dwell is the amount of time primary current flows through the ignition coil.

16. Set your controls to check secondary voltage, superimposed.   Completed ☐

17. Turn on the ignition system training aid or start the engine. If needed, connect a vent hose to the exhaust.   Completed ☐

18. Inspect the scope pattern. Since all of the cylinder patterns are stacked on top of each other, this pattern can quickly tell you if there are problems in any cylinder.   Completed ☐

Open Plug Wire

19. Shut off the trainer or the engine. Disconnect one spark plug wire, restart the engine or trainer, and recheck the pattern.   Completed ☐

> ⚠️ **Caution**
> Do *not* let the engine run for over a few seconds or it could contaminate the catalytic converter.

20. What differences did you notice in the secondary superimposed? _____

_____

_____   Completed ☐

21. To find which cylinder is bad, switch to parade. This compares all the cylinders side-by-side.   Completed ☐

22. Does your parade pattern show the disconnected spark plug wire? _____

    Explain: _____

    _____   Completed ☐

23. Shut off the trainer or engine.   Completed ☐

Fouled Spark Plug

⚠ **Caution**
If the engine is equipped with aluminum heads, allow the engine to cool before removing the spark plug.

24. Remove one spark plug from the engine or trainer. Close its gap until almost touching. Reinstall the plug and reconnect all plug wires. Recheck the parade pattern.   Completed ☐

25. Could you detect the closed spark plug gap on the parade pattern? _____

    Explain: _____

    _____

    _____   Completed ☐

💡 **Tech Tip**
A closed spark plug gap simulates an oil or carbon fouled spark plug. Less voltage would be needed to fire the plug.

26. How did the scope show that less voltage was needed with the closed gap?

    _____

    _____

    _____

    _____   Completed ☐

27. Remove and gap the spark plug properly.   Completed ☐

Other Analyzer Tests

Today's vehicle analyzers can perform a wide range of tests. They can analyze combustion efficiency, theoretical cylinder compression, charging system condition, starting system condition, trouble codes, computer datastream values, and many other functions.

If possible, use your vehicle analyzer to check the theoretical compression pressure in each engine cylinder. This can be done without removing the spark plugs. The ignition system is disabled and the engine is cranked over. The analyzer can then monitor starter current draw during each revolution of the crankshaft. If a cylinder has low compression, lower current draw will be present on that cylinder's compression stroke.

28. Using the specific instructions for your analyzer, connect the unit to a vehicle and check engine compression.   Completed ☐

29. Did the engine pass its theoretical compression test? _____

    Explain: _____

    _____

    _____   Completed ☐

30. If possible, print out the results of your engine analysis and turn it in with this job.   Completed ☐

31. Clean your work area and return all tools to the proper storage location.   Completed ☐

32. Ask your instructor to sign this job.

Instructor's Signature _____

Engine Bottom End Service

Name: _____

Date: _____

Instructor: _____

Score: _____

Objective: Given an engine short block and set of tools, you will learn to properly disassemble and reassemble an engine's bottom end.

Tools and Equipment: Check out a ridge reamer, hammer, safety glasses, ring expander, inside micrometer, outside micrometer, set of flat feeler gauges, ring compressor, engine oil, cylinder hone, low speed electric drill, ratchet and socket set, two short pieces of fuel line hose, torque wrench, and a shop-owned engine assembly.

Instructions: If not already briefed, ask your instructor for any added directions and for the location of the special equipment and engine to be used. This is a rather long and time-consuming exercise. If you see that time is running out, inform your instructor so the engine parts may be stored. Study text Chapters 14 and 48–50 before doing this job.

Engine Disassembly

If you are going to service only one piston and cylinder, position that piston at bottom dead center (BDC).

The crankshaft can be turned with a breaker bar and socket that fits the large bolt on the front of the crankshaft snout. A special flywheel tool may also be used to grasp the teeth of the flywheel for turning. If needed, a large pry bar can be wedged between the flywheel bolts to turn the crankshaft.

1. How did you position the piston to be removed at BDC? _____

   _____ Completed ☐

Inspect Cylinders

2. Inspect the engine cylinder for wear or damage (scratches, grooves, etc.). To check for excessive cylinder wear, rub your fingernail across the top of the cylinder. This will detect if a ridge has formed in the top of the cylinder.

   Completed ☐

   ⚠ Caution
   A ring ridge is formed by the wearing action of the piston rings. If a ring ridge is present, it must be removed before piston removal. Forcing the piston out of the cylinder and over a ring ridge can break the rings and damage the piston grooves and lands.

3. Is your cylinder scratched or scored? _____

   Explain: _____

   _____ Completed ☐

4. Does your cylinder have a ring ridge? _____

   Explain: _____

   _____ Completed ☐

Removing Connecting Rods and Pistons

5. To cut off the ring ridge, stuff rags into the bottom of the cylinder bore. Insert the ridge reaming tool into the cylinder, **Figure 1.**

   Completed ☐

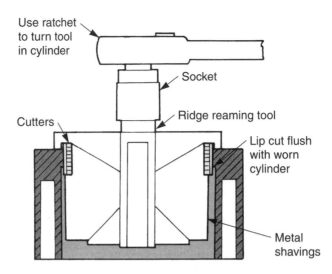

Figure 1. If the cylinder is badly worn, a ridge will be formed at the top of the cylinder wall. The ridge reamer cuts off this lip so the rings will not catch and damage the piston during removal.

6. Adjust the cutters out against the ridge. Then, turn the reamer with your ratchet and socket until the ridge is cut flush with the worn part of the cylinder wall. The newly cut surface must blend smoothly with the existing cylinder.   Completed ☐

7. Remove the rags. Blow out the block to remove metal shavings that might scratch the cylinder during piston removal.   Completed ☐

8. Loosen and remove the nuts holding the rod cap on the connecting rod. Keep them in order and right side up. It is desirable to replace the connecting rod nuts exactly as removed.   Completed ☐

9. Remove the rod cap and drive the rod and piston out of the cylinder, as in **Figure 2.** Remove the other rods keeping the caps on the correct rods.   Completed ☐

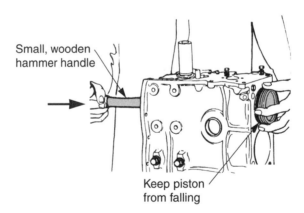

Figure 2. To remove pistons, first unbolt the rod cap. Use a wooden or plastic hammer handle to carefully tap the piston assembly out of the block. (Nissan)

10. After removing the piston and rod assembly, check it for markings. If the cap and rod are not numbered, mark the parts as needed. The numbers on the cap and rod should match to prevent them from being mixed up. An arrow can be marked on the piston head to indicate how it should be reinstalled on the rod and in the block.   Completed ☐

 Caution
During a complete service of all the pistons and cylinder, it is essential that all the caps, connecting rods, and related fasteners are installed in the same location.

Measuring Cylinder Wear

11. Measure the cylinder diameter with an inside micrometer, a telescoping gauge and outside micrometer, or dial gauge.

    A cylinder bore gauge can quickly check wear in a cylinder. Slide the gauge up and down. The indicator movement indicates the difference in diameter.

    Measure at the top, center, and bottom as well as sideways and forward in the block. This will let you detect taper and out-of-round.   Completed ❑

12. Take measurements at right angles to and along the engine centerline, near the top of ring travel. This will let you calculate how much the cylinder is out-of-round.   Completed ❑

13. When checking cylinder taper, use your micrometer to measure at the top and bottom of ring travel at right angles to the engine centerline.   Completed ❑

14. Cylinder oversize is determined by measuring the cylinder bore diameter at right angles to the engine centerline near the bottom of ring travel. Subtract the standard bore size from this measurement.   Completed ❑

15. Record your measurements in the following chart.   Completed ❑

Measurement	Result
Top of cylinder R/A	
Top of cylinder C/L	
Out-of-round	
Top of cylinder R/A	
Bottom of cylinder R/A	
Taper in cylinder	
Bottom of cylinder R/A	
Standard bore specs	
Cylinder oversize	

16. Calculate the out-of-round, taper, and oversize of the cylinder. Subtract the chart values. The difference will indicate these three conditions in your cylinder. The standard cylinder diameter will have to be obtained from your service manual or instructor.   Completed ❑

17. Is the cylinder within specifications? _____

    Explain: _____

    _____

    _____   Completed ❑

Honing Cylinder

18. To deglaze the cylinder, clamp a hone into a low speed electric drill. Install the hone in the cylinder bore. Squirt a moderate amount of hone oil in the cylinder and turn on the drill.

    Move the drill up and down the full length of the cylinder. However, be careful not to pull the hone too far out of the bore or damage may result. Move the hone up and down at a rate that will produce a 50° crosshatch pattern. This will help the rings seal during engine break-in. Hone more at the bottom than the top to help remove taper. Check manual and equipment instructions for how long to hone each cylinder.   Completed ❑

19. At about what angle are the hone marks in your cylinder?   Completed ☐

20. What kind of hone did you use? _____

_____   Completed ☐

21. After honing, clean the cylinder thoroughly. Any grit left in the engine will act as a grinding compound that can wear the engine's moving parts. Scrub the cylinder with soap and hot water and then rinse with clean hot water. Then wipe the cylinder dry with a clean rag.   Completed ☐

22. After washing and drying the cylinder, wipe it clean with an oil-soaked rag. Wipe until all of the grit is removed. The oil will help pick up heavy particles from inside the hone scratches.   Completed ☐

Checking Pistons and Pins

23. Using a large outside micrometer, determine piston clearance by first measuring the piston diameter across the skirts, even with the piston pin. Record the piston diameter in the chart below. Go back to the chart in step 15 and look up your cylinder diameter. Record it in the chart below.   Completed ☐

24. Subtract the piston diameter from the cylinder diameter to determine the piston clearance.   Completed ☐

> **Cylinder diameter:** _____
>
> *minus*   **Piston diameter:** _____
>
> *equals*   **Piston clearance:** _____

25. Is piston clearance within specifications? _____

Explain: _____

_____

_____   Completed ☐

26. To check the wrist pin fit in the piston, clamp the rod I-beam lightly in a vise. Try to rock the piston sideways (opposite normal swivel). Any detectable movement would indicate piston pin looseness. During an actual repair, this would require service (pin or bushing replacement).

Explain the condition of your piston and bushing. _____

_____

_____

_____   Completed ☐

Piston Ring Service

27. Position the piston and rod assembly in the vise so the piston skirt is resting on top of the vise jaws and cannot swivel. Clamp the jaw lightly around the connecting rod. Using your ring expander, remove the rings from the piston. To prevent ring breakage, open the rings only enough to clear the piston lands. Keep them in order and right side up. Use your fingers to remove the oil rings. Remove the rings from all of the pistons.   Completed ☐

28. Clean the carbon from the inside of your ring grooves with a ring groove cleaner. Select the correct width scraper for each groove and be careful not to cut too much. Ideally, you do not want to cut any metal in the groove, just remove the carbon.   Completed ☐

Tech Tip
If a groove cleaner is not available, an old broken ring can be used to scrape carbon from inside the ring grooves.

29. Measure the ring side clearance as shown in **Figure 3.** Fit a ring into the top and middle ring grooves. Determine the largest size feeler gauge that will fit between the side of the groove and ring. The largest size feeler gauge blade that fits equals ring side clearance. Your top piston groove will usually be the most worn.   Completed ☐

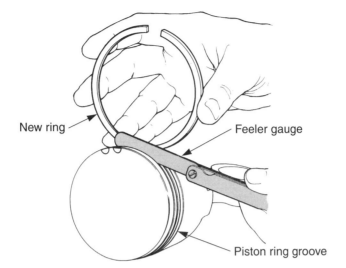

New ring

Feeler gauge

Piston ring groove

Figure 3. If ring side clearance is greater than specifications, the ring groove is worn or you have the wrong piston ring set. (Chrysler)

30. What is the top ring side clearance for your piston?_____   Completed ☐

31. What is the second ring side clearance for your piston?_____   Completed ☐

32. Determine your piston ring gap. Install the compression ring into the cylinder squarely. Push it to the bottom of ring travel with the head of your piston.   Completed ☐

33. Determine the largest size feeler gauge that will fit between the gap in the ends of the ring. To measure piston ring end gap, install and push the ring to the bottom of ring travel with the head of the piston. Use a feeler gauge to measure the gap. If too small, check the ring size or file ends. If too large, double-check the cylinder dimensions and rings.   Completed ☐

⚠ **Caution**
When a ring gap is too small, the heat of operation will cause expansion. This expansion could crush the ring outward against the cylinder wall with tremendous force, damaging or scoring the ring and cylinder.

34. What is your upper compression ring gap for one piston? _____
_____   Completed ☐

35. Is this within factory specifications for your engine? _____

Explain: _____
_____   Completed ☐

36. What is the second compression ring gap for your piston? _____
_____   Completed ☐

Checking Block Warpage

37. Main bearing bore alignment can be checked with a straightedge and a feeler gauge. Lay the straightedge on the bores; then determine the thickest feeler gauge blade that will slide between the straightedge and any of the bores. The size of this blade indicates the amount of main bearing bore misalignment.

Is the main bore misaligned? _____   Completed ☐

38. Cylinder block warpage can also be checked using a straightedge and a feeler gauge. To check for deck warpage, lay a straightedge on the clean block surface. Try to slip feeler gauge blades of different thicknesses between the block and straightedge. The thickest blade that fits indicates warpage. Check for deck warpage in different locations.

    Is your deck and main bore warped? _____

    Explain: _____

    _____

    _____ Completed ☐

Crankshaft Service

39. If one side of a crankshaft journal is worn more than the other, the journal is tapered. To measure journal taper, use an outside micrometer. Measure both ends of the journal. Any difference indicates taper.   Completed ☐

40. Using service manual specifications and the information in the text, is your crankshaft usable? _____

    Explain: _____

    _____ Completed ☐

41. Squirt a little oil on each main bearing. Then carefully place the crankshaft back into the block.   Completed ☐

42. If this were an actual rebuild, you would have to replace the main bearings and rear main oil seal. Torque the main caps to specifications.   Completed ☐

Installing Piston Rings

43. Now that you have cleaned the piston grooves and fit the rings, install the rings on the pistons. Take your time and follow the directions given in the service manual. See **Figure 4.** Start with your oil rings making sure that you butt the ends of the expander.   Completed ☐

Figure 4. Install the oil ring first. Fit the expander-spacer into its groove. A—Then spiral the bottom of oil rail around the bottom of expander-spacer. B—Spiral rail in groove. C—Double-check that expander-spacer ends are butted.

44. You may now either install your compression rings by hand or with your ring expander. The ring expander is faster and reduces the chance of ring breakage. The rings should be staggered and face the ends of the piston pin.   Completed ☐

>
> **Caution**
> If you must spiral the rings on by hand, be careful not to twist or expand the rings too much. Check that the rings are right-side up. They are sometimes marked with a dot or small circle on the top.

45. Are there any markings on your piston rings? _____

    _____

    _____   Completed ☐

46. How did you space the ring gaps?_____

    _____

    _____   Completed ☐

Installing Pistons

47. Oil the piston, pin, and rings generously. Then, tighten your ring compressor around the piston rings as shown in **Figure 5.** Check that the small indentations on the ring compressor are down near the bottom of the piston. These small lips prevent the compressor from sliding into the cylinder with the piston.   Completed ☐

Wooden hammer handle

Piston head

Ring compressor

Block

Figure 5. Use a wooden or plastic hammer handle to tap the piston and rod assembly into the cylinder block. The rod journal for the piston you are installing should be at BDC. Carefully glide the rod over the crankshaft as you tap the piston into cylinder. (Lisle Tools)

48. Install the bearing into your rod cap and on the rod assembly. Then, oil the outside surface of the bearing. Slide two pieces of rubber gas line hose (or other suitable protector) over the rod bolts to protect the crankshaft.

    Be careful not to let rod bolts hit and nick the crankshaft journals during installation. Sections of rubber hose or soft plastic tubing will protect the crankshaft.   Completed ☐

49. With the piston marking to the front of the engine, install the piston in the cylinder. Tap lightly on the piston head with a plastic or wooden hammer handle. Keep the compressor flat on the block. If the oil ring pops out between the compressor and cylinder, reinstall the compressor and try again.   Completed ☐

> **Caution**
> Do *not* hammer the piston to the bottom of the bore until you can reach under the engine to guide the rod over the crankshaft. If a rod bolt is hammered into the crankshaft, the crankshaft can be damaged.

50. While carefully guiding the connecting rod over the crankshaft journal with the bearing insert in place, tap the piston fully down into the cylinder. Double-check the piston and rod assembly are facing in the proper direction. Reversing the rod can cause bearing and crankshaft damage.   Completed ❑

51. How do you know that the piston and rod assembly is facing in the right direction?

_____

_____

_____ Completed ❑

Checking Bearing Clearance

52. Determine your rod bearing clearance using Plastigage. With the rod cap bearing insert clean and dry, lay a strip of Plastigage across the bearing. Then, install and torque the rod cap to specifications. Remove the cap and compare the flattened Plastigage to the paper scale provided with the Plastigage. Clearance must be within specifications.

    When the bearing clearance gets smaller, the width of the crushed Plastigage gets wider and vice versa. Also note, a 2 on the Plastigage scale would equal a bearing clearance of 0.002 of an inch (1 = 0.001″, 1.5 = 0.015″, etc.).   Completed ❑

53. What is your rod bearing clearance?   Completed ❑

54. Remove the flattened Plastigage from the rod insert carefully. Oil the bearing and crankshaft journal and install the rod cap. The rod identification numbers should be lined up. Torque the rod cap nuts to service manual specifications. Then, make sure the crankshaft will still rotate. Install the other pistons and torque the rods.   Completed ❑

55. What is your rod bolt torque specification? _____ Completed ❑

56. Measure the clearance between the side of one rod and the crankshaft. A feeler gauge is used to measure rod side play. If incorrect, measure rod width and journal width.   Completed ❑

57. What is the rod side clearance for your engine?_____

_____ Completed ❑

58. Clean your work area and return all equipment to the proper storage locations.   Completed ❑

59. Have your instructor sign this job for credit.

Instructor's Signature _____

Cylinder Head Service

Name: _____

Date: _____

Instructor: _____

Score: _____

Objective: Using the tools and equipment listed, you will learn to complete the inspections, tests, and measurements essential to cylinder head service.

Tools and Equipment: Obtain a valve spring compressor, brass hammer, power drill, rotary brush, valve guide cleaner, safety glasses, straightedge, flat feeler gauge, ruler, dial caliper or 0″–1″ (0 mm–25 mm) micrometer, dial indicator, and cylinder head assembly.

Instructions: During this job, you will completely disassemble, inspect, and reassemble an automotive cylinder head. Ask your instructor for any added details for the job (head location, engine make, etc.). Keep all your parts in a container. If you drop any of the small keepers, make sure that you find them. Inform your instructor if you lose anything or run into problems. You should study text Chapters 13, 49, and 51 before working on this job.

Checking Head Warpage

When warped more than specifications, a head must be milled or machined to straighten its deck surface. A warped cylinder head often results after an engine has been overheated. Warpage may cause the head gasket to blow, which may then lead to water, pressure leakage, and overheating.

A small amount of head distortion is acceptable, around 0.004″ (0.076 mm) on any 6″ (152 mm) area of the gasket surface. When machining, always check with service manual specifications for maximum amount of milling permissible.

When an engine is driven with a blown head gasket, serious head and block damage can occur. The surfaces next to the leak can actually be burned away by the hot, high pressure combustion leak. If the burned flaw area is not too deep, the cylinder head gasket surface can be milled at a machine shop.

1. Identify the cylinder head used in the job. List the following information.   Completed ☐

   Engine make: _____   Engine model: _____

2. Check the cylinder head for warpage. Lay a straightedge across its surface at various angles. Try to slide different size feeler gauge blades between the straightedge and the head. The largest blade that will fit between the straightedge and head indicates the amount of warpage. See **Figure 1.**   Completed ☐

Figure 1. Measure your cylinder head for warpage as shown.

3. Record your warpage measurements. Compare your measurements to manual specifications.

   (A) _____   (E) _____

   (B) _____   (F) _____

   (C) _____   (G) _____

   (D) _____   Completed ☐

4. Is there any damage on the deck surface of your cylinder head? _____

   Explain: _____

   _____ Completed ☐

5. What was the largest size of feeler gauge that would fit between the straightedge and the head?

   _____ Completed ☐

6. Explain the condition and resulting action that should be taken with your cylinder head. _____

   _____

   _____ Completed ☐

Head Disassembly

⚠ **Warning**
Make sure you are wearing your safety glasses.

7. Begin cylinder head disassembly. Using a brass hammer, so as not to damage the valve stems, strike the retainers to free them from their keepers. Completed ☐

8. Using a spring compressor, squeeze the valve springs and remove the keepers. One end of the compressor fits on the head of the valve and the other over the spring retainer. Hold on to the compressor firmly and keep it square. If it starts to slip, open and reposition the compressor. Completed ☐

9. After removing the keepers, open the compressor and remove the retainer, spring, and the seal. Place all the organized parts in a container. Do *not* remove the valves from the head at this time. Completed ☐

10. Repeat steps 7 through 9 on the rest of the valves. Do not lose any of the parts. Completed ☐

Check Valve Guides

11. With the springs removed, you should now check the condition of all the valve guides. Pull each valve open about 1/4″ (6.35 mm) and wiggle it sideways and up and down. The valves should *not* be excessively loose in their guides. If a valve wiggles excessively, wear is present in the guide or on the valve stem. Completed ☐

12. Use a dial indicator to measure valve stem-to-guide clearance. Measure with the valve pulled open about 1/4″. Mount the indicator stem against the side of the valve head. Wiggle the valve sideways and read the indicator. Check in different positions and compare to specifications.

    List the clearance for each valve guide in the space provided. Completed ☐

Valve	Clearance	Valve	Clearance
1		5	
2		6	
3		7	
4		8	

Inspect Valves

13. Remove one valve at a time, keeping them in order. Completed ☐

14. Inspect each valve and seat for wear or damage. Look for burn damage to the valves and seats. Also check for worn valve guides, pitted valve faces, and pits in the seats.

    A margin is a flat lip between the valve face and head. If the margin is gone and the valve is relatively sharp, the valve must be replaced. Also, look on the end of the valve stem and check for wear. Completed ☐

15. List the condition of each valve and seat in the chart below. Check the condition of stems, stem tips, margins, and faces. Indicate which are good (no detectable wear), fair (normal amount of correctable wear), and bad (unrepairable wear or damage).   Completed ☐

Valve or seat number	1	2	3	4	5	6	7	8 (4 cyl.)	9	10	11	12 (6 cyl.)
Stem condition												
Margin condition												
Face condition												
Seat condition												

16. Did you find any burned valves? _____

Explain: _____

_____

_____   Completed ☐

17. Did you find any burned or damaged seats? _____

Explain: _____

_____

_____   Completed ☐

18. Did you find any badly worn valve stems? _____

Explain: _____

_____

_____   Completed ☐

Grinding Valves

19. If this were an actual cylinder head reconditioning (valve job), you would grind the valves and seats at this time. If you are using a shop-owned cylinder head, go on to the next step of the job. If this is a real repair, check with your instructor for additional information.   Completed ☐

⚠ **Warning**
Never grind sodium-filled valves. Also, do not attempt to use valve grinding equipment without instructor's permission.

20. Use a ruler, dial caliper, or micrometer to measure the following dimensions.

Intake Valve Head Diameter: _____

Exhaust Valve Head Diameter: _____

Valve Length: _____

Valve Stem Diameter: _____

Valve Margin Width (Maximum): _____

Valve Spring Free Height: _____   Completed ☐

Cleaning Head Assembly

21. If this were an actual repair, you would have to clean the valves and head. A wire brush mounted in a drill will quickly clean gasket material and carbon out of the combustion chambers on cast iron heads. On aluminum heads, a dull scraper and solvent or scuff pads must be used. Wear eye protection.   Completed ☐

22. Check out a drill and rotary brush or scuff pads. Wearing your safety glasses, practice cleaning the combustion chambers and gasket surface.   Completed ☐

23. A valve guide cleaner and drill are needed to clean carbon from inside the valve guides. The drill is used to spin the tool while pulling up and down. Do not let the tool come completely out of the valve guide.

    Using the drill and the valve guide cleaner, practice cleaning the valve guides. Clean the head in a solvent tank and blow it dry.   Completed ☐

Reassemble Head

As you learned in the text, there are two types of valve seals in present use: umbrella and O-ring types. Naturally, the umbrella type is installed *before* the valve spring. However, the O-ring type seal must be installed *after* the spring and retainer.

24. You can now begin cylinder head reassembly. Oil the valve stems and install the valves into their original guides.   Completed ☐

Caution
If you install an O-ring seal before compressing the spring over the valve, the seal may be cut and damaged. The engine may smoke and burn oil.

25. Explain how you installed your valve stem oil seals. _____

    _____

    _____

    _____

    _____

    _____   Completed ☐

26. Reassemble the rest of your cylinder head. To seat the keepers in their retainers, tap the ends of the valve stems with a brass hammer. A steel hammer can damage the stems.   Completed ☐

Check for Valve Leakage

27. The head can be tested for compression leaks by pouring water or clean parts solvent into each of the ports. Place the head with the ports facing up and pour the water or solvent into the ports. If fluid leaks out around the head of any of the valves, the valve or seat must be reground or lapped. This operation can save you the unpleasant task of having to remove the head from the engine to repeat the valve job.   Completed ☐

28. Clean your work area and return all equipment to the proper storage locations.   Completed ☐

29. Have your instructor sign this sheet for credit.

Instructor's Signature _____

Universal Joint, CV-Joint Service

Name: _____

Date: _____

Instructor: _____

Score: _____

Objective: Using the listed tools and equipment, you will learn to properly disassemble, inspect, and assemble the parts of a propeller shaft universal joint and a ball-type CV-joint.

Tools and Equipment: You will need a basic set of hand wrenches, large brass or ball peen hammer, safety glasses, large screwdriver, pin punch, needle nose pliers or snap ring pliers, one small and one large socket, large driving punch, vise, and two drive shafts or two shop vehicles equipped with universal and CV-joints.

Instructions: Ask your instructor for the location of the drive shafts and joint assemblies to be used. It may be located in or out of the automobile. If you are removing the drive shafts from a vehicle, you may need more than one class period to complete this job. You should review Chapters 60 and 64 in your text before starting this job.

Review of Parts

A faulty propeller shaft universal or joint can cause a wide range of problems. It may produce a high pitch chirping sound similar to the sound made by small birds. If highly worn, a bad U-joint can also cause a metallic crunching or grinding sound which resembles the sound of popcorn popping.

A faulty constant velocity (CV) joint will make a grinding noise during turns. If highly worn, it will make this noise all the time, especially during acceleration. A faulty joint will also be a source of vibration during acceleration. Upon total failure, a universal or constant velocity joint may break and separate from the remainder of the drive train. As you can see, proper diagnosis, inspection, and repair of universal and CV-joints is very important.

The first step is to identify the type of joint you are dealing with. If you are dealing with universal joints, begin with step 1. If your vehicle has CV-joints, go to step 14. Check the service manual if you have any questions.

Remove Drive Shaft

1. If your propeller shaft is installed in a car, it is a very good idea to mark the mating surfaces of the differential yoke and drive shaft yoke. This will allow drive shaft reassembly in exact alignment and prevent possible imbalance and vibration.

   Completed ❏

2. Remove the bolts holding the rear joint. Some vehicles use two U-bolts while others have a flange, which connects to the differential yoke.

   Completed ❏

3. Pry the drive shaft away from its yoke and slide the drive shaft out of the car. Be careful not to scrape the transmission slip joint on the ground or drop the roller ends.

   Completed ❏

⚠ **Caution**
If you must clamp the drive shaft in a vise, make sure that you do not dent or bend the drive shaft. Shaft imbalance and vibration may occur when the shaft is returned to service.

Universal Joint Service

4. Lay your propeller shaft assembly on the back of a vise. Using a large punch or shaft and hammer, tap each roller inward to free up the locking rings. They may be located either on the inside or outside of the yoke.

   Completed ❏

5. Where are your lock rings located?_____

   Completed ❏

6. Place the drive shaft in the vise. Using the appropriate tools (pin punch, needle nose pliers, small screwdrivers, or snap ring pliers), remove your snap rings from the joint.

   Completed ❏

7. Push the rollers and cross out of the yokes. This operation is shown in **Figure 1.** Make sure the small socket is smaller than the roller and the larger socket is large enough to accept the full roller. If it is stuck, you may need to strike the tightened vise with the hammer to free the rollers.   Completed ☐

Tech Tip

Since they will be reused, keep your rollers organized so they can be replaced in the same location in the yoke. Also, do not drop or lose the needle bearings.

Figure 1. Check that the sockets are the correct sizes. Then press out the rollers.

8. Explain the condition of your rollers and cross journals. _____

_____

_____

_____

_____   Completed ☐

9. Reassemble your universal joint. Being careful not to knock any of the needle bearings loose, force the rollers into the yoke until flush, **Figure 2.** Then, force the rollers inward just far enough for snap ring installation.   Completed ☐

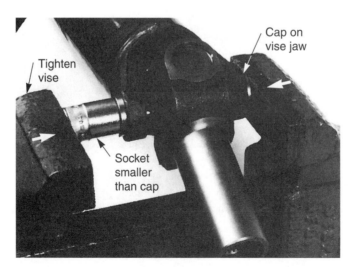

Figure 2. Use a vise to force the rollers inward until flush with the yoke lug surface. Do not tighten beyond this point.

> ⚠ **Caution**
> If you find it difficult to drive the rollers completely into position (clearing snap ring grooves), one of your needle bearings has probably fallen sideways in the roller. If so, remove the rollers and start over. Do not try to force the roller in with excessive force or damage will occur.

10. Refit your snap rings into their grooves. Needle nose pliers, snap ring pliers, etc. may be required.   Completed ❏

11. After installing your rollers and snap rings, center your rollers in the yoke by tapping on them until the joint swivels freely.   Completed ❏

12. If applicable, reinstall your drive shaft assembly. Check that the slip joint is perfectly clean and coated with a thin layer of grease. Check that both rollers are fitted inside their locating tangs.   Completed ❏

13. Have your instructor check your work and sign this sheet.

Instructor's Signature _____

Constant Velocity (CV) Joint Service

14. Check out the shop-owned CV axle with a ball-type joint.   Completed ❏

15. What make and model vehicle is the CV axle from? _____   Completed ❏

16. Remove the boot straps from the CV-joint.   Completed ❏

17. Slide the boot back and remove the C-clips or snap rings that hold the CV-joint together, **Figure 3.**   Completed ❏

18. Separate the joint. Refer to the service manual instructions, if needed. Light taps from a brass hammer may be needed.   Completed ❏

19. Remove the balls from the cage. This is done by pivoting the joint to free each ball.   Completed ❏

Figure 3. Removing a snap ring so the joint may be disassembled.

20. While wearing rubber gloves and eye protection, clean the CV-joint parts in a cold solvent tank or parts washer.   Completed ❏

21. Inspect the parts of the joint (bearings, housings, snap rings, ring grooves) for signs of wear. Look for pitting, marring, and other surface imperfections.   Completed ❏

22. Describe the condition of the CV-joint.

_____

_____

_____

_____

_____   Completed ❏

23. If this were an actual CV-joint rebuild, you would install a CV-joint repair kit containing new parts. Since this is an exercise, simply reinstall the old joint.   Completed ☐

24. How many ball bearings are used in this joint? _____ Completed ☐

25. Grease the bearing race, cage, and bearings with the appropriate grease.   Completed ☐

26. Reinstall the bearings and snap-rings in reverse order of removal.   Completed ☐

27. Fill the boot with grease. Then, reinstall the boot straps, **Figure 4.**   Completed ☐

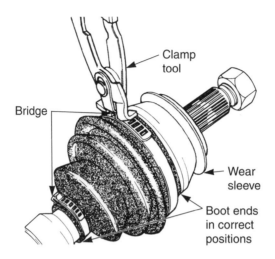

Figure 4. Installing and restraining boot straps with a special strap (band) and pinch tools.

28. Clean and return all of the tools to their proper storage location.   Completed ☐

29. Have your instructor check your work and sign this sheet.

Instructor's Signature _____

Tire Repair and Replacement

Name: _____

Date: _____

Instructor: _____

Score: _____

Objective: Given an old tire, a wheel, and the proper tools, you will learn to service and repair a wheel and tire assembly.

Tools and Equipment: You will need a wheel and tire assembly (tubeless), tire changer, valve core tool, tire plugging tool kit, wheel weight pliers, small steel ruler or tread depth gauge, soapy water, safety glasses, tire pressure gauge, diagonal cutting pliers, shop rags or paper towels, and steel wool.

Instructions: Ask your instructor for the tire and wheel assembly and all the tools needed to complete this job. You should have seen a demonstration on the safe and proper use of your shop's tire changer. Be sure to wear safety glasses, especially while inflating the tire.

Reading Tire Sidewall Information

1. Check out the tools, equipment, and wheel and tire assembly to be used for the job.

2. From the information printed on the sidewall of the tire, fill in the following data.

Brand name: _____

Tire size: _____

Tread plies: _____

Sidewall plies: _____

Aspect ratio: _____

Tread wear number: _____

Traction rating: _____

Temperature resistance rating: _____

Speed rating: _____

Construction type: _____

Load index: _____

Maximum inflation pressure: _____

Maximum load rating: _____

DOT serial number: _____

Checking Tire Wear

Tire wear patterns are indicators of suspension, inflation, alignment, and driving problems. Compare your tire's wear pattern to those shown in **Figure 1.**

Figure 1. Tire wear patterns will help you identify suspension, inflation, and alignment problems. (Chrysler)

3. What type of wear pattern does your tire have? _____

_____ Completed ☐

4. What is the most likely cause for the wear pattern? _____

_____ Completed ☐

5. Can you find any tire damage other than wear (cuts, cracks, etc.)? If so, describe the damage found.

_____

_____

_____ Completed ❑

6. As a rule of thumb, a tire is unsafe and should be replaced if the tread is less than 1/16″ (1.59 mm) deep at any point. Use a depth gauge or a steel rule to measure the tread depth at its deepest and shallowest points.

What is the tread depth at the shallowest point?_____

_____ Completed ❑

What is the tread depth at the deepest point? _____

_____ Completed ❑

Describe the tread condition of the tire. _____

_____

_____ Completed ❑

Removing a Tire

7. While wearing safety glasses, remove the valve stem core with your core tool. This will let the air out of the tire. Also, remove any wheel weights with your wheel weight pliers. Completed ❑

8. Use the tire changer to break, or push, the tire bead away from the wheel flange. Follow the specific instructions provided with the tire changer. Keep your fingers out of the way and follow all safety rules. If you are using a power tire changer, do *not* catch the bead breaker on the edge of the wheel. It can bend a steel wheel or break an alloy wheel. Completed ❑

9. Rub soapy water (or specified lubricant) on the tire bead and the wheel flange. This will ease tire removal. Then, use the proper end of the large steel bar of your tire changer to remove the tire from the wheel. Use one hand to *hold the tire down* into the drop center of the wheel while prying off the opposite side of the tire. Completed ❑

Caution
Be careful not to cut or split the tire bead when removing the tire. If you run into difficulty, ask your instructor for help.

10. After removing the tire from the wheel, inspect the inside of the tire for splits, cracks, punctures, patches, or repairs. List any problems found.

_____

_____

_____ Completed ❑

Repairing a Punctured Tire

In the past, tires were repaired by inserting a rubber plug in the puncture without removing the tire from the wheel. This practice is no longer acceptable. Tires must be repaired from the *inside* only. The following procedure is for repairing a puncture with a plug and a patch. If available, a one-piece head-type plug can be used. This type of plug eliminates the need for a separate patch. Follow the manufacturer's instructions.

11. After removing the tire from the wheel, remove the puncturing object and note the angle of penetration. Completed ❑

12. From the inside of the tire, fill the puncture with a plug or a liquid sealer. After filling the hole, cut off the plug (if used) slightly above the tire's inside surface. Completed ❑

13. Scuff the inside surface of the tire well beyond the repair area. Clean the scuffed area thoroughly.   Completed ❑

14. Apply cement to the scuffed area and place a patch over the damaged area. Use a stitcher to help bond   Completed ❑
the patch to the inner surface of the tire. See **Figure 2.**

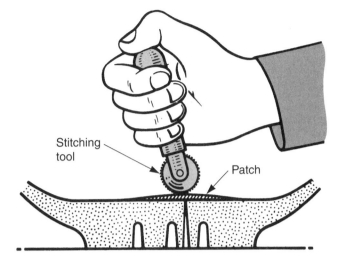

Figure 2. Use the stitcher tool to firmly roll the patch into contact with the cement. Roll over the entire surface of the patch.

Mounting a Tire

15. Clean the outer pressure sealing edge of the wheel as needed. Remove dirt with a rag or paper towel. If
the sealing edge is rusted or corroded, clean it with steel wool.   Completed ❑

16. Check the condition of the valve stem. Bend it sideways and look for weather cracks or splits. If this
were an actual repair, you would replace a cracked or weathered valve stem. Unless instructed to do so,
do not remove the valve stem.

Describe the condition of your valve stem._____

_____

_____   Completed ❑

17. To remount the tire, wipe soapy water on the tire bead and the wheel flange. Following the manufacturer's instructions, use the tire changer to pry the tire back on the wheel. While installing the tire, push
the tire bead opposite the pry bar down into the drop center of the wheel. If this is not done, the tire will
not go on the rim.   Completed ❑

18. With the tire on the rim, pull up on the tire while twisting it. The upper tire bead should catch and hold
on the upper safety ridge of the rim.   Completed ❑

19. Inject air into the tire. If you can hear air rushing out of the tire, push *in* lightly on the leaking part of
the tire. When the tire begins to take air, do not overinflate it and loosen the wheel holddown cone. Be
careful not to get your fingers caught between the tire and the wheel. If your tire will not take air and
expand, continue with step 20. If your tire holds air, skip to step 21.   Completed ❑

20. If your tire will *not* hold enough air to expand and seal on the wheel, you may need to use a bead
expander. Clamp the expander around the outside of the tire. This will push the tire bead against the
wheel flange. Again inject air into the tire.   Completed ❑

   Warning
As soon as the tire begins to expand, release the bead expander. If not released immediately, the expander
can break and fly off the tire with unbelievable force.

21. While inflating the tire, lean away from the tire to prevent possible injury. The tire could blow out. Do not inflate the tire to over 40–50 psi. Check that the bead ridge on the sidewall is even or true with the wheel. If it is not, remount the tire on the wheel.   Completed ☐

22. After the bead has popped over the safety ridges, screw in the valve core and snug it up.   Completed ☐

Checking Tire Pressure

23. Use your pressure gauge to check tire pressure. The tire pressure should be a few pounds under the maximum pressure rating labeled on the sidewall of the tire. As a tire is operated, it can heat up. This may cause the pressure in the tire to increase.   Completed ☐

24. What is the inflation pressure for your tire? _____

_____   Completed ☐

25. To check for leaks, pour water over the tire beads, puncture repair, and valve stem. Watch for bubbles. Air bubbles indicate a leak.

Is your tire holding air? _____   Completed ☐

26. Clean your work area and return all equipment to the proper storage locations.   Completed ☐

27. Have your instructor sign this sheet for credit.

Instructor's Signature _____

Wheel Bearing Service

Name: _____

Date: _____

Instructor: _____

Score: _____

Objective: Given the proper tools and equipment, you will learn to service both open and sealed wheel bearings.

Tools and Equipment: You will need a basic set of hand tools, torque wrenches, grease cap pliers, parts cleaning tank, wheel bearing grease, a stool creeper, lug wrench, air nozzle, cotter pins, ruler, shop rags, seal driver, and a hydraulic press with appropriate adapters.

Instructions: Wheel bearings must support the weight of the vehicle while spinning for tens of thousands of miles. Worn bearings can cause many problems including loose wheels, handling problems, erratic brake application, and ultimately, the loss of a wheel while driving.

Ask your instructor which vehicles and parts will be used during this job. You should have access to a vehicle with tapered roller bearings on the front or rear wheels. You will also need a steering knuckle with a pressed-in sealed bearing. The first part of the job is for a serviceable bearing that can be disassembled. The second section summarizes how to service a sealed bearing. Depending on your class situation, your instructor may choose to assign only one part of this job.

Review of Parts

1. Examine your test vehicle and fill in the following service information. Use a service manual if necessary.

   Make: _____

   Model: _____

   Year: _____

   VIN: _____

   Engine size: _____

   Transmission type: _____   Completed ☐

2. Look on the inside of the front wheel to determine whether your hub uses drum or disc brakes.

   What type of brakes are used? _____   Completed ☐

Remove Wheel and Brakes

3. Loosen the wheel lug nuts one half turn but *do not* remove them all the way. Then, raise and secure the car on jack stands. Block the wheels so that the car cannot roll off the stands.   Completed ☐

4. Before removing the wheel and tire, mark one of the lug studs and the wheel with chalk or crayon. This will let you install the wheel exactly as it was removed. If the wheel and tire were balanced on the car, it could be thrown out of balance if installed in a different position. Remove the lug nuts, then the tire and wheel from the vehicle.   Completed ☐

Remove Hub

Whenever a tire is removed, you should inspect the brake linings for wear. As a general rule, brake linings should be at least 1/8″ (3.18 mm) thick at their thinnest point. If the drum brakes use tapered roller bearings, you may need to remove the bearings before you can inspect the brakes.

5. What is the minimum measured thickness of your brake linings? _____   Completed ☐

6. Are your linings worn enough to need replacement? _____

   Explain: _____

   _____

   _____   Completed ☐

7. If you have disc brakes, you must remove the brake caliper before removing the rotor and hub. The caliper is usually fastened to the spindle with two or three bolts.   Completed ☐

> **⚠ Warning**
> Brake lining dust contains asbestos, which is a powerful cancer causing substance. Avoid using air to blow the asbestos dust off the brake parts. Instead, use a special vacuum or solvent machine if available. In any case, wear a filter mask to prevent the dust from entering your lungs. Use a rag to wipe the spindle clean.

Open bearings must be periodically serviced by disassembling, cleaning, and repacking with new grease. Sealed bearings must be replaced when worn and noisy. If you are servicing tapered roller bearings, proceed with step 8. If you are servicing a sealed bearing, go to step 24.

Tapered Roller Bearing Service

> **📄 Note**
> If you disassemble *both* front wheel bearing assemblies, keep your right and left side bearings separated. Wheel bearings are matched to their race. Placing a bearing in a different race can cause problems.

8. Using dust cap pliers or channel locks, remove the dust cap. Then use diagonal cutters to straighten and remove the cotter pin. Place all the parts into the bottom of the stool creeper, parts tray, can, or wheel cover.   Completed ☐

9. Unscrew and remove the adjusting nut and wiggle the rotor or drum sideways. This will make the safety washer and outer bearing pop out for removal.   Completed ☐

10. Thread the adjusting nut onto the end of the spindle without the safety washer and outer bearing. Slide the rotor or drum assembly briskly off the spindle while placing a slight downward pressure. This is an extremely fast and efficient method of removing the inner grease seal and bearing.   Completed ☐

> **◇ Caution**
> Some front rotors have toothed reluctor wheels for the anti-lock brake (ABS) system cast to the back. Exercise care when handling and servicing these rotors as damage to these wheels can affect ABS operation.

11. Submerse and clean your bearings in part cleaning solvent. Blow them dry with compressed air, but *do not* allow them to spin. If spun, a wheel bearing can explode with tremendous force. Remember to wear eye protection.   Completed ☐

12. Inspect your bearings and race for faults. Look at them closely. Rotate and inspect each bearing roller. Run your finger over the surface of the bearing races as you check for imperfections. The slightest amount of roughness can cause bearing noise and failure.   Completed ☐

13. Can you detect any problem with your bearings or races? _____

   Explain: _____

   _____

   _____   Completed ☐

14. Pack your wheel bearings with grease. Work grease into the bearing rollers with your fingers. Then, lay them on a clean rag or paper towel.   Completed ☐

15. Inspect the inner lip of the grease seal for splits or tears. To check the seal for wear, slide it over the enlarged portion of the spindle. The seal should fit snugly over the spindle. During an actual repair, you would normally replace a grease seal.   Completed ☐

16. Can you find any problem with your grease seal? _____

    Explain: _____

    _____ Completed ☐

17. If your instructor gives the okay, wipe out the inside of the hub to remove all the old grease. Coat the inside of the rotor or drum hub with new grease to a depth even with the bearing races. *Do not* overfill the hub or upon operation, the heat and expansion will force the grease out of the hub and possibly onto the brake linings. Completed ☐

18. Lay the greased inner bearing onto its race and use, if available, a seal driver and a ball peen hammer to install the inner grease seal. Lightly tap the seal squarely into place. Make sure you *do not* dent or bend the seal housing. Completed ☐

19. Slide the rotor or drum assembly onto the spindle. Install the outer bearing, safety washer, and adjusting nut. Be careful not to damage the grease seal on the threads of the spindle. Completed ☐

20. Following the procedure in **Figure 1,** adjust your wheel bearings. A torque wrench and socket will be needed to properly set the bearings. Completed ☐

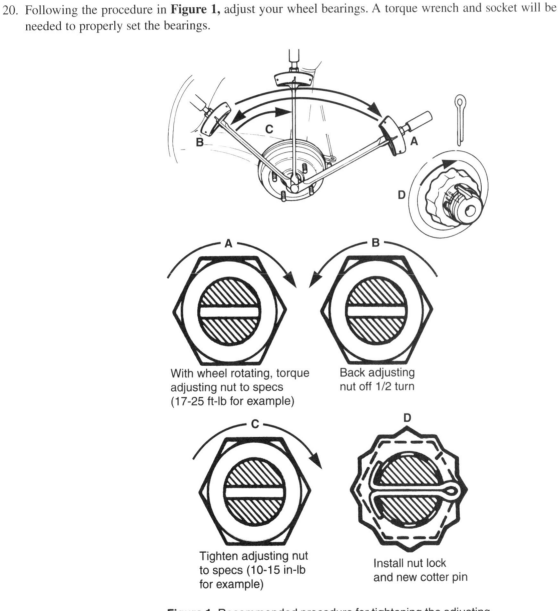

With wheel rotating, torque adjusting nut to specs (17-25 ft-lb for example)

Back adjusting nut off 1/2 turn

Tighten adjusting nut to specs (10-15 in-lb for example)

Install nut lock and new cotter pin

Figure 1. Recommended procedure for tightening the adjusting nut on a roller bearing assembly. A—Torque the nut to specifications. Rotate the hub. B—Back off the adjusting nut one-half turn. C—Tighten the adjusting nut to specifications (about one foot-pound or less). D—Install a new cotter pin.

21. Install a new cotter pin and bend it around the outside of the adjusting nut.   Completed ☐

22. Always double-check the installation of the cotter pin. If the cotter pin is left out or installed improperly, the front wheel of the car may fall off. Being careful not to dent it, tap the dust cap into the hub with a ball peen hammer. If you dent the cap, straighten it by hammering on the inside of the cap with a blunt driver and a hammer.   Completed ☐

23. What was the final torque value of your bearing adjusting nut before loosening? _____ Completed ☐

Sealed Bearing Service

Tech Tip
Since procedures for replacing sealed bearings vary between different makes and models, you will need to look up the correct procedures in a service manual.

24. Obtain a steering knuckle with a pressed-in sealed bearing from your instructor. Try not to remove a sealed bearing from a vehicle as knuckle removal would require front end alignment when reinstalled. Some vehicles have sealed front bearings and others sealed rear bearings.   Completed ☐

Caution
Some sealed wheel bearings contain speed sensors for the vehicle's anti-lock brake (ABS) system. Handle these connectors with care as damaging them will require bearing replacement.

25. Remove any dust covers or snap rings in the steering knuckle.   Completed ☐

26. In some cases, the sealed bearing and hub is bolted to the knuckle. However, in most cases, you will have to press the bearing from the knuckle. If the bearing is bolted to the knuckle, using the correct tools, unbolt the bearing and hub from the knuckle.   Completed ☐

27. What type of tools did you need to unbolt the bearing? _____

    _____

    _____   Completed ☐

28. Rebolt the bearing and hub to the knuckle.   Completed ☐

29. If the bearing must be pressed out, start by placing the knuckle in an appropriate press.   Completed ☐

30. Using the proper adapters, press the bearing out of the steering knuckle. See **Figure 2.** Take care to *not* press out the hub if it is still in the bearing.   Completed ☐

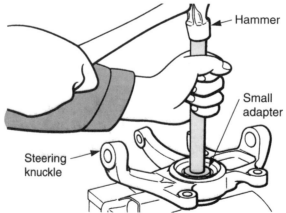

Figure 2. Remove the bearing from the steering knuckle with an arbor press and a special bearing adapter tool.

31. Clean the steering knuckle and study it for cracks and wear. Does the knuckle show signs of wear or damage? _____

    Explain: _____

    _____

    _____   Completed ☐

32. Inspect all parts removed from the steering knuckle. Replace worn or dented dust covers and wear plates.   Completed ☐

33. Position the bearing assembly on the steering knuckle.   Completed ☐

34. Using the proper adapters, press the bearing into the steering knuckle.   Completed ☐

35. Install snap rings or dust covers in the correct positions in the steering knuckle.   Completed ☐

36. In your own words, summarize the major steps for replacing the sealed bearings on this vehicle.

    _____

    _____

    _____

    _____

    _____   Completed ☐

37. Do you have to press out the CV-axle to replace the wheel bearing? _____

    Explain: _____

    _____   Completed ☐

38. According to the flat rate manual in your shop, how much time should it take to replace the sealed bearings?

    _____   Completed ☐

39. List any special tools needed to service the sealed bearings. _____

    _____

    _____

    _____   Completed ☐

Torquing Lug Nuts

40. Reinstall the brake caliper, if removed, and tighten to specifications. If applicable, line up your marks and install your wheel and tire. The tapered edge of the lug nuts should face the wheel. This centers the wheel on the hub.   Completed ☐

41. Snug the lug nuts with your lug wrench and lower the car to the ground using the reverse order used when raising the car.   Completed ☐

Tightening the Lug Nuts to Specifications

42. Proper lug nut torque is very critical, especially on some late-model cars using disc brakes.

    Overtightened lug nuts can cause the rotors to warp. Then, the car will vibrate when the brakes are applied. Use a torque wrench or torque sticks. Torque the lug nuts in a crisscross pattern. Go over all of the lug nuts two or three times to double-check their torque.   Completed ☐

43. How tight did you or would you torque your lug nuts? _____

_____ Completed ☐

44. Clean your work area and return all equipment to the proper storage locations.   Completed ☐

45. Have your instructor initial this sheet for credit.

Instructor's Signature _____

Disc Brake Service

Name: _____

Date: _____

Instructor: _____

Score: _____

Objective: Given the proper tools and equipment, you will learn to service an automotive disc brake assembly.

Tools and Equipment: Check out a basic set of hand wrenches, ruler or dial caliper, large C-clamp, two large screwdrivers, dial indicator, and safety glasses. If your instructor wants you to rebuild the caliper, you will also need an air nozzle, brake fluid, drill, cylinder hone, and, possibly, a special seal installation tool. Make sure you have safety glasses and gloves to keep brake dust and fluid off your hands.

Instructions: Ask your instructor whether or not you are to rebuild the caliper and also ask for the location of the disc brake unit to be serviced. If you have problems, ask for help. You should have studied Chapters 71–73 in your text before starting this job.

Disc Brake Disassembly

1. If the caliper is mounted on a vehicle, secure the vehicle on jack stands and remove the wheels. Use a large screwdriver or C-clamp to push the caliper piston back into its bore, **Figure 1.**   Completed ☐

End of screw
against
outboard pad

C-clamp

Caliper

End of clamp
against caliper

Figure 1. Use a C-clamp or large screwdriver to push the piston into its caliper bore.

2. Unscrew the caliper locating pins, stabilizer bolts, or bolts so the caliper can be removed. Since bolt locations and procedures vary, inspect the construction of the unit and decide exactly which fastener must be removed to free the caliper.   Completed ☐

3. How many bolts held the caliper in place? _____   Completed ☐

4. Lay the caliper on the upper control arm or a tie-rod. If necessary, hang the caliper from the suspension using a piece of wire. The weight of the caliper pulling on the rubber brake hose could damage the hose.   Completed ☐

5. How did you support the caliper? _____

_____

_____

_____   Completed ☐

Caution
Exercise care when working around anti-lock brake (ABS) wheel speed sensors. The sensors and trigger wheels can be easily damaged.

6. Remove the brake pads, retaining clips, anti-rattle clips, etc. If anti-rattle clips are used on the pads, note how the clips are installed.   Completed ☐

7. Does your brake assembly use anti-rattle clips? _____   Completed ☐

8. How do they fit into place? _____

_____

_____

_____

_____   Completed ☐

Disc Brake Inspection

9. Inspect the condition of all the parts to be reused (clips, bolts, retainers). Look for wear, breakage, distortion, etc. Also, look around the edge of the caliper piston. If leaking, the caliper must be rebuilt or replaced. **Figure 2** shows some common troubles.   Completed ☐

10. Describe the condition of your rotor.

_____

_____

_____   Completed ☐

11. Are your brake pad linings reusable? _____

Explain: _____

_____

_____

_____

_____   Completed ☐

Figure 2. Check for disc brake problems. A—Check for excessive pad lining wear. The wear indicator clip will produce a loud squeal when the linings wear enough to let the clip touch the rotor. B—Check rotor for heat checking, cracks, and deep scoring. C—Also check for leaking piston seals and missing clips. (Cadillac and FMC)

12. Measure rotor thickness with a micrometer or dial caliper. If a rotor is worn too thin, it must be replaced, **Figure 3.**

Completed ☐

Figure 3. A—Measuring disc runout using a dial indicator. B—An outside micrometer will detect any thickness variations. If the readings are not the same or within specifications at different locations around the disc, turn or replace disc. (EIS)

13. What is the minimum and maximum thickness of your rotor?_____

_____   Completed ☐

14. Is this thickness within specifications? _____

Explain: _____

_____   Completed ☐

Rebuilding Caliper

If you have your instructor's approval, you may disassemble and rebuild the caliper. If not approved, skip over, but read, steps 15 through 23 of this Job.

15. Disconnect the brake hose at the caliper, not at the steel brake line. Be careful not to lose the special sealing flat washer on the end of the hose fitting. Drain the fluid from the caliper.

Completed ☐

16. As in **Figure 4A,** position rags or a small block of wood inside the caliper. Then, *keeping your hands out of the way,* slowly apply air pressure to the inside of the cylinder.

Completed ☐

⚠️ **Warning:**
Too much air pressure can cause piston to shoot out of the caliper with tremendous force.

17. If the piston is frozen and will *not* come out with moderate air pressure, tap on the piston lightly with a soft hammer or mallet and try again. In extreme cases, you can reinstall the caliper and try to force the piston out with brake system pressure.

Completed ☐

18. Remove the dust boot and piston seal from the caliper. During a real repair, these parts would always be replaced. See **Figure 4B.**

Completed ☐

Figure 4. A—Air or brake system pressure can be used to push the piston out of the caliper. B—Screwdriver and hook type tool will allow boot and seal removal.

19. Inspect the condition of the caliper cylinder bore. Check it for scratches, pits, and scoring. Crocus cloth may be used to clean up minor imperfections (gumming, discoloration, etc.). You may also need to hone the cylinder. If excessive honing is required, the caliper must be replaced. After honing, clean the cylinder.

Completed ☐

20. Using a ruler or dial caliper, estimate the diameter of the caliper cylinder.

Caliper cylinder bore diameter. _____

Completed ☐

21. Lubricate the caliper bore, piston, and seal with clean brake fluid. Then, fit the seal into its groove in the cylinder. If the caliper is a training aid, reuse the seal and boot.

Completed ☐

22. Slide the piston into place. Then, hold the piston and boot over the bore and use your fingers to work the boot bead into place, **Figure 5.** A driving tool may be needed.

Depending upon the type of brake system, you may need to change your procedures slightly. If you are having problems, ask your instructor for help or refer to a service manual.

Completed ☐

Figure 5. Slide the piston into place. The boot should seal in the caliper and in a groove in the piston.

23. Push the piston fully into place. You may need to use a C-clamp.

Completed ☐

Caution
Be careful not to cock the piston sideways during installation or it may be damaged.

Bleeding Brakes

24. If applicable, bleed the system of air as described in the service manual or textbook. With the system pressurized or with someone pumping the brake pedal, open the bleeder screw until all the air bubbles are removed from the system. The jar and rubber hose will help prevent a mess on the floor and reentry of air.

Completed ☐

25. Fill the master cylinder with fluid and check that you have a solid brake pedal.

Completed ☐

26. Clean your work area and return all equipment to the proper storage locations.

Completed ☐

27. Have your instructor check your work and sign this job for credit.

Instructor's Signature _____

Drum Brake Service

Name: _____

Date: _____

Instructor: _____

Score: _____

Objective: Given the proper tools and equipment, you will learn to service a typical drum brake assembly.

Tools and Equipment: Safety glasses, goggles, plastic or cloth gloves, brake vacuum machine, brake retracting spring tool, hold-down spring tool, some high temperature grease, brake adjusting spoon, a ruler, small screwdriver, a brake adjusting gauge, a lug wrench, drill, brake fluid, wheel cylinder hone, and a shop vehicle.

Instructions: Ask your instructor whether or not you will do the wheel cylinder rebuilding portion of the job. Also, inquire about the location of the brake assembly. Before starting this job, make sure you have read Chapters 71–73 in the textbook. If class time is running out, place all of the parts in a can or tray so they will not be lost.

Drum Brake Disassembly

1. Remove the wheel, tire, and brake drum. If the drum will not come off, you may need to back up the star wheel, **Figure 1.** The adjustment may be too tight or the drum may be grooved. Some brake drums contain wheel bearings, which may need to be removed along with the drum.

   A stuck rear brake can also be caused by rust between the axle flange and the drum. To free a rusted drum, lightly tap the drum with a hammer. Only strike the drum on the edge nearest you. The inner edge is not supported and will break easily.

   Completed ☐

Figure 1. Backing off the star wheel will sometimes allow drum removal. A—Using a hole in the backing plate, hold the lever and turn the star wheel as shown. B—Turning star wheel using an access hole in the drum. (Bendix)

2. Did you have to back off the brake adjustment to remove the drum? _____

   Explain: _____

   _____

   _____ Completed ☐

3. Using a closed vacuum or solvent wash system, clean the rear brake assembly. If solvent is used, allow the brake assembly to air-dry.

   Completed ☐

   Warning:
   Never blow off brake parts with compressed air. Brake lining dust may contain asbestos—a cancer causing agent.

4. Inspect how all the brake parts fit together, especially the automatic adjuster mechanism and springs. A few minutes here can save a lot of time later. If you were performing an actual brake job, it is recommended that you take apart one side at a time. This way, you can look at the other brake assembly if you do not remember where a particular part belongs.   Completed ☐

5. How many springs are on your brake assembly? _____   Completed ☐

6. Measure the dimensions of the following components.   Completed ☐

   Primary lining length: _____   Lining width:_____

   Secondary lining length: _____   Lining thickness: _____

7. Using your brake spring tool, **Figure 2,** remove the upper (primary and secondary) return springs, adjusting cable or lever, etc. Keep the front and rear springs and other parts separate to simplify reassembly.   Completed ☐

📄 **Note**
The springs may have different tensions, even though their physical appearance is similar. Always replace the brake springs in the exact same location.

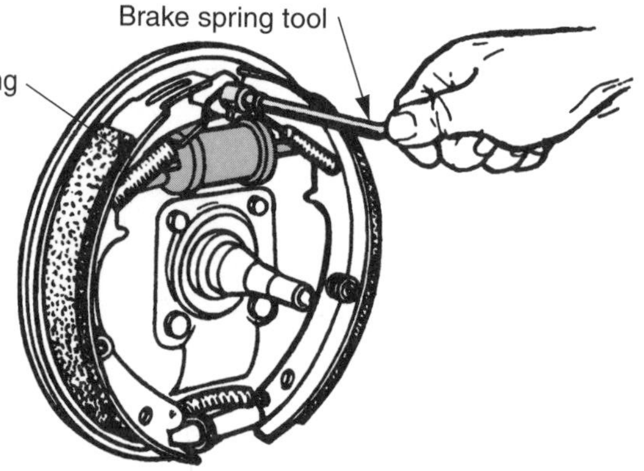

Figure 2. Use a spring tool to force the retracting springs off the anchor.

8. Remove the hold-down springs with your hold-down spring tool or with pliers. See **Figure 3.** To remove the hold-down springs, you must use one finger to hold the pin tight against the inside or rear of the backing plate.   Completed ☐

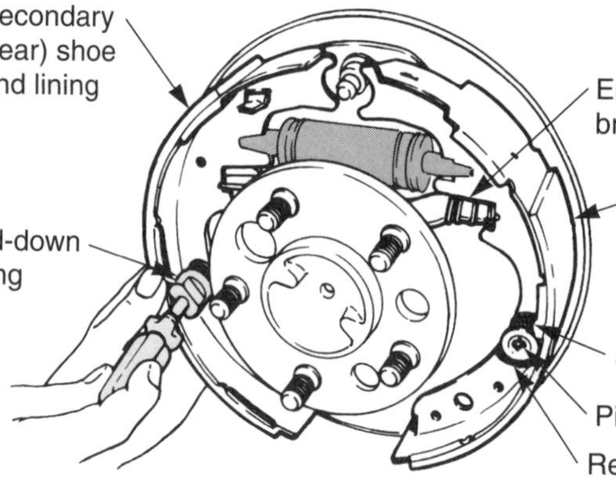

Figure 3. Push in and turn the tool to remove the hold-down springs. Use your finger to hold the pin on the rear of the backing plate.

9. The brake shoes, star wheel, and lower return springs can now be removed as one unit.   Completed ☐

10. If you used solvent to wash the brake assembly, use a rag to clean off any remaining fluid and dust from the backing plate.   Completed ☐

Inspect Brake Parts

11. Check all components for damage (stretched springs, bent parts, frayed cables, etc.). Look for the problems shown in **Figure 4.**   Completed ☐

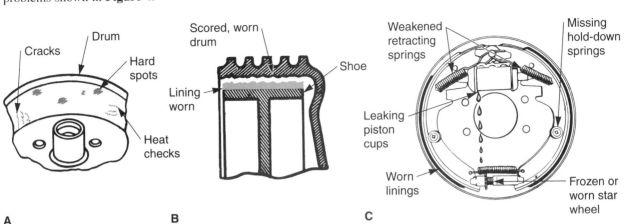

A   B   C

Figure 4. Drum brake problems. A—Check drum for cracks, heat checks, and hard spots. B—A badly scored drum must be machined. If worn too much, it must be replaced. C—Check for leaking wheel cylinder, worn linings, and missing or damaged parts. (Bendix and FMC)

12. Are the shoes too worn to be reused? _____

   Explain: _____

   _____

   _____   Completed ☐

13. Is the drum in good condition? _____

   Explain: _____

   _____

   _____   Completed ☐

14. Is any wheel cylinder leakage present? _____

   Explain: _____

   _____

   _____   Completed ☐

15. Are the teeth on the star wheel or ratchet worn? _____

   Explain: _____

   _____   Completed ☐

16. Apply a light coat of high-temperature grease on the star wheel threads and the raised pads on the backing plate. This will help reduce excessive friction, squeaks, and the possibility of an inoperable automatic brake adjusting mechanism.   Completed ☐

Rebuilding Wheel Cylinder

17. If your instructor has given you permission, remove and rebuild the wheel cylinder. After disassembly, check the inside of the cylinder surface for wear, pits, scratches, and scoring. The slightest scratch or score may require cylinder replacement. As described in the text, hone the cylinder with your drill and a small hone. Be extremely careful not to pull the hone too far out of the cylinder. The hone could break.   Completed ☐

18. After honing, clean the cylinder with denatured alcohol or brake fluid and wipe dry. Wear your goggles.   Completed ☐

19. What is your wheel cylinder cup size? _____ 　　　　　Completed ☐

20. Is the inside of the wheel cylinder in good condition? _____

    Explain: _____

    _____

    _____ 　Completed ☐

21. Reassemble the wheel cylinder. Then, reinstall the cylinder on the backing plate. During a real repair, you would always use new wheel cylinder cups and boots. 　　Completed ☐

Reassembling Brake Parts

22. Place the shoes into position on the backing plate and secure them with their hold-down springs. Check that the smaller primary lining is toward the *front*. Check that the shoes are completely up into position. 　Completed ☐

23. Fit the anchor pin plate, adjusting cable or link, and primary and secondary springs into place. You will need to stretch the springs with a brake spring tool. With a cable-type adjuster, the cable guide must be installed under the rear or secondary return spring. 　Completed ☐

24. Is your brake mechanism a link or cable type? _____ 　　Completed ☐

25. After screwing it in most of the way, slip the adjusting screw or star wheel between the bottom of the shoes. 　Completed ☐

26. How does the star wheel face? _____

    _____ 　Completed ☐

27. Fit the short hook end of the lower return spring into its hole in the primary shoe. The half-hook on the end of the spring must fit (lock) in the lower portion of the shoe. If the hook is installed incorrectly, the spring can easily come off and jam against the rotating brake drum. 　Completed ☐

28. Attach the other end of the lower spring to the adjusting lever (cable type) or to the other brake shoe (lever type). Complete the assembly of the remaining parts. 　Completed ☐

29. Do your springs have half-hooks? _____ 　　　　Completed ☐

30. When you pull on the adjusting cable or arm, does it turn the star wheel? _____

    Explain: _____

    _____ 　Completed ☐

Measuring Drum Diameter

31. If a drum is worn too large in diameter, it must be replaced. Generally, a drum should not be worn over .060″. Measure your drum diameter, **Figure 5.** 　Completed ☐

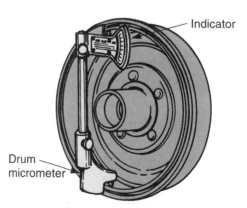

Figure 5. A special micrometer or caliper can be used to check drum wear.

Name _____

32. What is the drum's diameter and condition?_____

_____

_____

_____ Completed ☐

Adjusting Drum Brakes

33. Adjust the brakes by setting the lining-to-drum clearance. Install the special gauge into your brake drum, **Figure 6A.** Then, spread the gauge to the maximum inside diameter of the drum and lock it.   Completed ☐

34. Use the palms of your hands to tap the brake shoes from side to side. This assures they are completely seated on the anchor pins and centered on the backing plate.   Completed ☐

35. Fit the adjusting brake gauge over the linings, **Figure 6B.** Then, adjust the star wheel until the linings touch the gauge.   Completed ☐

36. Fit the brake drum into place. The linings should almost touch the drum if they are adjusted properly.   Completed ☐

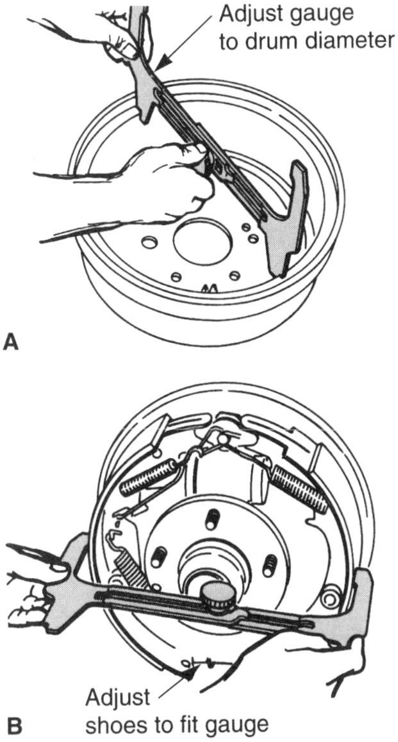

Adjust gauge
to drum diameter

A

Adjust
B   shoes to fit gauge

Figure 6. Study drum brake preadjustment. A—Fit the gauge into the brake drum and lock into position. B—Fit the gauge around the outside of the brake shoes. Adjust the shoes until they just touch the gauge. (Pontiac)

Bleeding Brakes

37. If the wheel cylinder or any other hydraulic component was removed, you will need to bleed the brakes to remove air from the system. As described in the text, have someone pump the brake pedal as you open and close the bleeding screw. A pressure tank or brake bleeder may also be used. Follow operating instructions.   Completed ☐

38. After air bubbles have stopped coming out of the bleeder fitting, snug the fitting and check the feel of the brake pedal. If needed, bleed the entire system. Also, fill the master cylinder with brake fluid. Wear your safety glasses at all times.   Completed ☐

Caution
Do not press the brake pedal with the drum removed or the wheel cylinder will pop apart.

39. How do you bleed brakes? _____

_____

_____

_____

_____ Completed ☐

40. Remove the brake drum and ask your instructor to check your work. If wheel bearings were removed
to access the brakes, repack and reinstall the bearings. Completed ☐

41. Turn in your tools and clean your work area. Completed ☐

42. Ask your instructor to check your work and sign this job for credit.

Instructor's Signature _____

Wheel Alignment

Name: _____

Date: _____

Instructor: _____

Score: _____

Objective: Given the needed tools and equipment, you will be able to realign all four wheels of a vehicle.

Tools and Equipment: You will need a basic set of hand tools, front end machine, and a car or light truck.

Instructions: Proper wheel alignment is critical to the driveability and dependability of modern vehicles. After getting your instructor's approval, align the four wheels on the vehicle. Study Chapter 74 of the text first.

Service Manual Information

1. Using the appropriate service manual, read the service information on four-wheel alignment. Completed ❑

2. What are the alignment specifications for your vehicle? Completed ❑

Front wheels

Caster: _____

Camber: _____

Toe: _____

Rear wheels

Camber: _____

Toe: _____

Steering and Suspension Inspection

3. Position the vehicle on the alignment rack. Have someone help guide you as you drive the vehicle up onto the rack. Completed ❑

4. Once in position, place the transmission in park or in neutral and block the rear wheels. Completed ❑

5. What kind of alignment equipment is in your shop? _____
_____ Completed ❑

6. Have someone turn the steering wheel right and then left while you check for worn steering system parts. Use the chart on page 496 to record any problems. Completed ❑

7. Summarize the condition of the following steering parts. _____

Tie-rods: _____
_____

Steering linkage: _____
_____
_____

Steering gear or rack-and-pinion assembly: _____
_____
_____

Power steering belt and pump: _____
_____
_____ Completed ❑

8. Check the suspension system for wear.   Completed ☐

9. Summarize the condition of the following suspension system parts.

Ball joints: _____

_____

Struts and/or shock absorbers: _____

_____

Springs: _____

_____

Control arms and bushings: _____

_____

Engine cradle or frame: _____

_____

Sway bars and links: _____

_____

Other parts: _____

_____

_____

_____ Completed ☐

10. Inspect the tires for signs of wear, **Figure 1.** What does the tire wear pattern tell you about the vehicle's wheel alignment?_____

_____

_____

_____ Completed ☐

	Rapid wear at shoulders	Rapid wear at center	Cracked treads	Wear on one side	Feathered edge	Bald spots	Scalloped wear
CONDITION	1. / 2.						
CAUSE	Underinflation or lack of rotation	Overinflation or lack of rotation	Underinflation or excessive speed	Excessive camber	Incorrect toe	Unbalanced wheel / or tire defect	Lack of rotation of tires or worn or out of alignment suspension
CORRECTION	Adjust pressure to specifications when tires are cool, rotate tires			Adjust camber to specifications	Adjust toe in to specifications	Dynamic or static balance wheels	Rotate tires and check alignment

Figure 1. Tire wear patterns can indicate suspension, steering, and alignment problems. (Chrysler)

Name _____

11. Since the steering and suspension system must be in good condition before wheel alignment, must any parts be replaced? _____

Explain: _____

_____

_____

_____

_____ Completed ❑

Measuring Alignment Angles

12. Install the wheel alignment equipment on the vehicle. Since equipment varies, refer to the user's manual for details.   Completed ❑

13. How did you prepare the equipment to measure the vehicle's alignment angles? _____

_____

_____

_____

_____ Completed ❑

14. Many of today's alignment machines are computerized. They will give instructions, specifications, and even pictures of what should be done to align the wheels. Is your alignment machine computerized? _____   Completed ❑

15. Read through the operating manual for your machine. How many pages are in the manual? _____   Completed ❑

16. How did you mount the alignment machine's attachments (heads) on the vehicle? _____

_____

_____

_____

_____ Completed ❑

17. Take your readings for four-wheel alignment and record them. Then, center the steering wheel and install a steering wheel lock. Apply the parking brake or install a brake pedal lock.

Front wheels

Caster: _____

Camber: _____

Toe: _____

SAI: _____

Rear wheels

Camber: _____

Toe: _____

Thrust angle: _____

Completed ❑

18. How much do these readings vary from specifications?

Front wheels

Caster difference: _____

Camber difference: _____

Toe difference: _____

SAI difference: _____

Rear wheels

Camber difference: _____

Toe difference: _____

Thrust angle difference: _____

Completed ❑

Adjusting Rear Wheel Alignment

19. When performing a four-wheel alignment, the rear camber and toe can be adjusted on most newer vehicles. On older vehicles with rear-wheel drive, these rear angles are fixed. If a rear camber and toe adjustment is available, correct these first before any front angles as they will affect the vehicle's thrust angle. If no rear wheel adjustments are available, proceed to step 23. If the camber or toe on a fixed rear suspension is out of specifications, you may have a bent frame or suspension part. Completed ☐

20. If available, adjust rear camber. How would this be done on this vehicle? _____

_____

_____

_____

_____ Completed ☐

21. If available, adjust rear toe if not within specifications. How do you adjust toe on this vehicle?

_____

_____

_____

_____ Completed ☐

22. How did adjusting these angles affect the thrust angle? _____

_____

_____

_____ Completed ☐

Adjusting Front Wheel Alignment

When adjusting the front wheels, always adjust caster first, if available and if needed. This is the best way to correct any pulling condition. Adjusting caster sometimes will also correct an out-of-specification camber or toe reading. Once caster is correct, adjust the camber, if needed, finishing with a toe adjustment.

23. Adjust caster if available. Explain the adjustment methods on this car or truck. _____

_____

_____

_____

_____ Completed ☐

24. If needed, adjust camber. How would this be done on this vehicle? _____

_____

_____

_____

_____ Completed ☐

25. Adjust toe if not within specifications. How do you adjust toe on this vehicle? _____

_____

_____

_____

_____ Completed ☐

26. How did adjusting these angles affect the thrust angle? _____

_____

_____ Completed ☐

27. Is the steering wheel centered with the front wheels straight ahead? If not, how would you correct this problem? See **Figure 2.**

_____

_____

_____ Completed ☐

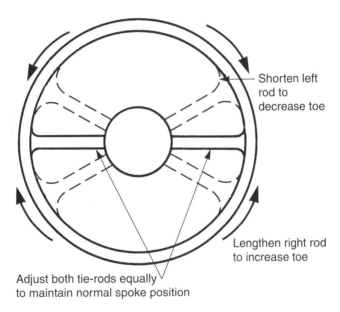

Shorten left rod to decrease toe

Lengthen right rod to increase toe

Adjust both tie-rods equally to maintain normal spoke position

Figure 2. After adjusting toe, the steering wheel should be in the center position. This shows how each tie-rod can affect the position of the steering wheel. (Ford)

28. Make sure all steering and suspension system fasteners are retorqued to specifications. Road test the vehicle to check your work. Completed ☐

29. Clean your work area and return all tools to their proper storage location. Completed ☐

30. Ask your instructor to check your work and sign this job for credit.

Instructor's Signature _____

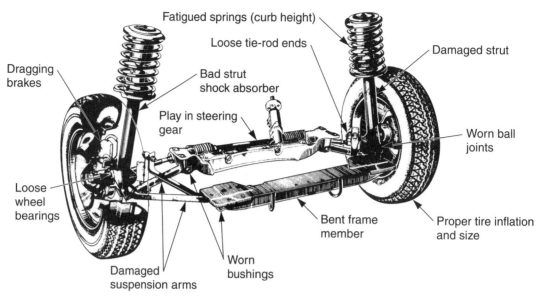

Fatigued springs (curb height)

Loose tie-rod ends

Damaged strut

Dragging brakes

Bad strut shock absorber

Play in steering gear

Worn ball joints

Loose wheel bearings

Bent frame member

Proper tire inflation and size

Damaged suspension arms

Worn bushings

Alignment Inspection Report Form

Name_____ Date_____, 19____

Address_____ Phone: Bus._____ Home_____

Make_____ Yr. and Model_____ License_____ Odometer _____

Tire and wheel checks

			Comments:
Tire condition-	Inspection	OK: LF__ RF__ LR __ RR__	
Tire pressure		OK: LF__ RF__ LR __ RR__	
Wheel bearings-	Adjustment	OK: LF__ RF__ LR __ RR__	
	Roughness	OK: LF__ RF__ LR __ RR__	
Runout-Lateral		OK: LF__ RF__ LR __ RR__	
Radial		OK: LF__ RF__ LR __ RR__	
Wheel balance		OK: LF__ RF__ LR __ RR__	
Shock absorbers-Operational		OK: LF__ RF__ LR __ RR__	
	Leakage and	OK: LF__ RF__ LR __ RR__	
	Bushings	OK: LF__ RF__ LR __ RR__	
Riding height		OK: LF__ RF__ LR __ RR__	

Suspension checks

		Comments:
Tracking	OK:__	
MacPherson-type struts	OK: LF__ RF__	
Ball joints	OK: LU__ LL__ RU __RL__	
Front control arm assembly	OK: LU__ LL__ RU__ RL__	
Strut rod and bushing assembly	OK: L__ R__	
Stabilizer (or sway) bar,		
mounting brackets,	Front: OK__	
and links	Rear: OK__	
Leaf spring assembly	OK: L__ R__	
Rear coil spring assembly	OK: L__ R__	
Rear control arm assembly	OK: LU__RU__LL __ RL__	
Track bar and bushings	OK:__	

Steering linkage checks

				Comments:
Tie-rod end	OK: ____	L__	R__	Comments:
Tie-rods and inner ball/stud				
sockets	OK: ____	L__	R__	
Steering arms	OK: ____	L__	R__	
Tie-rod adjusting sleeves	OK: ____	L__	R__	Comments:
Relay rod	OK: ____			
Pitman arm	OK: ____			
Idler arm and bracket	OK: ____			
Steering shock absorber and				
bushings	OK: ____			
Steering gear mountings	OK: ____			

Manual steering gear – inspection

		Comments:
Lubricant leakage	OK: ____	Comments:
Operation	OK: ____	
Sector shaft and bearings	OK: ____	
Adjustment of gear	OK: ____	
Lubricant level	OK: ____	

Power steering gear – inspection

		Comments:
Fluid leakage	OK: ____	Comments:
Power steering hoses	OK: ____	
Power steering pump	OK: ____	
Fluid level	OK: ____	
Pump belt	OK: ____	
Power steering operation	OK: ____	
Steering gear adjustment	OK: ____	
Sector shaft and bushings	OK: ____	
Pinion shaft and bearings	OK: ____	
Control valve	OK: ____	

Front alignment check

	Reading	Manufacturer's standard	OK
Caster	L__° R__°	L__° R__°	
Camber	L__° R__°	L__° R__°	
Steering axis inclination	L__° R__°	L__° R__°	
Turning radius	L__° R__°	L__° R__°	
Toe	In__ Out__	In__ Out__	

Air Conditioning Service

Name: _____

Date: _____

Instructor: _____

Score: _____

Objective: Given the needed tools and equipment, you will be able to recover, evacuate, and recharge an automobile's air conditioning system.

Tools and Equipment: You will need a basic set of hand tools, set of gauges, recovery station, charging station, thermometer, leak detector, safety glasses, and gloves, and a shop or customer vehicle.

Instructions: We have seen recent changes in automotive air conditioning systems in an effort to reduce air pollution. R-134a has been assigned as a replacement for R-12. This is because R-12 has been found to contribute to the depletion of the earth's ozone layer. As a result, you must be aware that two different refrigerants are now in use. It is important to remember that these two refrigerants cannot be interchanged. You must also recover old refrigerant to keep it from entering and harming the atmosphere. After getting your instructor's approval, obtain the needed tools and equipment. Find out which shop-owned or customer car you will use and proceed carefully. You should have studied Chapters 75 and 76 in the text.

Service Manual Information

1. Read the service information for your vehicle's air conditioning system.   Completed ☐

2. What type of refrigerant does your vehicle use?_____   Completed ☐

A/C System Inspection

3. The first step is to perform an A/C system performance test. Start the engine. Turn the A/C on high cool. Allow the system to run for about 10 minutes with the windows up. For a more accurate assessment of the air conditioner's performance, test the vehicle outside the shop.   Completed ☐

4. Using a thermometer, measure the air temperature leaving the center vent.   Completed ☐

5. What was the vent temperature reading? _____   Completed ☐

6. Is this temperature normal or out of specification?_____

   Explain why. _____

   _____

   _____

   _____   Completed ☐

7. Inspect the air conditioning system for signs of obvious troubles.   Completed ☐

8. Summarize the condition of the following:

   Compressor drive belt: _____

   _____

   _____

   Compressor and clutch: _____

   _____

   _____

Condenser: _____

_____

_____

Radiator fan: _____

_____

_____

Fittings and hoses: _____

_____

_____

Switches and wiring: _____

_____

_____

Dash controls: _____

_____

_____ Completed ☐

9. Which part(s) do you think might be in need of service or replacement? _____

_____

_____ Completed ☐

Refrigerant Recovery

10. Connect a charging station to the vehicle. Follow the equipment manufacturer's instructions and wear
    eye protection and gloves, **Figure 1.** Completed ☐

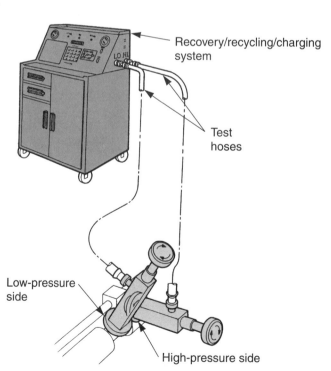

Figure 1. Charging station connections to an air conditioning
system. (Snap-on Tool Corp.)

11. Where are the service ports located?_____

    _____

    _____

    _____   Completed ☐

12. Recover all the refrigerant into the charging station. Set the machine to filter and ready the refrigerant for re-use.   Completed ☐

13. Was there any refrigerant in the vehicle's air conditioning system? _____

    Explain: _____

    _____   Completed ☐

14. Using the information in your textbook. explain what could happen if refrigerant sprayed into your unprotected face and eyes._____

    _____

    _____

    _____   Completed ☐

Evacuating and Charging

15. Evacuate the system. Describe how this is done. _____

    _____

    _____

    _____

    _____

    _____   Completed ☐

16. After pulling a vacuum, the system should maintain its negative pressure to show there are no leaks. Is your system leaking? _____

    Explain: _____

    _____

    _____   Completed ☐

17. Now, charge the system. Meter the correct amount and type of refrigerant into the system. What are your service manual specifications for this? _____

    _____

    _____

    _____   Completed ☐

Gauge Readings

As you charge the system, you should monitor gauge readings and compare them to specifications.

18. What should the gauges read with a properly charged and functioning system?

    _____

    _____   Completed ☐

19. Monitor vent temperature as an aid to proper system charging.   Completed ☐

20. What does your thermometer read after charging? _____   Completed ☐

21. Leak test the system. Move your leak tester around all potential leakage points (fittings, compressor seal, condenser, evaporator), **Figure 2.**   Completed ☐

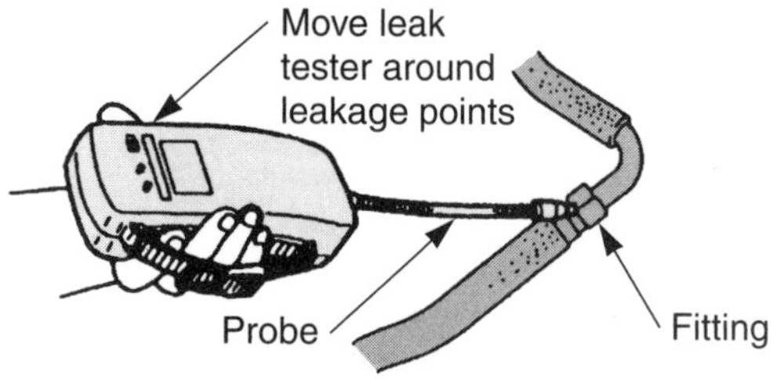

Figure 2. A leak detector will make an audible signal if refrigerant gases are present. (Snap-on Tool Corp.)

22. Did you find any leaks? _____

     Explain: _____

     _____

     _____

     _____

     _____   Completed ☐

⚠ **Warning**
If the system is leaking, immediately recover the refrigerant so it does not leak into the atmosphere.

23. Clean your work area and return all tools and equipment to their storage areas.   Completed ☐

24. Have your instructor check your work and sign this job for credit.

Instructor's Signature _____